THE CAPTAINS
AND
THE KINGS

Edith Benham Helm
WHITE HOUSE SOCIAL SECRETARY
FOR TWENTY-FIVE YEARS

WITH A FOREWORD BY

Mrs. Franklin D. Roosevelt

G. P. PUTNAM'S SONS   NEW YORK

Copyright, 1954, by Edith Benham Helm

All rights reserved. This book, or parts thereof, must not be reproduced in any form without permission.

Published on the same day in the Dominion of Canada by Thomas Allen, Ltd., Toronto.

Library of Congress Catalog Card Number 54-8705

MANUFACTURED IN THE UNITED STATES OF AMERICA

Edith Benham at 18.

Foreword

I FIRST CAME TO KNOW Mrs. Helm well on shipboard. She was secretary to Mrs. Wilson, and my husband was Assistant Secretary of the Navy. As the daughter of an admiral and later the wife of an admiral everything that touched the Navy had interest for Mrs. Helm and she soon recognized in my husband a kindred soul. We had tea together in our cabin and plenty of talk. My husband and I, of course, saw something also of President and Mrs. Wilson, but with Edith Helm it was a very much easier and less restrained relationship. She told us of her time in Paris and London with President and Mrs. Wilson and, since she was a good storyteller, every incident gained in the telling.

During our stay in Paris I had gone with her and Mrs. Wilson to several hospitals and I had noticed everywhere how thoughtful Mrs. Helm was, how helpful to Mrs. Wilson and how self-effacing. She always seemed to remember the right things, and I think I realized for the first time what a difference it can make if you have someone with you who is tactful, who remembers what you forget and feels at ease in the most difficult situations. At that time I had no idea I would come to know Mrs. Helm very well indeed in the future, but I was grateful for her friendliness because I was still somewhat shy and in awe of the great people in whose orbit my husband's work sometimes drew us.

In the years that followed we kept in occasional touch with each other, so that when Mrs. Helm heard we were going to Washington she wrote and offered her services for the first few days, saying that she could perhaps help us to get settled. How grateful I was, but when her letter came I did not realize how grateful I was going to be as time went on!

To really know the ins and outs of Washington I think you must have lived there a long time, and Mrs. Helm could qualify as one of the "cave dwellers." She knew protocol and what one should do, and after being with us for the first few days in the White House and straightening us out in our first difficulties, she decided she would stay on to help us with the social side of our problems. It was quite evident from the amount of mail piling up on Miss Thompson's desk that she would not have time to think of official entertaining. These letters that were pouring in dealt with every problem that faced the American people in that particular year of depression, 1933. I wish that the part of this book which deals with the White House years under my husband's administration could have been written, as was once intended by Mrs. Helm, with my secretary, Miss Malvina Thompson.

They always had a wonderful relationship together and in different ways their sense of humor lightened many a situation which might have become difficult or touchy. In all the years they worked together there was never a misunderstanding, but of course these years are only a few of the years that are touched on in this book, for Mrs. Helm's life of travel and contacts in various parts of the world began at a very early age. Her story covers many periods of great historical interest. I have always felt that it is the story of individuals and their lives which really illuminates history. This story is a part of history.

I am sure I was at times a trial until Mrs. Helm came to know me better, for her social conscience where dinners and official functions were concerned was far more pronounced than mine. I tended to feel that when you had to seat dinners according to protocol you could leave it all to the State Department, and when you had to shake hands with so many people all you needed to do was to be sure there was enough food and that you were glad to see anyone who came. But Mrs. Helm felt that a little more thought should go into one's decisions on matters of society. She would come with great determination every morning to make me go over my duties of the day, and liked me to be prepared to play my part as well and as understandingly as possible.

I am sure readers will find in these pages many anecdotes and stories which illustrate the time in which Mrs. Helm lived and paint vivid pictures of the people whom she met. This may well serve also to explain some of the things that happened during these years which are not always easily understood. In any case, I am sure you will find this life history both entertaining and interesting, and I recommend it to you as a book well worth your attention.

ELEANOR ROOSEVELT

February 9, 1954

Acknowledgments

To ALL THE FRIENDS who encouraged me to write these recollections of a long life, go my thanks. The list is long and I can choose only a few to name here.

Foremost come Mrs. Franklin D. Roosevelt and Mrs. Harry S. Truman, who urged me to make the difficult start in writing this book.

Also to Martha Strayer and Bess Furman, veteran Washington newspaperwomen and my personal friends, I am deeply indebted for arranging in readable form my notes and letters.

To Miss Ida Andrews, for her patience and skill in secretarial work.

To Mr. Adrian S. Tolley, of the White House Social Office, and Mr. Howell G. Crim, Chief White House Usher, for their generous aid in giving me details of the intricacies of traditional White House entertaining and operation, which were outside the scope of my own experience.

And to my publishers—and in particular to Mrs. Virginia Carrick—for their courtesy and friendly guidance.

E.B.H.

Contents

	Foreword *by* Mrs. Franklin D. Roosevelt	v
1.	With All Humility	3
2.	A Kiss from General Grant	5
3.	A Four Hundredth Anniversary	14
4.	When Father Rolled to Rio	29
5.	Blazing a Trail to the White House	41
6.	Romance and Great Adventure	56
7.	Path of Glory	72
8.	The League Is Born	86
9.	The Lonely Figure	99
10.	The Price of Glory	109
11.	A Washingtonian of the Minority	126
12.	After Many Years—Again the White House	134
13.	Staging State Dinners, High Teas and Deb Dances	153
14.	I Meet the Press—and Enter Picnic Politics	169
15.	The Social Secretary Is Invited Out	180
16.	King George and Queen Elizabeth Come Visiting	186
17.	Royal Refugees; Churchill; and Madame Chiang	207
18.	In Comes the Mail, Out Go the Souvenirs; On with the War	224

19.	The End of the Roosevelt Road	240
20.	White House Lights Go On Again	250
21.	Big Doings in Little Blair House	264
22.	An Old-New White House	279
23.	An Old-New Home and a Farewell	293
	Index	301

Miss Edith Benham—Aged 18, frontispiece

Sixteen pages of photographs will be found following page 116

THE CAPTAINS AND THE KINGS

Chapter 1

WITH ALL HUMILITY

Looking back on the years I have lived through, I often think how fortunate I have been to have known and worked with so many men and women who have played important roles in the history of our times.

I have seen three of our war Presidents weather the storms of war and peace. A fourth is a fleeting memory of my childhood. I have dined with royalty and slept in palaces. I have ridden in cavalcades with kings and queens, met Majesties and great military leaders, seen them (I think) for what they were, as men and women.

I have watched the unrolling of great moments of history.

In October, 1918, just before the Armistice that ended the First World War, I wrote a friend: "This is the tensest day I have ever known in the White House. These are days when atmosphere can fairly be felt. The door of the President's study, usually open all the time, has been closed all day. I suppose by tomorrow we shall all know if he has decided to entertain some sort of peace parleys. . . ."

On January 16, 1942, after Pearl Harbor, I saw a pile of gaily wrapped packages lying unopened in the second-floor sitting room at the White House. President Roosevelt had not opened his Christmas gifts that fateful year. . . .

In the autumn of 1948, I came out of my office one day and met President Truman on his way to the little outside sunroom on the third floor of the White House, where he always lunched with his family. It was at a time in his campaign for President when I could see absolutely no chance that he would be elected. I said, "How are things going?" His face lighted, he smiled and told me he was confident of election. . . .

I am sure I never would have believed it if anyone had told me when I was a girl that I would see what I have seen. Looking back, it seems almost like a dream.

Chapter 2

A KISS FROM GENERAL GRANT

ONE THING HAS ALWAYS PUZZLED ME: why do autobiographers when they take pen in hand to describe their own lives feel it necessary to write the thousand uninteresting details about childhood? Nearly all of us have had measles, mumps, or whooping cough. Many of us have dreamed strange dreams. Those of us who go back far enough have frightful collections of photographs. If male, they are scowling little boys dressed in ugly kilts. The feminine contingent unearth photographs of themselves with waspy waists and bulgy hips and busts. In a moment of frenzy, after reading the autobiography of one lady of quality, I destroyed all of my photographs of tender years and of tougher ones also, allowing only one to survive.

The decks now being cleared for action, I can state that my first recollection was climbing laboriously up and down a ladder on a boat. This must have been when I was about three years old, my brother about eleven. My father, a naval officer, was on duty in Charleston, South Carolina. This must have been in the late Seventies and feeling was very high against all Northerners.

The family, consisting of my father, mother, brother Harry and me, had boarded with a family on the Battery. After my brother had had several bloody encounters with other little boys, it was decided that it was better for us all to move on board the lighthouse tender so that my brother would not be utterly annihilated.

My father was Andrew Ellicott Kennedy Benham, born on Staten Island, a seafaring son of a seafaring father. He was thus lengthily named for an old friend of his father, who was supposed to leave him some money—but didn't.

My mother was the great-granddaughter of Captain John Kortright, whose sister, Elizabeth Kortright, married James Monroe, who became the fifth President of the United States. Indeed, my mother was descended from two colonial New York families, the Kortrights and the Seamans, whose intermarriages among distant cousins so confused my family chart as to make it almost unbelievable. For Captain John Kortright married Katharine Seaman; and their daughter Hester Mary Kortright married Billopp Benjamin Seaman; and their daughter Katharine Sarah Seaman married Henry John Seaman; and their daughter, Emma Hester Seaman, my mother, married Andrew Ellicott K. Benham, a young officer of the U.S. Navy, causing punsters to remark that here was still another seaman in the family. It is scarcely any wonder that my earliest memories centered on a ship's ladder to which I was driven by a peculiar and belated aftermath of the Civil War.

At intervals all through my childhood our family went home to the old house at Richmond, Staten Island, where I was born. My memories of it are varied—and satisfying. It was a lovely old place, a huge stone house built by my grandfather, Commander Timothy Green Benham. Why he put so much money into this house has always been a mystery to me. Probably he thought he was immortal and could live on and on and save enough to leave a very large family comfortable. Fate decided otherwise and he died in 1861, leaving a widow and numerous children.

Life was rather patriarchal in this old house. My father was the head of the family and on him for many years fell the task of helping to support his mother, brothers and sisters.

Though we were very near New York City, and Staten Island now forms a part of it, communication was primitive. We went by ferry to a point along the shore on Staten Island. Then we took a train which puffed and wheezed its way as far as Tottenville.

Our station was Giffords. There we were usually met by a nondescript vehicle designated in those days as a carryall. This consisted of two seats. The back seat was so close to the front that adult knees were tucked up under the chin. The horse was usually an old and eminently safe animal, although my aunts occasionally gave way to dark suspicions that Philly might run away. Philly was never known to have shown any tendencies in this direction, but the thought lent a certain awful horror to the three-mile drive from the station to the old house.

One of the treasures of my grandfather's house was John James Audubon's great life work, *The Birds of America*. This beautifully illustrated tome was considered so important it was kept upstairs and brought out only on rare occasions. As a child, I was told that Audubon was a friend of my grandfather's, and that he had tramped all over Staten Island in his study of birds. And when I was shown the picture of the marsh wren, it was with the information that it had been painted right there on Staten Island near the old house.

I can still see the little bedroom that was always mine, the apple-green furniture painted in gay-colored flowers, the bed which I strongly suspect had a feather bed on it in winter. Usually those abominations abounded throughout the house, and one which my mother inherited from her side of the family, a down article, followed us to China, came back via the Isthmus of Panama, went to Portsmouth, New Hampshire, then to New York, and now is cut up into cushions for my sofa in Washington. So the mighty have fallen!

The dining room had a mahogany table in it. On the sideboard were two silver pitchers and two silver cups presented to my grandfather by the County of Richmond for gallantry in the Mexican War. The inscription is quaint and reads as follows:

Presented Jany 1st 1848
To
Lieut. Timothy Green Benham
U. S. Navy
by his fellow citizens of Richmond County in token of their Esteem for his distinguished services and nautical skill on board the war schooner Bonita during and subsequent to the attack on Vera Cruz March 24th & 25th 1847 and of their admiration of his deportment in private life

It is interesting to speculate on how many of the dramatic bits of our country's history may have been thus inscribed on silver, preserving names and places—and the names also of proud and patriotic friends.

In a scrapbook kept by my mother I found, undated and unidentified as to what publication it came from, a newspaper clipping which gave details of the presentation of these vases. According to this account, the reception to my grandfather, when he visited his home shortly after the Mexican War, was "one of the greatest social events in the history of Staten Island"; and "The village of Richmond was the scene of a large concourse of people from all over the country. Distinguished navy and army officers, statesmen and citizens were present. The court room of the County Court House was densely packed and hundreds were unable to gain entrance to the building." Information was also given that "The presentation speech was made by Minthorne Tompkins, son of ex-Vice-President Tompkins"; and that "After the presentation ceremonies, very many of those present repaired to the Benham mansion, about a mile distant, where a royal banquet was held."

The dining table at my grandfather's house was long, always filled on Sundays, sometimes with friends, sometimes with other members of the family who came down to the old house to visit.

An old Franklin stove in winter furnished cheer. The window seats in this room were always littered by a collection of almanacs, old newspapers, and what have you. The seat near the fire was very much sought after on the cold days, and I remember one of my aunts' somewhat gloomy habits was to tell me that if I sat too near the fire I would melt the fat around my kidneys. This worked for some time until I noted the tendency on her part to expose that section of her anatomy to the blaze, and it began to dawn on me that my aunt's seeming deep interest in my welfare was only a clever trick to maneuver me away from the fire.

Through all these recollections of Staten Island there runs a very golden thread of memory. The memory of my father. It was he who taught me the love of the outdoors. I can't remember when our excursions first began, but my earliest memory of them is going along with him to look for arbutus in the spring. Then came the early strawberries, and later other seasonal fruits and flowers. I remember the thrill of finding the first mushrooms in September, and the nuts later in the autumn.

It was my father who first formed my taste for reading. He would not allow any trash and I can remember him reading aloud Pope's translation of the *Iliad* and then giving me a child's version of this classic.

I am afraid that discipline from my father was rather lax and all of that burden fell on my mother. She it was who managed expertly our family expenditures. It was miraculous what she accomplished. Time to sew, time to teach me, and time for play; the burdens of family responsibilities, relatives to be taken care of—but we never had the specter of debt to haunt us.

It must have been very shortly after the Charleston experience that I remember a somewhat stuffy boardinghouse in Boston and preparations afoot for going to China and Japan. We went up to Boston because the frigate *Richmond*, which my father was to command on a three-year duty tour to the Far East, was fitting out at the Navy Yard. His was to be a remarkably ceremonial cruise, for he was to pick up General and Mrs. Ulysses S. Grant, then nearing the close of a trip around the world, and take him through his final triumph in China and Japan.

Probably no ex-President ever had as spectacular a world trip as Grant. Shortly after he finished his eight years in the White House, the Secretary of State of the Hayes administration sent a letter to all diplomatic and consular offices of the United States telling them that General Grant was going abroad "to secure a few months of rest and recreation after sixteen years of unremitting and devoted labor in the military and civil service of his country." The letter stated that it was the wish of President Hayes that the diplomatic and consular officers of the Government make his journey a pleasant one should he visit their posts. So happily did they perform this duty that the Grant party was feted in every port, and in every capital by every ruler. The "few months" lengthened into three years, 1877, 1878 and 1879. My father's orders took him by way of the Atlantic, the Mediterranean, and the Indian Ocean to the Orient.

My mother, brother, and I were to follow in leisurely fashion, going across the continent to the West Coast, thence by the Pacific Ocean to meet my father in Japan. This trip was made possible by an old friend and neighbor of my mother's, Mr. William Henry Vanderbilt. When he had married, against the wishes of the family, the daughter of a Brooklyn clergyman, his father, Cornelius Vanderbilt, cut his son off from the family's financial kingdom, at the same time presenting him with a seventy-acre farm on Staten Island. There his four sons and his four daughters were born. He and my mother had belonged to the same set, had gone to the same "sociables." But when William Vanderbilt was past forty his father relented and made him vice-president of the New York and Harlem Railroad. Soon Mr. William Vanderbilt had control of a nationwide network of railroads, and he and all his sons and daughters lived in Fifth Avenue mansions.

One day shortly after my father got his orders to command the *Richmond,* my mother met Mr. Vanderbilt in New York. She told him my father was going to China, but that we could not accompany him because the price of tickets for such a long trip was prohibitive.

He promptly said: "I will give you passes for yourself and your children across the continent."

I remember little of the trip across the country except that we carried food along with us in lunch baskets and the bread became unpleasantly stale after a few days. It took us a long time to cross the Pacific. We went on an old side-wheel steamer on her last trip and I think it took nearly a month to get over.

I have a distinct recollection of entering the harbor of Yokohama, of someone smelling very strongly of tobacco, and a bushy beard brushing my face, which I did not like. In later years I was told that I behaved very badly whenever General Grant kissed me, so I think that this must have been he.

A day-by-day account of my father's part in the Grant adventure, both before and after we joined the Grant party in Yokohama, was told—and with full descriptions, maps, and profuse illustrations—by John Russell Young, the newspaperman who accompanied General Grant. The dispatches which he sent to the New York *Herald* were later published in a two-volume set entitled *Around the World with General Grant*.

My own memory-glimpses of our life in Japan are far different from Mr. Young's accounts of the sophisticated goings-on of the adults. I remember the little bungalow we had in a tiny garden with three exciting little hills in it. And an earthquake, when the huge wardrobe in our room swung back and forth and Mitz, our Japanese manservant, came rushing in with a blanket to take me out in the open air. The Japanese servants had said that a severe earthquake was imminent that day because a hen had crowed in one of the crowded quarters of the town. I have a memory of going to Miyanoshita, a watering place, with hot springs, up in the hills. We went part of the way in jinrikishas, part of the way in kangas, a species of litter swung from the shoulders of two Japanese coolies. The little hotel in Miyanoshita had sliding paper screens for partition walls. There was a lovely rushing stream and hot and cold water from the springs.

A winter in Shanghai in a hotel was marked by the difficulties my mother had in getting a nurse for me—not that there were not plenty of applicants for the place, but they were all of the upper class with bound feet. I was an active child and finally she had to get a peasant woman whose feet could allow her to travel with me to the lovely gardens of the city.

Back again in Japan, we began preparations for the journey home. In the old days of the Navy the admiral or the captain was allowed to take his wife and family aboard. Happily this rule has been abolished because enthusiastic women must have made life miserable for the officers. My mother and I were almost the last women to travel aboard a man-of-war. I can remember our starting from the harbor of Yokohama. My father was an old-fashioned seaman and he always pined to sail. The *Richmond* was an auxiliary steamer and we could not carry enough coal in the hold to last us on the long trip from Yokohama to Panama. The decks were piled high with coal. We had on board some sheep. Those were the days long before cold storage was dreamed of and the tinned provisions were very poor. It must have looked like a Noah's Ark, because there was a goat aboard, a dog or two, and numerous cats. For days before, the crew had been busily making a homeward-bound pennant and I can still see this long slim piece of bunting floating from the mast way behind the stern of the ship after we steamed out of the harbor. The *Richmond* was built for a flagship and we were very comfortable on this return trip because we had the admiral's quarters to live in as well as the captain's.

I remember long days of calm when the ship was almost still and the crew got up turtle and we could feast on turtle soup. My brother had a turn for zoology and he was constantly dropping buckets overboard to get up the queer nautiluses with their little membrane sails. Occasionally flying fish would come aboard and the crew would catch lovely-colored tropical fish.

Many old-fashioned sailormen were among the crew. One specimen of the old Navy who obviously felt that women and ships didn't mix, and who was rebuked by one of the officers for his picturesque profanity in my mother's hearing, retorted contemptuously, "I don't care a g—— d—— for the skipper or the skipper's wife."

It was a cruise almost without incident. Once something went wrong with the navigator's reckoning just before we were to stop at the Galapagos Islands for fresh provisions, and all we saw of them was a blue cloud on the horizon. Then there was a terrifying night in the Gulf of Panama when a hurricane struck us and the wind shrieked through the rigging.

I think life on this cruise must have been like any other long journey when people are together for some time. Except for that one storm, it was harmonious in every way. My mother always said she regretted reaching Panama.

Our trip across the Isthmus must have been extraordinary. I remember a most inadequate railroad with people coming aboard all the time to sell tropical fruits. We picked up various pets along the way besides those we had started with from Japan, and when we reached the Atlantic side, loaded down with bird cages, we must have looked like a zoo as we went aboard the ship taking us to New York. The old *Richmond* stayed behind to take another crew on board and return to the Orient, but the Benham family went back to New York and to the old stone house for a time.

There my mother found places for all the treasures she had purchased overseas. To this day, I take many a meal from the china which my mother bought in the Orient on that trip which started when I was four years old—and on which my welcome to Japan was a kiss from General Grant.

Chapter 3

A FOUR HUNDREDTH ANNIVERSARY

THE NEXT TREK OF OUR Navy family was to Portsmouth, New Hampshire, for three years, 1882 through 1884, at the Navy Yard there. The Portsmouth waterfront was a place of delightful mystery to me. At one end was a collection of old wooden ships and my father used to take me down there and point out the different ones lying in what was called "Rotten Row." Some of them had figureheads. They all had a little touch of the eerie about them. I remember one most hauntingly, the *Sabine*. She had had frightful cases of yellow fever aboard. That was always the plague of the old wooden ships of that time.

The house we lived in was an old one, and haunted. Unhappily we never saw any of the haunts. Perhaps we were too prosaic a family, though my mother did have a bad fall and was supposed to have seen the ghost of a Mrs. Young who had hanged herself in a closet on the third story.

There were riotous days for me with three boon companions, daughters of naval officers at the Yard. And cousins came to stay with us, sometimes for lengthy visits. My mother was always fond of young people and the Portsmouth Navy Yard was a gay place—informal dances and ships coming and going.

In the old town of Portsmouth there was constant social interchange. Nearly all the old families there had married into the Navy or had sons in it. It had fond memories for my mother who had come there for a short time when she was a bride. She had married at the close of the Civil War when my father came to Boston unexpectedly and telegraphed her to ask if she were willing to be married. She started off with her mother and the clergyman of their old church, St. Luke's in New York, and was married in Boston, going later to Portsmouth. She always said it had caused very deep disappointment among the Portsmouth girls. They had thought my father was another bachelor and it was very depressing to have him arrive with a perfectly good wife.

In the summers Seavey's Island was a favorite spot for our numerous berrying excursions. On a rocky point there, we stood one windy afternoon watching the *Constellation,* with midshipmen aboard, sail out of the harbor back to the Naval Academy. For many years the *Constellation,* famous old sister ship of the *Constitution,* was used by the Academy as a training ship so that the young officers would know how to manage a ship under sail. The *Constellation* came in every year and it was quite an event of the social season to have the gay young boys come ashore for the dance. Of course they seemed a prodigious age to me, yet it was not long before my brother went to Annapolis to round out the family tradition.

My grandfather, Timothy Green Benham, had been appointed midshipman in 1814. There was no Naval Academy then. My father, Andrew E. K. Benham, was appointed to the Naval Academy at Annapolis in 1847 and was graduated in 1851. My brother, Henry K. Benham, was appointed to the Naval Academy in 1884, which was for that reason and for other unexpected events a notable year for our family.

About this time, through Lieutenant Charles Harlow, a friend from Japan days, my mother met Mrs. Livingston Mason of Newport and her friend, Miss Katherine Butterfield of New York. Mrs. Mason was a brilliant woman, far in advance of her time, who had been educated in Europe. If there had been as much money in the family at that time as there was earlier, she might have had a real salon. Mrs. Mason asked us to visit her that autumn in Newport and I remember the thrill I had on going away for our first visit. There I met the Mason children, Earl and Edith, and later Marguerite and Lion. From that time, whenever I was near them I would go to spend a part of the summer with them and these were the happiest days of my life. I did not have many young companions and the Mason family took me in and made me feel that I belonged to them.

The Masons owned a large place, Halidon Hall, on the Bay side of Newport. It was an inconvenient old stone house and there were two cottages on the place. Occasionally the family rented out one or the other of these places. In consequence, sometimes the family lived in the stone house, and sometimes in one of the cottages. The stone house was filled with relics brought back from a trip Mrs. Mason had made to Yucatan, and there were pets galore. They were great fun at first but later became the bane of our existence because we had to clean bird cages and exercise animals.

After three happy years at Portsmouth, my father was ordered to Staten Island. The Navy then had charge of the lighthouses in the country, and this Third Lighthouse District was very desirable duty. My father and mother had wanted to go back to Staten Island for a long time, so she seems to have tried some bribery and corruption on old Admiral J. Grimes Walker, who was the head of the Lighthouse Board. He always came to visit us at Portsmouth, and once he admired a silk patchwork quilt that my mother was making. My mother promptly said, "If you will order Ken [my father] to the Third Lighthouse District, I will make you one." He said, "I will hold you to that promise," which was taking a mean advantage because he had the orders then in his pocket. But he got his quilt and we journeyed down with the feather bed to Tompkinsville, Staten Island.

It was wonderful to be back on the Island which for so many years had been home to both my father and mother. My father's people had lived there the year around in the old Benham Place. My mother's father, Henry John Seaman, spent his summers on

Staten Island as so many other New Yorkers did. It seems incredible now, in view of the somewhat tumble-down condition of the Island, but in those days it was filled with beautiful places, particularly along the shore, and life was very pleasant.

My Grandfather Seaman owned an old family place of about two hundred acres a mile or so from the Benham place. After his death my grandmother sold it. As a little child, I can remember driving past this old house, which has since been torn down, and I can still see it, low and rambling. My mother and others of the family said it was haunted. She had had a psychic experience there of feeling hands passed over her face while asleep. One of my great-aunts had a similar experience.

Grandfather Seaman had dabbled in politics and started his career as secretary to Governor King at Albany. Then he went to Congress, serving from 1845 to 1847. Our only relic of this congressional experience was a cane which was presented to him by Mr. Bodisco, a picturesque figure, who was the Russian Minister in Washington at the time. Old Mr. Bodisco married a very young and beautiful Georgetown girl who queened it over Washington society for twenty-five years.

During my grandfather's stay in Congress, he secured an appropriation for old Fort Wadsworth at the entrance to the Narrows. In consequence of this I always had a strong proprietary feeling for the Fort. Years later when I used to visit the beautiful old Austen home near there, I still felt that the Fort belonged to me.

The naval officer in command of the Third Lighthouse District had an old boat which was large enough to accommodate his family and in which he could make inspection tours of the lighthouses along the coast as far as Montauk Point and up the Hudson River. Years after whenever I saw an extraordinary-looking vessel on inland waters or at Newport or Boston, I at once could recognize it as a lighthouse tender. These lighthouse tenders certainly were not designed for beauty. They probably were built that way to accommodate the buoys they had to carry from place to place. The old *John Rodgers* was the one assigned to this District and many were the happy excursions we made on her. My father always found it convenient to inspect the lightship off Sandy Hook when the International Cup Races took place. The tender could tie up alongside the lightship and from that vantage point we could see the two beautiful yachts as they rounded the lightship on their return journey.

Every September the great event of our lives took place. Harry, my brother, came back from the Naval Academy bringing with him an assorted group of midshipmen. With some young ladies, cousins and friends we all climbed aboard the *John Rodgers*. How we ever got sorted out there and tucked away I cannot imagine. But youth does not mind discomforts and we would sail up the Hudson on a leisurely cruise, my father inspecting the lights as we went along, going all the way up to Albany. About Newburgh we would take aboard Captain Jake Schemerhorn, a tyrannical old pilot who made everyone's life, as well as his own, miserable aboard ship. Another year it would be a trip along Long Island Sound to inspect the lights there. A small-boy cousin and I were the only children aboard, and in those days children were seen and not unduly heard. Youthful individualities were not cherished as they are nowadays, and mine was frequently assisted by the maternal hairbrush or slipper.

The last year of our stay on Staten Island we moved away for a few months from this pleasant old house to one we rented at Clifton, Staten Island, for the winter. In the spring of that year my father, who had been promoted to rear admiral, was ordered to the Mare Island Navy Yard, California.

The previous spring we had gone down to see my brother graduate and though I was much too young, I was allowed to go to the June Ball. My card was made out for me just as though I were grown up, and then I fell in love for the first time in my life. He was a second or third classman, William A. Moffett. Unhappily, he never knew of this hopeless passion which gnawed at me for a couple of years. I don't think I even told him of this many years after when I met him in Washington and he had become head of the Naval Aviation Service, specializing in craft that were lighter than air. He was killed in the crash of the Navy dirigible balloon *Akron,* off Barnegat, New Jersey, in 1933.

June Week then at the Academy was a small affair. Graduating classes were about a tenth the size of the present ones and it was more like "old home week" than anything else. The Academy in those days was a charming old place with shady walks and somewhat ramshackle buildings which had not been rebuilt since the Academy was founded. My mother met any number of old friends and she had two young-girl cousins with her, who had a wonderful time. My life was somewhat clouded by having people say, "and this is Edith and how she has grown!"

My father went ahead of us to Mare Island and we followed, going by the Canadian Pacific.

For the first time in our lives we had no relatives with us. The admiral at the Yard received sea pay because so many people had to be entertained for the night and these expenses had to come out of his budget. As a matter of fact my future husband, James M. Helm, was one of the young officers entertained by my father there. When years later we compared notes on this, I had little recollection of him and he remembered me only as a long-legged girl scampering about Mare Island.

This was the first time the family was ever able to save anything to speak of and we felt like millionaires in the fine house which was later destroyed by an earthquake. Servants were supplied by the government, and an extraordinary vehicle drawn by two horses, more like a Black Maria than anything else, was allotted for the use of the commandant of the Yard.

I quickly made friends with the numerous children on the Yard, with whom I had a marvelous time riding over the hills on the Island on my own horse and swimming in the icy cold waters of the Bay. My crony there was Alice Cutts, a descendant of the sister of Dolly Madison, and later the wife of General John T. Myers, U.S.M.C. We went to school in the little town of Vallejo on the mainland adjoining the Island, carrying our lunches with us in substantial wicker baskets. I can't say either of us learned very much at the school and we must have made the life of the unhappy Methodist clergyman who kept the school a burden. We were very young for girls of fourteen and turned what intellects we had to displays of insubordination during the school hours.

About that time the first epidemic of influenza swept the country and my father and mother were both in bed with high temperatures, when the survivors of the disastrous hurricane at Samoa came back to Mare Island. Two ships of our Navy, the *Trenton* and the *Vandalia,* were there. The hurricane came up suddenly. The British ships at anchor in the harbor had coal aboard and steam up and they were able to sail out. The *Trenton,* the flagship, was being pounded to pieces on the rocks but as the British ship steamed by the American crew cheered.

Those who came back from this terrific experience, fortunate enough to be washed ashore or to get ashore in boats, showed lines of care and terror from what they had been through on that day when they clung to the rigging of the two ships.

They were invited to lunch at our house but neither of my ill parents could receive them, so my mother told me that I must act as hostess. It was probably a good experience for me, though someone must have helped me in this. We had several of the survivors stay at the house. In fact, there were always people from one place or another staying with us.

Another event about this time was the christening of the old cruiser, *San Francisco,* on October 27, 1889. Mary Scott, the daughter of the head of Union Iron Works where the ship was built, and I were chosen as sponsors. All I remember of this is standing on the platform built around the bow of the vessel and clinging to my bottle of champagne decorated with red, white and blue ribbons, which was hung from the side of the ship. However, the San Francisco *Chronicle* contemporaneously gave a full description, including the fact that the day was rainy, muddy and altogether disagreeable.

"The prospect would have disgusted an enthusiastic duck hunter equipped with the mighty boots of his calling," that paper said, "but the daintily shod fair ones never quailed." The *Chronicle* also stated that efforts of the ladies to avoid the quagmire resulted in "a display of feminine anatomy along four blocks of Kentucky Street that would have appalled the most reckless variety show."

Up on the platform the Mare Island Band played patriotic airs. Mary Scott was described as "dressed in blue" while "Miss Edith Benham, the twelve-year-old daughter of Commodore Benham, was attired in cream white, with a broad-brimmed white hat caught up at the side and trimmed with garnet." I was really fifteen at the time. The *Chronicle* estimated that ten thousand voices cheered as "the great vessel, moved by the impetus of the girlish blows, receded from the platform." The *San Francisco* was the last word in size, 328 feet long overall, 300 feet, 9 and ¾ inches at the waterline—smaller than a destroyer nowadays!

The people of San Francisco had enormous civic pride and the state had united with them in presenting a gorgeous silver service with solid gold bears, the emblem of the State of California, to this cruiser. My brother, who had returned from a two-year cruise in the Mediterranean and had just received his commission as an ensign, made his first cruise in her; many years later, my father made his last cruise in her when he hauled down his flag in the West Indies.

These happy three years at Mare Island came to a close all too soon. My father was detached and we went to Santa Barbara for the summer while he was awaiting orders. It was a primitive enough spot in those days. The streetcars were drawn by little burros with long flapping ears. There were many of the old Spanish adobe houses still in the town. I remember going out to a ranch in the country owned by one of the Diblee families. It seemed to me a colossal size, ten thousand acres, but they told me they owned another ranch of forty thousand acres.

Fortunately, living in a boardinghouse in Santa Barbara had prepared us for the little apartment we were able to afford in Brooklyn, New York, where we stayed while my father was fitting out to go in command of the South Atlantic Squadron. I was given the choice of going to Miss Porter's school in Farmington or getting some serious education at the Packer Institute in Brooklyn. I chose the latter and for two years took some special courses there to make up for the many deficiencies in my education.

We made great preparations for this cruise of my father's. He was to have the *Newark* as a flagship and he invited a certain lieutenant commander of the Navy to be his chief of staff. This gentleman declined because he could not stand the South Atlantic and the lack of desirable social contacts there. Finally, Lieutenant Commander Kilbourne accepted and as a very practical joke on the first man, the orders were changed and the *Newark* and the *Bennington* went to Europe to represent the U.S. at the festivals in Spain and Italy celebrating the four hundredth anniversary of the discovery of America.

Never did anyone miss out on so much high social life as did the lieutenant commander who scorned the South Atlantic Squadron. For the four hundredth anniversary of the voyage of Christopher Columbus was one of the most tremendous and prolonged multi-national patriotic celebrations of all times. It blossomed in the fall of 1892 in Spain, Italy, and New York City, where the Columbus Circle statue was dedicated on October 12th, with parades both naval and military. The next spring it continued in Havana, Cuba, the Virginia Capes, and New York City, building up to a mighty climax in the great World's Fair, the Columbian Exposition, in Chicago. My father had a leading role in the celebrations both abroad and in this country.

From Italy I have this letter from my father describing the festivities there:

U.S.S. Newark
Genoa, Sept. 21st, 1892

My dear little girl—

When Dar gets my letter of night before last she will be just too proud and haughty to live with, for I told her that the Duke of Genoa inquired after her and desired to be remembered, but she will get way up on her toes to hear that the Princess of Monaco admired her photo very much—as she did also those of you two little snips which I showed her. What strange tastes some women have! The Princess and her husband were on board for fully an hour and seemed to enjoy the visit very much, especially the Princess, who is very chatty and pleasant. Since then I have met them very often, and on Sunday afternoon went on board their yacht to an afternoon tea, where there were a lot of our set, Marquises, Counts, etc. and my friend the Duke of Genoa. Among the Marchesas (you would call it Marchioness in English) was the Marchesa of Spinoli whose father, T. J. Page, was the First Lieut. of the first ship I went to sea in. She is about fifty but a very handsome woman and must have been a beauty when young. Dr. Page at Mare Island is no doubt some relation of hers. Her father resigned on the breaking out of the war to join the Rebel navy. He is an old man now—84—and totally blind. They live at Florence where she gave me a most cordial invitation to come which, however, I can't accept on account of lack of time and a slight stringency in the money market.

I wish you could have been on board the French battleship Formidable and the Italian ship Lepanto to see the splendid receptions for the King and Queen. That aboard the Lepanto was rather ahead of the other because she is the larger ship, being nearly four times the size of the Newark or San Francisco, and has a magnificent deck for such purposes. The floral decorations combined with the different flags draped overhead as well as around the sides made a brilliant picture. There were about three thousand people there with a large sprinkling of the aristocracy. In fact, Marchionesses were so thick that it was necessary to shoo them away so as to get along from our end of the ship to the other. I was fortunate enough to be assigned to the Marchioness Razzi Martini who speaks English perfectly but was rather too popular for comfort as she stopped to chat with nearly every mother's son of the entire three thousand. So by the time I got her back to where she belonged my collar was wilted and I was in a state of partial collapse. Prior to these receptions two large parties were given on shore—one by the Marchioness Pallavicini, the other by the Prince Centurioni. The Pallavicini Palace is considered one of the handsomest in Genoa, inside; outside it doesn't show much better than dozens of others.

The frescoing though is splendid. There are also many very fine pictures. At the back is a beautiful garden which is reached by a sort of bridge from the reception rooms in the second story and contains lots of shrubs, flowers and some trees, together with grottoes, statuary and such like things. All our set was there except the Monacos.

The Centurioni palace isn't so handsome but the party was quite as brilliant. These two are perhaps the oldest families in Genoa and have, of course, lots of pretty things that have been handed down and added to.

I hope you will get on with your French. Who knows? The Lord may be good to us yet and give us enough money to allow of a trip over here after I have retired. Then you'll be glad enough of even a limited stock of French. It will freshen Dar up too to help you along with it. There is one thing certain, if I should come to Europe with you, one or the other would have to do my talking for I make an awful fist of it. I ask a fellow if he speaks French and when he says yes I get so awfully demoralized that I can't recall a word. Some of the people I have been thrown with are deserving of pity in being compelled to listen to my mixture of French, Spanish, Japanese and pigeon English I have fired at them when goaded to desperation by the necessity of saying, or trying to say, something, but the poor devils had to make believe they understood me too! One of these chaps always crosses the street when he sees me coming.

Now, young woman, that's enough of a letter for one as young as you.

Your loving old Pops

P.S. I expect to get away from here very soon but don't know when we shall go. You will most likely see the orders in the paper by the time I get them.

Little did I think that years later this would somewhat identify me in Rome with the King of Italy's uncle, the Duke of Genoa. Of course we could not afford to go to Europe and to travel from Italy to Spain meeting the ships at different ports, so we stayed on in Brooklyn, going occasionally to Annapolis, which I was old enough to enjoy then as a young lady.

Early the next Spring my father came back from Europe towing the three Columbus caravels used in the Spanish celebration at the Port of Palos—exact duplicates of the *Santa Maria, Pinta* and *Niña*. They had been built the year before in the shipyards of Barcelona and Cadiz, the United States government paying for the *Niña* and the *Pinta*, and the government of Spain giving the *Santa Maria* as her part of the celebration.

The caravels, trailing behind the ships of my father's squadron, took the same route to the New World that Columbus had taken, landing at Havana. There my father left the little Spanish ships, to join with three modern Spanish ships in helping Havana celebrate the coming of Columbus. This festival included the placing of new sculptures at Columbus' tomb in Havana. The caravels were later to come to Columbus celebrations at the Virginia Capes and New York City. Finally, through inland waterways, they would grace the Columbian World's Fair in Chicago.

My mother and I went down to Old Point Comfort to meet my father. We stayed at the Hygeia Hotel, a low wooden structure somewhat decrepit even then, but a proud place and considered very fashionable in the summer.

The great Naval Rendezvous made the old Hygeia the most famous hotel in America from April 9 through April 25, 1893. In that interval, thirty-two warships of nine nations, including the three little Columbus caravels, gradually gathered in Hampton Roads, to go on up to New York for the Naval Review of April 27, 1893. Every day we saw naval maneuvers in the Roads. Every night there was dancing at the Hygeia, which was popularly called "High Gee."

The first foreign ship in from the sea was the Russian cruiser *General Admiral*, arriving on the morning of April 9th. In two days it was joined by another Russian ship, the *Rynda*. These two wooden cruisers were strange-looking, with high black hulls and gracefully rigged masts. Later their flagship, the *Dmitri Donskoi*, arrived, and we went aboard to various parties. That was my first experience of seeing tea drunk from glasses. In the cabin of the flagship a samovar was always on the table with the tea glasses beside it. I was not a little surprised to see one night quite a large number of young men in sailors' uniforms coming into the ballroom of the Hygeia. They were obviously foreigners and I asked how they happened to allow the enlisted men in the hotel. One of the Russian officers laughed and said that with them their midshipmen always wear a sailor's uniform. I found that one of these "sailors" was Prince Yourievski, a big, good-natured boy whom I later knew quite well. He was the son of the Czar and his morganatic wife, the Princess Dolgorouky, who was living then on the Riviera with her numerous brood of children.

The British sent five ships, and I promptly deserted the American navy for the British. My father, in charge of the First Squadron, which included, besides the *Newark*, the *San Francisco* (my brother came in on her), the *Baltimore*, the *Atlanta*, the *Bennington* and the *Bancroft*, acted as sort of a special host to the British ships. Each of the ships under him was paired with one from the British.

All the ships in the Roads had parties aboard. There were three American admirals at Hampton Roads, and I happened to be the only girl in any of their families, so I had the lion's share of the entertaining. Then Father and Mother had a dance aboard the *Newark* for me—I suppose it was a debut party really. I can't say that this festivity was a particularly joyous one for me, because my mother never allowed me to dance until I saw that every other girl had a partner, and the usual number of sticky people with whom no one wanted to dance were there. I would approach some officer and ask him if he had met so-and-so. A wild look would come into his eye and he would say that he already had met her, and if he had a mean nature he would indicate some other man who he felt should have his turn of suffering.

The metropolitan press was well represented at the Rendezvous, and each day the New York newspapers would carry the news of the increasing fleet and of the social events at the Hygeia. One day it was reported that "200-odd representatives of the great species of American summer girl is now quartered at, or near the Hygeia." Norfolk staged an elaborate ball for the officers from the fleet, and a New York correspondent quipped: "It is whispered by the belles at the Hygeia that the Norfolk committee will attach three to five coupons to their ball tickets entitling the holder to 1 dance with a Naval officer—American, English, Russian, Turk or Prussian—so that the Norfolk girls can have one sure chance at the delights they have been monopolizing for two weeks." The Inaugural Ball for President Grover Cleveland, when he took over from President Benjamin Harrison, had been staged the month before, and it was boasted that the tickets to the Norfolk Ball cost more than did the tickets to the Inaugural Ball in Washington.

As the time approached for the fleet to go to New York there began to be fears that the three little Columbus caravels would not arrive from Havana. Word even went out that they might have to go directly to New York. Then on April 23rd, in they came to the Roads—"The Spanish Squadron and Their Three Tows." It was a sight which deserved the eye-witness account given in a newspaper that day:

"Before 10, all three Spanish men-of-war came plainly into view, each with a tiny ship, high-pooped and lateen-rigged like a painted property-piece from some fifteenth-century marine setting, dancing and tugging at the end of a long rope.

"These fantastic tows were the reproductions of the Niña, Pinta and Santa Maria, the ships of Columbus' first fleet of discovery, built with archeological exactness and constructed with infinite pains across the ocean to exhibit by contrast with modern vessels.

"The low, white-hulled cruiser Infanta Isobel, flagship of the squadron, led the way, towing the caravel Pinta, the ship of Columbus' hardy lieutenant, Pinzon. Next in line came the little torpedo boat, Neuva España, with the tiny Niña; while half a mile or more behind, the big, black-hulled protected cruiser Reina Regenda steamed tardily in, dragging at her stern Columbus' flagship, the heavier and more seaworthy Santa Maria."

Next day, Secretary of the War Herbert arrived aboard the yacht *Dolphin,* ready to make the trip to New York really official. It had already been arranged that the President and Mrs. Cleveland would board the *Dolphin* in New York Harbor to review the fleet, after which Mrs. Cleveland would return to Washington and the President would go on by special train to Chicago to open the Columbian Exposition.

My mother and I went on up to New York for the big review and the many social festivities that followed it. I remember that we were not allowed aboard the American ships, but the British said they had no such restrictions. So we had the proud privilege of taking actual part in this review from the British armored cruiser *Australia* as the ships steamed up the North River, the bands playing, their crews lining the deck, and the whistles of all the small boats in the harbor shrilling wide open.

At eight A.M. on the big day, they hoisted colors; at nine a cordon of patrol boats formed around the fleet; at ten-thirty President Cleveland was supposed to have reviewed them, but a sudden downpour of rain caused him to postpone it until one o'clock. Amazingly enough, the skies cleared, and he did board the *Dolphin* and ride up and down the river between the "two columns of floating steel." That night there was a searchlight exhibit from the ships; a banquet at the Waldorf honoring the fleet officers on the anniversary of General Grant's birthday; and at eleven P.M. the Naval Ball at Madison Square Garden.

The Madison Square Garden Ball that night was called "perhaps the most notable social gathering New York has ever seen." President Cleveland occupied a box, and so did Vice-President Adlai Stevenson. There were boxes for all the Admirals from this country and abroad. Even the Commanders of the Spanish Caravels had a box—Number 9. It was noted in the newspapers that there were four hundred present at the exclusive dinner which preceded the ball; and that Ward McAllister was at neither function, and no one even had a chance to ask if he'd had a chance to decline a place on any of the committees. New York was still smarting at his remark, made the year before, that even if Mrs. Astor's ballroom held only four hundred people it was big enough, since there were only about four hundred people in Society. There were about eight thousand people at the Naval Ball, which was otherwise made notable by crimson and gold decorations and flags galore—and one hundred singing birds trilling in the Grand Entrance on Madison Avenue.

There came a day, May 11, 1893, when the British vessels had to leave. It was a tragic day for me when I had to say good-by to the British fleet. My heart was evenly divided between two officers, and I know I wept when the *Australia* passed out to sea.

Chapter 4

WHEN FATHER ROLLED TO RIO

MY FATHER TRANSFERRED HIS FLAG to the *San Francisco*, which I had christened and on which my brother had served, and was off on another tour of duty, leaving my mother and me in Jamestown, Rhode Island, that little place dear to the hearts of Navy people.

However, at eighteen, I found nearby Newport a greater attraction. I spent a great deal of that summer in Newport with a friend, Mrs. Schuyler Hamilton, whose husband was a direct descendant of Alexander Hamilton. She was living in one of the cottages of Halidon Hall, where I had spent so many happy hours in childhood.

As my first introduction to any save Navy society, my family had a dance for me aboard the *San Francisco* in Newport Harbor when the ships came in. Soon I was in the full swing of Newport in the Nineties, having a wonderfully good time. I accumulated an admirer with a coach and four, and tried to look natural as we drove along world-famous Bellevue Avenue, that street of mansions called cottages. There lived the Vanderbilts, the Belmonts, the Goelets.

Most of the houses on Bellevue Avenue, as a matter of fact, were overimpressive in that they had comparatively little ground for the size of the house. But I did not notice for I was Cinderella riding in her coach.

Those were the days of fine horses, victorias with a coachman and a footman on the box—their coats folded just so. No vehicle was ever more flattering than a victoria to the lovely ladies with large hats and sweeping skirts who reclined therein, holding up their little ruffled parasols and looking very bored. As for livery, the color schemes went to all lengths, even to deepest mourning. I recall a contemporary of mine and her hatchet-faced mother swathed in long black veils, their coachman and footman in black, and black cockades at the blinders of their horses.

My own family had their friendships with the families in the old town of Newport itself, and there was where my father went to pay his respects on one of the matriarchs, Mrs. Breese. Halidon Hall was in a newer neighborhood—one of several fashionable places on the Narragansett Bay side of the island of Newport. Next door to the Hamiltons lived Mrs. Ludlow, great-aunt of Eleanor Roosevelt. The ultra-fashionables, like the Vanderbilts, were over on the ocean side. My grandmother, whose Staten Island family had been losing wealth as their former neighbors, the Vanderbilts, were making millions, was not overimpressed by my new friends. When I told her that I had been entertained on a yacht by one of the Lorillards, a family whose fortune came from tobacco before the Duke fortune did, my grandmother dryly commented, "Oh, yes, those snuff people who had a little shop on the Battery."

I was quite out of my element with the enormously rich people I was thrown with, a rank outsider really. Still, it was a heady experience. Tennis week came along, and people went to see Mrs. O. H. P. Belmont, a determined-looking dowager, and her daughter by her former marriage, Miss Gladys Vanderbilt, whose small head was set on a very long neck. The lowly also gazed upon Mrs. Ogden Goelet, and Mrs. Stuyvesant Fish. It was my impression that they all wanted the common herd to see them and admire them, and would have been very much disappointed if the common herd had not had a chance to look at them.

That summer my mother pasted in her scrapbook some New York society column accounts of the comings and goings of her daughter which noted that the Grand Duke Alexander of Russia was being lionized at the Newport garden parties. One article, describing Miss Benham "in an airy costume of white mull," closed with this devastating sentence: "Her mother has a cottage at Jamestown, but that is such a hopelessly dull place that Miss Benham much prefers Newport."

In retrospect I suspect that my family had the idea I was taking glamour and its attendant match-making too seriously, for suddenly it seemed imperative that I see the World's Fair in Chicago and take on a round of gaiety in New York.

Then orders came for my father to go to South America with the ships, as there was trouble brewing in Brazil. My brother Harry was sent to Alaska. It was decided that Mother and I would go to Paris, far from Newport, for my further education.

We crossed in a vile little steamer of the Red Star line. It took us days to get across the Atlantic and the only comfortable moment I knew was when we pulled into still waters on the trip up to Antwerp. The first landing in a strange country leaves an indelible impression—sights, sounds and smells are all different. We stayed in a tiny hotel near the Cathedral and I tried to stay awake all night listening to those lovely chimes. We did some sightseeing there, also in Brussels, and finally reached Paris, where we stayed for nearly two years in a *pension* on the corner of the Rue Boccador and the Avenue de l'Alma.

We had a few friends in Paris already and Mother had letters to the American Ambassador, Mr. Eustis, and to General and Mrs. Meredith Read. Mrs. Read turned out to be an old school friend of my mother's. The Reads were very kind to us all the time we were in Paris, and I remember many delightful parties at their apartment, which seemed to be swathed in tapestries.

Another friend we made in Paris was Mrs. Edward Drake. She was American, he English, and they had a lovely apartment on the Avenue du Bois de Boulogne with a ballroom and I remember many happy parties there. One night Mrs. Drake sent her carriage for us to go to a dinner followed by a dance. We were to stop for Mr. and

Mrs. Samuel Clemens (Mark Twain). I am sorry to say that he had an attack of gout and was in frightfully bad humor, so my memories of him are not as happy as they are of his books.

Of course, all was not gaiety in Paris. I studied French diligently and instead of the usual English-French translations, my teacher gave me those textbooks which the French children in the grammar schools used at the time. Then there were lectures at the Sorbonne and the Collège de France. At that period of ladylike history every young woman was supposed to play, sing or paint. My voice was a somewhat reedy affair, but I took lessons in a dark little apartment at the Cours Masset, up interminable flights of stairs, where a teacher from the Conservatory struggled with me. It did give me a taste for music which I am glad to have, but I can't say that it was a very useful accomplishment.

Some time that year, President Carnot was assassinated. We had called at the Ministry of Marine and we were sent cards from there requesting us to wear black and to view the funeral cortege as it passed by through the Place de la Concorde. At that time the statue representing the "lost Province" of Alsace-Lorraine was always draped with black. After the troops and the funeral bier with the horses swathed in black trappings had passed, there came the representatives sent by the foreign governments to attend the funeral. These walked on foot and I remember one magnificent man, six feet or more in height, dressed in a white uniform. As he passed and the crowd recognized him, they hissed him. He was a Uhlan, the Kaiser's representative, and the most hated of those Germans who had overrun France in 1870. He gave back in his steady insolent indifference hate for hate as he walked along behind the dead President's body.

Years later when I went to Paris with President and Mrs. Wilson and stood with Mrs. Robert Lansing on this same balcony of the Ministry of Marine, looking down on the cannon captured from the Germans during the war and watching the French troops as they formed the escort for the American President, I remembered this scene of years ago. The crepe was taken from the Strasbourg statue. *"Le revanche,"* of which I heard so much even in those days of the Nineties, was accomplished.

After a quiet summer spent in Normandy, we returned to Paris for the winter. A very much talked-of person that year was Miss Anna Gould, whom I used to see very often at Mrs. Drake's. Two French titled gentlemen were supposed to be vying for her hand and fortune and Count Boni de Castellane was the winner.

One morning, my mother and I were very much startled to see my father's name emblazoned in the cable dispatches of the Paris *Herald* and other papers. One example, in the long headlines of the day, shows the tenor of these articles: "Admiral Benham Teaches Brazilians a Lesson—American Shipping Fired Upon—Benham Remonstrated and Da Gama Very Curtly Refuses to Cease Troubling Merchant Vessels—Hostile Display on the Part of the Insurgents Brings a Shell from the Detroit—Insurgent Admiral Would Have Surrendered but for His Officers." In Rio harbor the first gun fired in hostility since the Civil War had sent a six-pound shot across the bows of the *Guanabara,* of the insurgents' fleet, on orders from my father.

A revolution had been on in Brazil for some time. An insurgent fleet, under Admiral da Gama, had become increasingly irritating to foreign shipping as well as to the Brazilian government. Admiral da Gama had issued an order that incoming merchant vessels could proceed to the docks only on certain days. As a regular blockade was not in force this was a somewhat high-handed proceeding. My father's squadron, on duty in Rio harbor to protect American shipping, was working under difficulties. Yellow fever was rampant, and he would transfer his flag from one ship to another, sending off all that could be spared so that there would be no yellow fever aboard them. The insurgents increased in aggressiveness from day to day, until they had incoming ships of all nations practically under their orders. The other countries had tacitly acquiesced to this situation but Admiral Benham decided the United States should not do this. He ordered the *Bennington,* commanded by Captain Willard Brownson, to convoy two American sailships into the harbor. The Brazil insurgents' flagship fired a blank cartridge at these ships, to which Captain Brownson promptly replied. After this interchange the *Bennington* and her convoy proceeded to the wharves and Admiral da Gama came aboard the *Newark* and virtually surrendered to my father.

For weeks my father was the hero of the headlines, and for the rest of his life any mention of Admiral Benham was linked with "that famous shot at Rio."

My mother and I suddenly became people of consequence in the American colony in Paris. The little salon which we had in our boardinghouse became crowded on Sunday afternoons. Everybody wanted to see the latest lion's relatives. Of course, we were very anxious for a time, not knowing what would happen, but we knew he had done the right thing. The only comment I remember that my father made was to send us a newspaper clipping that "Admiral Benham will soon be as famous in America as Jim Corbett."

After affairs had quieted down in Brazil he came with his ships to the West Indies. There I think the saddest moment of his life came when he had to haul down his flag. He had reached the retiring age of sixty-two. A friend on board wrote to me about it and said how much the officers hated to see his flag come down, and that, instead of the usual boat's crew to man the Admiral's barge to take him to the mail steamer which would bring him North, the young officers took the place of the bluejackets.

That autumn my father joined us in Paris. We studied French history vigorously and Paris from the antiquarian and historic viewpoints. We roamed around through the old quarter of the Marais; we read Victor Hugo's *Notre-Dame de Paris* and hunted in that quarter for reminiscences of the intriguing old palace of St. Pol.

My family became prime favorites with my young friends in the Latin Quarter and we would journey over there sometimes, riding on the top of omnibuses and sometimes, just to splurge, taking one of the little one-horse cabs to the different parties they gave.

This happy year drew to a close and we went to London for two months. Someone suggested that I should be presented at Court but that was out of the question on account of the expense connected with it. I was terribly homesick for Paris and the good times there and was not particularly sorry when we sailed for home, though I would have much preferred going back to Paris to live on and on.

Arriving in this country we went, of course, to the old house on

Staten Island. We were making plans to go to Washington to live. New York was out of the question and we had a number of friends in Washington, so we took some china, a few chairs and tables and moved into a little furnished house on Corcoran Street.

These first impressions of Washington were not very happy ones. Lindsay Poor, whom I had known in Paris, had come out the winter before. I had seen all of the lovely clothes she had bought and I remembered that my mother and Mrs. Poor had gone to the Bon Marché together and bought Bonnet silks. They were supposed to be the last cry in middle-aged elegance. They were a species of brocade and lasted for years. My mother's figured as a dress, then as a slip and finally a petticoat—for me, I think.

Lindsay Poor was very kind to me, brought several of her friends to see me, among them Belle Hagner, of an old Washington family who was destined to become the first social secretary at the White House. She was very handsome and one of the most popular girls who ever came out in Washington. Just the same, it was difficult coming to a perfectly strange place with no schoolgirl associations, no family associations and no money, and I wonder that I had as good a time as I did.

It was the last year of the Cleveland Administration. With other high-ranking officers of the Navy, we were invited to a reception. I think it must have been the Army and Navy Reception. This was, of course, some years before the Theodore Roosevelt remodeling of the White House, which cleared out much old clutter and made possible several entrances for incoming guests. But at that time, everybody came in at the front door. Facing that door was a terrible screen of colored glass which divided the front from the middle corridor. There were a few racks for coats but these were filled speedily. My father and brother had to put their uniform capes on top of some others on the floor and we left our evening wraps folded up in them.

I cannot remember where the President and Mrs. Cleveland stood. I don't remember even seeing them. I can recollect only the horrible mob, people walking on one's feet, dresses almost torn off the backs of their wearers, and after we had been shot through in front of the President and his wife I noticed that my father's epaulet was twisted over one ear. This one experience of a White House reception lasted us for some time.

We did not go again until the McKinley regime, when an old friend from New York, Mrs. Livingston Best, came down and implored my father to take her to the Diplomatic Reception. This may have been less crowded, because I do know we stood in what is now the long hall between the dining room and the East Room. There was a large staircase, later taken out by Theodore Roosevelt to enlarge the State Dining Room, which came down from the upper hall not very far from where the elevator is now. It was an impressive black walnut affair with, I think, a red carpet on it. We stood and watched the President and Mrs. McKinley come down, she very pretty and frail, followed by members of the Cabinet and various relatives. There was one lady, I think the wife of the Military Aide, who was upholstered in a creaking red satin dress. Miss Mabel McKinley, who was lame, carried a cane with a shepherdess crook at the top.

In the spring of 1897—it was the night of April 26th—the old Benham house on Staten Island was burned. My father had gone to New York for the dedication of Grant's Tomb. While he was on the train, a telegram came to us saying that the house had burned but my aunts and cousins had escaped with their lives and a few possessions. We did not try to catch my father on the train. We thought it best to let him have a few hours of pleasure before the devastating news reached him. Newspaper articles of the day listed some of the valuable historical collection destroyed by the fire—the rare souvenirs of my grandfather's early voyages, old records of Staten Island, and all my father's papers. My father went down immediately and found that the cottage on the place, happily, was unoccupied and that his sisters and brother had moved into it. Our dreams of bringing our own furniture to Washington had to be changed.

We took a lease for two years on the residence of friends who were going abroad, thus settling down into the I Street home of Jefferson Davis when he was Secretary of War. The library at the back had formerly had a back staircase leading down to the yard below, which in turn opened onto a small alley. Tradition had it that the Southern sympathizers used to come in through this alley up the back stairs to the library for conferences with Jefferson Davis. On the corner of our block lived Mrs. Harriet Lane Johnston, President Buchanan's niece and his very successful hostess in the White House. She was still a beautiful and gracious figure, and I do not wonder that she was so popular in London as hostess to her uncle when he served as United States Minister at the Court of St. James.

We settled down to the slow-moving social life that was Washington at the turn of the century, walking, driving, cycling, above all making social calls.

An extract from a letter from General Jackson to Mrs. Jackson in 1823 on a visit to Washington says, "There is nothing done here but vissitting and carding each othir—you know how much I was disgusted with those scenes when you and I were here, it has been increased instead of dimishing." Certainly it reached its apogee in the Nineties. Calling was almost a sacred rite. Every afternoon families and flocks of families could be seen starting out with white gloves, cardcases in hand, stern determination written across their countenances to call or die. Everybody had days "at home." Cabinet members were always at home Wednesdays and some of them had quite elaborate refreshments which attracted many hungry constituents. Other people had days at home, too. I think our section of the town had Thursday and I was planted behind the tea urn with cakes and sandwiches, and we felt very unhappy if quantities of people did not come.

Transportation was by foot or horse car for those who were not fortunate enough to own carriages. There was an extraordinary vehicle in use then, originally imported from Boston, called a "herdic." I do not see why one of these vehicles has not been enshrined in the Smithsonian Institution. They were square boxes on two wheels and the driver sat in front. They were upholstered in red velvet. There was a little box in the front window just behind the driver's seat where one deposited the money for the driver's fare. I think twenty-five cents was the usual price from place to place. The herdic opened at the back and when one drew up to a house for a call or an evening party, the horse always backed in and one got out that way. We were always allowed to go alone with the herdic drivers. They were supposed to be "so safe."

I do not known whether any other part of the country enjoyed the herdics. We even had large ones which plied up and down Sixteenth Street. They must have had a special breed of horses for them for they were all uncommonly fat and uncommonly lazy.

A woman's club had been started at 1710 Eye Street and I became a member of that. It had a current events class and the members rehashed the newspapers for their own and their neighbors' benefit. There were also card clubs within this club. In those days it was supposed to be quite intellectual and quite exclusive and characters were carefully scrutinized before admission. In the ballroom of this old house, annually, two cotillions were given that might be called "the last stand of the Aborigines." I refer, of course, to the "cave dwellers"—a race apart, born in Washington of unimpeachable lineage.

We had secured entrance to some of this charmed collection through the good offices of one of them, Mrs. Edward Very, daughter of a former commandant of the Marine Corps, who had lived in Paris for years. Her cousins and relatives called upon us and I remember hearing it said that one of these ladies always kept her grandmother's visiting list and only the descendants of that lady's contemporaries were admitted on her own visiting list. Of course there must have been some latitude because we were there. I suppose someone had died off and there were no eligible descendants at the moment to fill up the membership.

For the two cotillions the lists were carefully scanned and it was said that names with too recent a taint of trade were obliterated from consideration. I can see now the row of ladies forming at the reception committee, most of them in dresses of daring décolletage showing as far as the collarbone. One exception to this list was the Countess Esterhazy, née Carroll. She was a very charming person with a lovely voice and must have been a great beauty when young.

An amusement which really started somewhat earlier than this was bicycling. In Paris we had seen the first lady bicyclists who, I am afraid, were denominated "hussies" by my parents, because the real enthusiasts appeared in knickerbockers and coats. For some time

I was not allowed to ride. Then my brother arrived and overrode their objections, so an extraordinary costume was made by my mother and me. It was what was called a "divided skirt" and had long flowing petticoats on either leg, which was supposed to be very modest and give the illusion of skirts while riding the bicycle. I think I also had another skirt, short, with pants underneath.

Every Sunday in Washington, a large party started off, sometimes as many as twenty of us. Often we would go to Great Falls. The road was not finished then beyond Cabin John and it was rather rough riding to the Falls, but lovely. At Cabin John Bridge was an inn in the worst style of Queen Anne. There we would get very good chicken dinners and waffles. Other times we carried our luncheon along with us tied to the backs of our seats in neat little parcels.

Part of our route lay past the Chesapeake & Ohio Canal, that historic landmark, whose tow-path became the delightful meeting place of all who loved long walks. In later years it was a lovely walk to go down the Canal, either by motoring out to Great Falls and walking down to Cabin John, or going to Rockville, thence to Pennyfield's Lock and walking down from there to Great Falls. Pennyfield's was quite an institution. Here President Cleveland often came for bass fishing, rest and relaxation. Mrs. Pennyfield was a character. No matter when we arrived she would always say, "I haven't a thing for you to eat, but walk up the Canal a little ways and I'll see what I can find." When we returned there was an enormous meal—fried chicken, a ham, sometimes the Pennyfields' homemade sausages and several kinds of preserves on the table, and pie. It is hard to imagine how we ever had the strength to walk the eleven or twelve miles down to Great Falls after this feast. After President Theodore Roosevelt issued his famous order requiring officers of the Army and Navy to walk or ride a certain number of miles each month, I used to take these walks with different friends.

Still later, some enterprising spirits started a club in the old Lock Tavern Inn at Great Falls. This I joined and we could spend the night there or go out for the day and rent canoes and paddle up and down the Canal. Comparatively few Washingtonians really knew this Canal or enjoyed walking on it. It was almost a fraternity, these walkers on the Canal. One would meet people one had never seen before and suddenly plunge into unexpected discussions of art, literature and nature, as the Canal boats drawn by mules and their sometimes profane drivers passed by. If my picture of the Canal in those bygone days seems to suggest an atmosphere of romance as well as nostalgia, I should have to admit its truth. During the early 1900's, I spent many happy hours there with the man who was later to be my husband.

While in the Eye Street house my brother Harry married a beautiful girl, Elizabeth Riley, of Washington. One newspaper termed the ceremony at St. Thomas Church, near Dupont Circle, "the most brilliant of all weddings of the post-Lenten season," and "the ushers, all brother officers of the bridegroom, were, like him, in full uniform." When Harry and his bride came back from their wedding trip we had a reception for them, and shortly after that he went to the West Indies.

The family whose home we had been occupying came back from Europe and we had to find another place to live. We bought some furniture and moved into a house whose number certainly spelled ill luck and we had it there—1313 Twentieth Street. We had not been there very long when a telegram came one morning saying that Harry, who was in command of the *Truxtun*, was stricken with appendicitis at Key West and very ill. Later, another telegram came that he had died. This was the first break in this happy family circle. It seemed unbelievable. There is always incredulity when a young person comes face to face with death. This sort of thing had happened to other people, but we did not see how it could happen to us. A year later my father died of nothing else but a broken heart, and so ended that phase of my life and another existence began for my mother and me.

Chapter 5

BLAZING A TRAIL TO THE WHITE HOUSE

OF COURSE I HAD REALIZED that when my father died I should have to do something to earn a living. Nowadays people are more farseeing and girls start careers earlier. But in 1905 comparatively few careers were open to women.

However, my working life began at a fortunate time—for one of my background and experience. That autumn, Nellie Hunt, the pioneer of the social secretaries of Washington, had announced her engagement. She really started this line of work, others, like Belle Hagner, Helen Squire and Laura Harlan, following in her footsteps. Nellie turned part of her work over to me. Two months after my father's death on August 11, 1905, I had started my first business contacts as social secretary.

Nellie Hunt had told me what I should ask when I went to be looked over by Mrs. Ion Perdicaris, wife of the man whose capture by brigands under Raisuli in Morocco had startled the whole world, and had caused President Theodore Roosevelt to instruct Secretary of State John Hay to send that famous cable to the Sultan of Morocco, "Perdicaris alive or Raisuli dead."

Mr. Perdicaris, the son of naturalized American parents born in Greece, had gone into a career which took him overseas. He had married in London a widow with two children, and for a time they made their home in Tangiers, in a country place just outside the walls. It was there that the bandits broke in and carried off Mr. Perdicaris, an American citizen. The Republican National Convention of 1904 happened to be on when word of his case reached this country. Theodore Roosevelt, running for the nomination, proceeded to give a dramatic illustration of how he protected American citizens in foreign lands. In less than three days after the cable was sent, Mr. Perdicaris was released without payment of the ransom demanded by the bandits, and he cabled his thanks to the State Department. But the experience of having been carried off and held for weeks was a shattering one for a delicate man. They had therefore come to Washington for a change and had an apartment at Stoneleigh Court.

Like a condemned criminal I gave my name at the desk and with shaking knees went upstairs for the interview. A tall, elderly gentleman with a beard streaked with gray met me and he seemed as embarrassed as I. Some months afterward when I told them how frightened I was, he confessed that he was equally so at interviewing a lady secretary. I presented my credentials and then he asked what salary I expected. I told him and nearly added, "But I am not worth half as much as that." But they took me, and my duties were to accompany Mrs. Perdicaris, who was somewhat of an invalid, when she went to tea, to drive with her and to look out for her affairs, including the drawing of checks. This first check-drawing was a terrible performance. I had never written one in my life, but I stood shamelessly over her and watched her as she drew one and then raced down to the bank to get a little instruction on the subject.

There never was a happier winter, never kinder people than these two. They treated me like their own child and certainly my lines fell in happy places when my working life started with these two dear friends. One of my most treasured possessions is an autographed photograph from Mr. Perdicaris with the inscription, "A brave heart is the most precious endowment."

I had other interesting employers.

Senator Murray Crane of Massachusetts, who ran his state, was a great political figure but I remember him as a little man who came to the sitting room I used as my office, each morning shortly after I arrived at nine o'clock to report for work as social secretary to Mrs. Crane. He always appeared wearing slippers, sat down in front of the wood fire, and said, "Well, Miss B., what do you think of the political situation?"

Theodore Shonts, engineer who first tried to "dig" the Panama Canal, for whose wife I was social secretary at another early stage of my career, is a shadowy figure in my memory. But I remember his wife, a woman of great wealth, who entertained lavishly for their two daughters. One daughter is now the Duchess of Chaulnes. Their Washington home was the handsome house on New Hampshire Avenue which is now the Woman's National Democratic Club.

A new Russian ambassador came to Washington, Baron Rosen, who had known my family in Japan. He and Baroness Rosen wanted someone who would walk with their young daughter, Elisabeth, and also do some secretarial work.

Elisabeth was an extremely pretty girl with lovely reddish-blond hair, and brown eyes with arched eyebrows which she told me came from a Georgian ancestor. She was full of temperament and most amusing. When her father and mother went out to dinner I used to dine with her. Sometimes we read, but she was always more anxious to learn about current affairs. Like most European girls, her reading had been strictly supervised and I remember squirming uncomfortably when she spoke about Shakespeare and said, "Now, Peter [her pet name for me], I want to know the truth about Lucretia." I told her it was an old scandal and she had better not rake it up.

The Russian Embassy was then at 1634 I Street, not a particularly comfortable house. It was built on the site of the house in which Secretary of the Navy and Mrs. Benjamin F. Tracy lived, and in which Mrs. Tracy and two daughters were burned to death in 1890. In those days the Russian Embassy was run on really regal lines. They had a wonderful chef and the door was usually answered by a tall Russian in Cossack uniform with various deadly-looking weapons stuck in the belt which confined his blouse. I remember years later a certain Mrs. Malaprop among the staff of the White House, speaking of this man or his successor, saying: "I saw Madame Bakhmetieff with her Cassock or Hassock!" Another time, apropos of one of the military aides, she said, "I hear that he has charge of the profligating gardens down on the Potomac!"

Every day the Embassy staff, following a custom peculiar to the Russian diplomatic service, lunched with the Ambassador and his wife. Baron Rosen really loved America and Americans. He said that his dream had always been to come back as Ambassador to the United States, ever since the days when he had been Secretary of Legation under Baron Struve. He spoke English perfectly, could even understand American jokes, and really did like us tremendously.

In the following spring Baroness Rosen asked me to come up North with them and stay as long as I wanted, just as a friend and for rest and change. It was an interesting and exciting experience, this life conducted in a strictly Russian household and in Russian ways. When I sat down to write my first letter from there the letter paper of the Imperial Russian Embassy seemed St. Petersburg transported to the United States.

Every morning we had the usual continental breakfast. At eleven o'clock the Ambassador and anyone who wanted could have sandwiches and with them were served various kinds of distinctly hard liquor. They had a French cook and at luncheon or dinner one was sure of having delicious French dishes. The Russian Embassy chef was French, but a cook was discovered who knew all the Russian dishes and for the first time I had borsch. With that were served little pastries which one does not have in the ordinary so-called Russian restaurants nowadays.

My happy associations at the Russian Embassy lasted for two years. Then Baron Rosen was recalled to go on the Conseil d'Etat in Russia. They left with great reluctance, particularly Baron Rosen. I do not think the Baroness ever cared as much for this country, and she was eager to return to Europe so that her daughter might "come out" there. They went to St. Petersburg, where Elisabeth was named one of the ladies of the Court, and I heard from them only occasionally. Happily, they were in Paris when the Russian Revolution broke out. Everything they had was swept away. They came later to this country and Baron Rosen published his recollections.

Through Mrs. Cowles, sister of President Roosevelt, I started work at the British Embassy with the wife of the Ambassador, James Bryce, later to be Viscount Bryce. For two years I climbed the Victorian black walnut staircase, passed under the portrait of the young Queen Victoria up to a singularly cold room over the porte-cochere where I worked very pleasantly on calling and reception lists for Mrs. Bryce. I remember she once said that at times it was rather embarrassing to have people consult her husband on questions of American politics. One story she told me was that one of the perennial visitors said she had been calling on all the Cabinet and had to see Mrs. Bryce—probably as the wife of a minister without portfolio. And of course it was true that he knew this American Commonwealth of ours better than many of us do. It was long before he was Ambassador that he wrote *The American Commonwealth*, still considered one of the greatest books on the subject ever written.

The Bryces lived as simply as their position would allow. Mr. Bryce arose at a very early hour and walked briskly around the British Embassy before his breakfast. They did not entertain very extensively—two large receptions a year and some dinners. I remember pouring tea one afternoon for a Canadian group and being told very firmly by one of the ladies not to "give us any American slops."

I remained on the Embassy staff when the Bryces were succeeded by Sir Cecil and Lady Spring-Rice. Lady Spring-Rice was the daughter of Lord Lascelles, who had been the British Ambassador to Germany at one time. She was a very sweet-looking woman of a delicate blond English type, with two little children.

I was going along very happily in October of 1915 and had made all my arrangements for my winter's work. I had to go to New York and on the train I read the announcement that Belle Hagner, the White House Secretary, had just announced her engagement. Somehow that struck a cold chill to my heart. I had a premonition that she might ask me to take her place. I kept saying to myself that it was all nonsense, that there were many others of her friends who were much better fitted than I for the position. But when I got home my mother told me that Belle had called up, and my heart went down deeper still. President Wilson's engagement to Mrs. Edith Bolling Galt had just been announced and Belle's engagement came at about the same time.

I did not want this work at all because the pay was very small and it meant a continuous job all the year round, whereas I could make almost as much in the winter and could have the summer for myself. Then I knew the endless demands on a White House secretary and how much blame was always attached to her about things with which she had nothing to do. It always seemed to me that to be a White House secretary one could paraphrase the inscription over Dante's Hell to read, "All ye who enter here leave friends behind." Belle spoke to me about the work and I pointed out all the other eligibles. There seemed to be various reasons why they could not take the job and Belle could not be married unless I took it, and so, bleating feebly, I entered into the position for a two weeks' trial.

Belle Hagner had been brought in by Mrs. Theodore Roosevelt as social secretary to help with the greatly increased entertainment problems which followed the 1902 remodeling of the White House. Miss Hagner remained throughout the Taft administration, and then saw President Wilson and his first wife through the White House weddings of two of their three daughters. Then Mrs. Wilson died, and Margaret Wilson had little appetite for the duties as hostess, in which she had the help of the President's cousin, Miss Helen Bones.

When I joined the White House Staff I did not know any of the White House family save Miss Bones, and her very slightly. Mrs. Galt I had never met but I knew her by sight—a very beautiful woman who sat near us at church.

As I recollect, the vocal reactions of Washington society when President Wilson was elected and before I went to the White House were many. The Republicans had been in power since President Cleveland. It was felt that a college professor, one who was supposed to entertain radical ideas toward big business similar in many respects to those of Theodore Roosevelt, would be socially upsetting.

Probably most of the older generation have forgotten the storm that arose when President Wilson declined honorary membership in the Chevy Chase Club. This was cited as a proof of social radicalism. In reality he was averse to accepting honorary membership in anything, preferring to pay his dues in the clubs which he might wish to join.

Although I had had a good deal of experience over eight years, the White House job was entirely different from the ordinary social secretary job. I had to learn to dictate and Mr. Ralph Magee, who was then my stenographer, was kind and patient to my faltering tongue as I tried to put ideas on paper through his clever fingers. The mail seemed perfectly terrible. Requests for clothing, requests for work, announcements of babies, and, at this time, congratulations to be answered for Mrs. Galt. I was sitting at my desk one day struggling over all this mail when I looked up and I saw Miss Bones with a tall, very lovely person whom I recognized as Mrs. Galt. She was very sweet and gracious to me and I felt at once that I should like nothing better than to be with her. For the six years that I was at the White House, the association was a very happy one for me.

After the marriage of President Woodrow Wilson and Mrs. Galt at her home in December of 1915, we had to start in with the social program, which had to be varied very much on account of the war. There could be no Diplomatic Reception with the members of the Embassies of the warring countries pitchforked in together into the Green Room. There was, however, a Pan-American Conference going on at that moment and it was decided to supersede the Diplomatic Reception with a reception to this Pan-American body.

I had been told that my duties consisted of making out only the social list; that the official lists would all be given me by the State Department and the office of the Secretary to the President. I have never known just what happened to the other lists. Apparently everyone who asked for an invitation received one, and the night of the reception a goodly percentage of the six thousand people who were invited stormed the East Entrance and the South West

Entrance. When I came downstairs the noise from the lower halls where the crowds had congregated sounded like a gigantic beehive broken loose. The crush was terrible. The enormous curiosity to see the second Mrs. Wilson had brought the crowd. The President and Mrs. Wilson stood for hours shaking hands.

After that experience the President sent me a note to say that I was to take over all the lists, that all requests for invitations would be referred to me. The official requests—those from senators and representatives—were referred directly to him.

At that time, following the custom inaugurated by President Taft, somewhat elaborate refreshments were served—salad, sandwiches and the like—and the crowds literally stampeded the tables in the dining room. Also, the sacred "behind the lines" custom existed. That was one of the most undemocratic forms of White House protocol. The President and his wife received in the Blue Room; the Vice-President and the Cabinet and their wives stood in a line beside them and one was supposed to shake hands or bow to each one of these people. A red rope or cord was stretched in front of this line and the same rope was stretched across the two entrances of the Blue Room. To be behind the line was considered a mark of great social distinction, and many were the heartburnings and fights of those who were not asked in, or who tried to force an entrance into the Blue Room and stand behind the President and his wife and the Cabinet and watch the people go by.

An aide was usually stationed at the door between the Red Room and the Blue Room to admit those entitled to entrance to this sacred spot. Ex-Ambassadors would come up and announce in important tones who they were and insist that they were entitled to the privileges of the Blue Room; and other Ex's and Is's would also tell those poor young men who they were and demand admittance. Of course, the female of the species was more deadly than the male and the White House Social Secretary was always being summoned to arbitrate the claims of ladies and their spouses, or ladies alone. One day Mrs. Wilson called me in for a conference and "behind the lines" was quietly abolished.

Diplomatic relations in Washington were very tense when the social season opened in the winter of 1916. Instead of one Diplomatic Dinner, two had to be given. The first, on January 21st, was to the Allies, with the neutrals favorable to them among the South American and European countries also invited; the second, on January 25th, was to the Central Powers, with the countries favorable to *them* invited. The balance had to be very finely kept. One dinner could not be more important than the other and the countries sending their representatives to this last dinner had to make as good a showing as to the first, although I think most of the countries were more inclined to the Allies than to the Central Powers.

The lists of the dinners show how carefully they were arranged. The State Department, as usual, did all of this fine work, and on Mr. Charles L. Cooke's shoulders fell most of the responsibility for the actual seating. There was no office of Protocol at that time. One of the Assistant Secretaries of State, usually Mr. William Phillips or Mr. Breckinridge Long, arranged for the seating of these dinners, but the list of precedence was given as always by the State Department.

No Diplomatic Reception could be held at this time, as it was not possible to separate the guests as was done by giving two Diplomatic Dinners. So instead of four state receptions, only three were given, starting with the one to the Judiciary which usually followed the Diplomatic; next came the Congressional, and then the Army and Navy.

About this time the dancing mania struck the country. Fathers, mothers, uncles, aunts and grandparents fell victims to the craze. Joints going rheumatic cracked under the two-step and hesitation waltz. To accommodate the devotees an "Administration" dancing class was formed. I think the originators were Mr. and Mrs. Huston Thompson and a small group. Margaret Wilson, Helen Bones and I all joined and I am amused now when I think of the various gentlemen of the Senate and House and prominent Government officials who were members and who plodded through the new steps.

In looking over the engagement book for this winter, I find that things must have been very gay for Miss Wilson, who was here all during the winter, and for Miss Helen Bones, the President's cousin. There were a great many dances and dinners given for them. The President and Mrs. Wilson seldom went out socially, but did attend a reception given by the Congressional Club, an organization composed of the wives of Senators and members of Congress.

The President and Mrs. Wilson went to the theater a great deal, and a few friends like Mr. and Mrs. Cleveland Dodge and Colonel and Mrs. Edward M. House came to stay in the house. Mrs. Wilson's large family, of course, were there a great deal.

As the war threatened to come close to our shores, various reserve officers' camps were opened, and there even was a National Service Training School started in which various enthusiastic ladies of the capital enrolled. It was a frightful sight to behold one's contemporaries in most unbecoming uniforms which emphasized every lumpy spot. We had had a decent camouflage before short skirts came along. These uniforms tore away many pleasing illusions. I recollect that this school was moved out on the road to Cabin John, where the ladies encamped and with enormous energy learned wigwagging and other arts peculiar to the military service. This was really more an outlet for patriotism than anything else.

In the spring of 1916 Mrs. Wilson inaugurated the teas for the graduating classes of schools in and around Washington, for the evil of bringing children to the night receptions had been steadily increasing and there seemed absolutely no way to cope with it. Little girls from eight years on were brought by adoring parents to shake the hand of the President and his wife, and the private schools published in their prospectuses that the pupils would receive invitations to the White House during the winter. They usually appealed to their senators and representatives for such invitations.

Prior to World War I it was customary to have four musicales in addition to the State Dinners. There was usually music after the State Dinner. The musicales were on other nights and separate invitations were sent for them. So that there should be no favoritism behind the four musicales, and the four garden parties which come in May, the names were taken alphabetically and people divided in four parts, which gave them a pleasing sensation of being sure that they would see their fellow alphabetists.

There was one terrible night when everything seemed to go

wrong. Paderewski was the artist. A special piano had been brought in, as either his contract did not allow him or he did not wish to play on the White House gold piano. After several crashes and clashing chords every aide seemed to drop his sword and people knocked over chairs. Paderewski, who was extremely sensitive to noise, nobly paid no attention to this. But the crowning episode was when a congressman, who had dined well but not wisely, arose, called out to the President, and asked if Paderewski could not play something cheerful, mentioning some popular air of the time. It was also at this same terrible musicale that a scion of one of the South's most distinguished families was taken ill and I had to escort her downstairs and remove a species of armor which she wore around her neck. I found afterward it was a pair of shoe buckles, placed on a velvet ribbon, which once belonged to George Washington.

At that time it was customary for people wishing to meet the President's wife to write notes asking if she would receive them. There was no particular distinction drawn about who should or should not write. It was not a widely known custom, and the number of people whom the President's wife had to receive in 1916, and prior to that time, was comparatively small. Mrs. Wilson usually received at tea in the Red Room. She stood at the door with an aide beside her, and the small group of twenty or thirty people who came were given tea by me at a tea table in one corner of the room.

In those days the President and his wife went to the house of each member of the Cabinet once during the season for a dinner. Of course, after our entry into the war all official entertaining ceased.

I attended that fateful session of Congress when President Wilson delivered his war message. For days—and nights too—afterward, I spent any spare hour that might come along in the gallery of Congress, hanging on every word of debate about the war and its conduct.

Like all the other women in official life, I turned to patriotic service. Mrs. Franklin D. Roosevelt, then wife of the Assistant Secretary of the Navy, and some other women had organized the canteen service of the Red Cross. It was really under semi-military discipline and it seems rather amusing now to think that these ladies had titles, major, etc., but it had to be done in this way because they took regular tours of duty, and every woman was assigned the hours she would have to report. She was also subject to call in case either someone had failed to appear or an extra number were needed to take care of the men passing through Washington on the large troop trains.

I had comparatively little to do at the White House, but I had to be there during the day and then, of course, there were home duties with my mother. So late afternoon and night were the only times I could be on duty. The head of the canteen, Mrs. Mason Gulick, very kindly allowed me to take duty at this time and I served as a high private in the rear ranks, without officer's uniform or any of the other insignia of rank, which of course I did not deserve as I did not do the work these other women did.

My services started in the late winter of 1917 or early spring of 1918. For security reasons it was not possible to hire cleaning women to keep the place in order. Margaret Wilson started to work about the same time and I think that both she and I shone as floor scrubbers and dishwashers. Later Mrs. Wilson herself joined up with this canteen, carrying to the troop trains trays of cigarettes, picture post cards and other articles.

Our headquarters was a small frame building situated between the railroad tracks about a mile and a half from Union Station. We had to scramble down a steep hill to get to this place, which was fearfully cold and drafty in winter and equally hot in summer.

The hut consisted of two or three rooms. The largest was for the preparation of sandwiches which we cut and spread with various jams, and a field kitchen—the most infernal contraption I have ever seen—which the Army had loaned to the canteen service. It ate the most enormous quantity of wood and required constant feeding. We had to drop huge bags of coffee into the boilers over the fires—at great danger to life and limb. When our superior officers were notified that a troop train or one of the drafts was coming through, we had to start our preparations for coffee and jam sandwiches. Occasionally requests came for ham or some other food from the officers commanding these trains. The men were on them for a long time in transit from the various training camps, and the coffee and sandwiches were most welcome.

We also had a small room where we sold, at cost, cigars, cigarettes, chewing tobacco, picture postcards and candy bars. Here Mrs. Roosevelt shone. We had to make change at quick order when the men were lined up buying these supplies and we were supposed to turn over our finances in perfect order to the incoming shift. In all my experience there were only two women whose financial affairs were in perfect condition. One was Miss Mary Patten and the other, Mrs. Roosevelt. I remember the latter evolved a scheme for accounting for the money. I do not know how successful it was, but I was very much impressed by it and also by her efficiency. I am always amused when people seem to think that Mrs. Roosevelt sprang suddenly into usefulness, either as the President's wife or as the wife of the Governor of New York. In reality she started her career of usefulness and efficiency years before those days, and added to it as time went on, enlarging her interest in things concerning women and in civic matters with the years. My remembrance of her in those early years was as a delightful person to work with.

Starting in April of 1917, a series of Allied Missions came to this country—British, French, Italian, Russian, Canadian, Japanese. These Missions came to present their needs, financial and economic. What they needed, of course, as we have since found out somewhat to our own cost, was money, materiel and foodstuffs. Liberty Loans were floated to provide for the costs of war not only for us, but for our Allies.

The British and the French Missions came practically together. The British Mission, which was headed by Mr. Balfour, had its dinner first, with the Chief Justice of the Supreme Court, the Speaker of the House, the Cabinet and the entire Mission. This was a men's dinner and included the Chiefs of Staff of the Army and Navy, the aides and some of the assistant secretaries.

We were all thrilled when we saw the first horizon blue of the French army on the streets, and the whole city went wild when the French Mission arrived. People lined the streets of the city. Of course, Marshal Joffre was the great hero, although Mr. Viviani, the former French Premier, headed the Mission. The popularity of Marshal Joffre was a constant source of unhappiness to Mr. Viviani.

With all the Missions as they came to this country trips were made down the river to Mt. Vernon on the Presidential yacht, *Mayflower*. French speaking was at a premium and the men who passed through the barrage of frightful French that was delivered to them must have been ready for the first-line trenches afterward.

The next Mission was the Italian—a somewhat more ornamental affair which did not, I think, excite the same interest as the British and French. The Italians had come later into the war and we were not as sympathetic with them as with the others. It was headed by Prince Udini, a cousin of the King of Italy. Women were excluded from most of the dinners to the Missions, since the members of the Belgian, Russian, Japanese and Serbian Missions were not accompanied by women.

Washington had been very quiet socially since we entered the war, and people were glad to have this opportunity, not only to entertain our Allies, but to entertain themselves as well. I find various notes and letters about the dinners and other events of that summer. A somewhat amusing dinner I went to was given by Secretary of State and Mrs. Robert Lansing for the members of the Russian Mission. They had landed at Seattle, I think, and were met there by representatives of the State Department, one of whom told me that as he watched them coming down the gangplank he made mental note that this one should have his hair cut, that one should get a suit of clothes. Evidently they had not had time to do this when they came to the Lansings' dinner. I remember one who was in a white uniform, evidently self-designed. The Czarist government, of course, had fallen and this was the interim government headed by Kerensky. There had been no time to arrange for diplomatic uniforms, so this man had on a short white jumper effect, somewhat like a mess jacket. The original purity of the white was somewhat marred by a voyage across the Pacific and the trip across the continent. Another man had evidently been taken out to buy a dress suit. He found one ready-made which fit around the middle section of his anatomy but left the sleeves dangling uncomfortably over his finger tips. At dinner I was opposite these gentlemen and I was fascinated at the technique displayed when they ate their soup. One tucked his napkin into his collar and his spoon had the lifting effect of a water mill as he conveyed it with rhythmic scoops to his mouth.

Sometime in summer of 1918 was held the first garden party for those who had been wounded in the war. Mrs. Wilson had made many visits to the Walter Reed and Naval Hospitals, and both she and the President wanted, if possible, to bring a little pleasure into some of these wrecked lives. This garden party was for those who were able to come to it. It was a tragic enough affair. There were men whose legs had been shot away, men who had to be almost carried onto the grounds, but they were the most cheerful. The Red Cross attended to the transportation and the housekeeper, Mrs. Jaffray, supplied unusually large, thick sandwiches with ample slices of ham or tongue between, as well as ice cream, for male appetites were not used to the wafer-thin articles provided at afternoon teas. This first party was a great success and it has been carried on nearly every spring since.

That autumn, even before the Armistice—both the false one and the real—there were rumors that the President might go abroad for the peace negotiations.

Thinking back on the Armistice and the false report that it was signed November 7th, I can see myself in my Ford car, part of a delirious crowd, going down Pennsylvania Avenue. A bluejacket and a soldier jumped aboard my car and asked if I would take them to Union Station as their leave was over and they had to be back in Philadelphia at a certain hour. During the war it was the unwritten law to pick up any man in uniform and take him wherever he might want to go, and I can see myself chugging along Pennsylvania Avenue, part of that throng which cheered its throat out on the day the false Armistice was announced. I think we were so worn out on the real day, November 11th, that we could do nothing more than utter hoarse cheeps.

Chapter 6

ROMANCE AND GREAT ADVENTURE

It has always seemed to me the most difficult thing in the world for a woman to write about her marriage and her married life. If the marriage has been a happy one, many tender memories are too intimate to be shared with others.

I have always felt that the love letters of Elizabeth and Robert Browning were written with an eye to publication and were not examples of spontaneous affection. They were too studied. I would have liked the Brownings better—and their heirs also—if those letters had never been published.

Of course I could not write my memoirs and leave out my husband, Rear Admiral James M. Helm. But it is difficult for me to try to put into words what he meant to me and the part he played in my life. We had only seven happy years of marriage before his death in 1927. In them I have had my full share of happiness.

My first memory of my husband was at Mare Island, when he was a young lieutenant and my father was commandant of the Yard. That was (as my husband always said) when I was a "long-legged girl of 14." I recollect him then as a big man with a blond mustache which fortunately disappeared later in life.

My father's Mare Island tour of duty ended, and I went on to New York, Newport, Paris, London and Washington. The young lieutenant I had known at Mare Island also went on with his Navy career. It was not until many years later, when he was on duty in Washington, that we became engaged. Circumstances delayed our marriage until I was in my middle forties. I have always said that being married at that ripe age gave heart to many another old maid and several other happy marriages resulted from this pioneer venture of mine, for which I am truly grateful.

Admiral Helm was always extremely modest about what he had done. I think he allowed himself a feeling of pride only in his record at the U.S. Naval Academy, which he entered in 1871 as a boy of sixteen, coming from the little town of Athens, Tennessee, where his family had moved from Grayville, Illinois, when he was four. In speaking of his first year at the Academy, he always said he was sure the officers pulled him through out of the kindness of their hearts, because he was so poorly prepared for the Academy's strict requirements. But after the first year he found what it was all about and was graduated second in his class.

Of course the classes were not as large then as they are now, but that really meant a great deal for a country boy whose parents had very little money and nothing to spare for any tutoring or any other help to prepare him for the rigors of Academy life.

He saw action in the Spanish-American War—and strangely enough, even for that long-past conflict, in a little sailing ship, the *Hornet,* of which he was captain. His Spanish-American War citation describes "eminent and conspicuous conduct in battle," for which he was advanced five numbers in rank on February 11, 1901.

It was on June 30, 1898, that his little ship met the enemy. The citation's terse words tell the story: "On the occasion of the conflict between a flotilla of U.S. gunboats and a Spanish flotilla and shore batteries at Manzanilla, Cuba, when the vessel which he commanded, 'The Hornet,' was disabled from moving by a shot received through her main steam pipe, and was much embarrassed by the escaping steam. Consequently upon injury, he continued his effective and active fire upon the enemy until at the expiration of about half an hour from the time of the damage to the steam pipe, he was towed out of action by 'The Wompatuck.'"

In 1909, he was commander of the battleship *Idaho*. That was the year of the now long-forgotten Hudson-Fulton celebration commemorating the one hundredth anniversary of Robert Fulton's first steamboat, *The Clermont*, and the three hundredth anniversary of Hendrik Hudson's discovery of the river which bears his name.

The *Idaho* was in New York Harbor for the review and sent men ashore to take part in the parade. Captain Helm and the other commanding officers were sent tickets to the reviewing stand. My mother and I went to New York to join Captain Helm and see the show, but we had no parade tickets.

In Washington we had acquired a rather odd friend, Representative Timothy D. Sullivan, whose district comprised Staten Island, who was one of the Sullivan clan of Tammany Hall. Those were the days when Tammany ruled, so Tim Sullivan came to Congress. It was Tim who made the famous remark, "A congressman in Washington is something to hitch horses to."

My mother, with her usual resourcefulness, called Tim Sullivan and told him of our ticketless plight. Tim duly "came across"; he arranged for us to go to a friend's apartment opposite St. Patrick's Cathedral, on the line of march. We went, with Captain Helm as our escort.

That was the first time my mother, who always wore a small bonnet with ribbons tied under her chin, hair neatly parted, had ever been in direct contact with Tammany Hall and its ladies. She provided a striking contrast to the feminine contingent in the apartment of Tim's friend, who were blond as to hair and somewhat noisy as to voice. One of them looked at Captain Helm and said, "Aren't you in the militia?" When he replied that he was not, she told him: "Well, a big fine-looking man like you ought to be in something like that."

In 1911 Captain Helm received his commission as a Rear Admiral. In 1916, as senior member of a Commission on Establishment of Additional Naval Stations, Admiral Helm made trips to Atlantic, Gulf and Pacific ports, and the recommendations of that

Commission were largely followed in the establishment of naval bases.

During the First World War, he commanded the Fourth Naval District. This won him the Navy Cross . . . "for exceptionally meritorious service in a duty of great responsibility."

He had a deep-rooted objection to wearing his medals, which he was supposed to put on when in uniform. Once he nearly got himself into difficulty with a commanding officer who saw he had nothing on his blouse and said, very pointedly: "Helm, I think you were once in a war."

It was Admiral Helm who helped me plan my Great Adventure —my two peace conference trips to Europe with President and Mrs. Woodrow Wilson after the First World War.

On an autumn day in 1918, Admiral Helm took me to lunch at Pennyfield's Lock, on the old C. & O. canal above Washington, where we so often walked. On the banks of the sleepy canal, over a delicious luncheon, Admiral Helm and I held our own pre-Peace Conference.

That very day a clever newspaper reporter had guessed in the newspapers that President Wilson might go abroad for peace negotiations after the Armistice. Already, Mrs. Wilson had dropped a word or two indicating that the President was thinking of making the trip. And only a few days before I had heard a comment from Mr. Wilson, who apparently was nettled by some remark made by Mr. Lloyd George, British Prime Minister: "When I see him I shall remind him of the facts."

So I assumed the rumor was correct. Admiral Helm and I talked it over. While crows gossiped in a nearby field and a horde of autumn insects added their music to the symphony, ways and means were considered by the two of us. It was a very serious problem. Even if I could manage it financially, I still was responsible for my mother who lived with me. And in the peace of that quaint old place, we worked out a solution—a happy thought of a friend who would stay with Mother in my apartment.

The President had not yet made a public announcement of the trip. I wondered if he and Mrs. Wilson would take me along. I knew if the President went he certainly would take Mrs. Wilson. But would the social secretary be included?

One morning about the middle of October, Mrs. Wilson came out of her room with the usual mail in her hand—requests for money; requests for interviews; cards from the Smiths and Joneses, announcing the births of the "firsts" (seconds usually were not honored unless they were twins); requests for the President's wife to be patroness for deserving charities; requests for appointments; requests for old clothes; paeans on the worth of the President's wife —perhaps to be rewritten later to another White House chatelaine; and the usual sheaf of manuscript music and homespun poems of the kitchen-garden variety which made up the White House mail.

After going over all these with her usual care, Mrs. Wilson told me the great news: the President had decided to go to the Peace Conference. Could I go with them?

Fortunately there had been Pennyfield's and I could say, "Yes."

I had only two weeks to make all preparations for the trip. I didn't know whether or not to buy clothes in Washington; it seemed like carrying coals to Newcastle, when I was going to Paris. And at first everything had to be done in secret, because the President still was not ready to let the country know of his plans.

Finally the ban of silence was lifted and I could make my preparations in the open. Kind friends did all they could to help me. The gown I wore to dinner at Buckingham Palace was a gift from one of them. Another friend gave me a fur coat—and I think I would have perished that bitter winter in Paris without it.

The White House began to hum with preparations.

Colonel House, who was already in Paris, had written that it was almost impossible to get stationery there. An enormous quantity had to be ordered and packed for the trip.

We learned that the Prince and Princess Murat had offered their Murat Palace near the Parc Monceau on a side street close to the Etoile as the Presidential residence.

The days became a nightmare of haste and worry. I felt the trip was real only when my luggage was pasted with official labels— "Trip of the President to Europe."

The President was to go as the guest of the French Republic and he did not want to take more people along than were absolutely essential. I would go as Mrs. Wilson's secretary. His own secretary, Mr. Joseph Tumulty, was staying in this country and Mr. Gilbert Close would go in Mr. Tumulty's place. Admiral Cary Grayson, the President's physician, would act in a much wider capacity than that; he had charge of many delicate negotiations for President Wilson. Also there were the President's stenographer, a detail of the Secret Service, and Mr. I. H. Hoover, the famous "Ike Hoover," the head usher of the White House staff, who had come in as an electrician with the initial wiring of the White House in the Harrison Administration.

It was really a very small party to accompany a President of the United States, with consequent heavy duties on each member. Traveling sovereigns or Presidents of other countries usually have very much larger entourages.

Admiral Helm suggested that I keep a regular diary. I said I could not do that but I would write down each night, in longhand, the experiences of the past day. I was sorry I had never learned to type, but I did make a copy of these longhand letters by putting a carbon sheet between two pieces of paper. The carbons I sent to Admiral Helm from time to time, in the White House mail pouch. The originals I kept, to avoid any danger of loss, for of course we both fully realized that I would be having a close-up view of highly important history.

Thinking over the circumstances in which these letters were written, I am amazed that they ever were done at all—or deciphered. Most of them were written in bed, after long and exhausting days, toward the small hours of the morning, when a New England conscience permitted me to take that much time off for myself.

Admiral Helm was deeply interested in the President's great adventure. He had traveled widely, would be able to visualize the places I described, and many of the personages. He would catch all the nuances of political give and take.

In this autobiography I am including extracts from my letters about both trips which I believe are of general interest, even after all the years that have passed since December 3, 1918, when we left Washington by train on the first lap of our great adventure.

I shall add no words to those I wrote so long ago.

December 4, 1918

We were all up early and Secretary Tumulty and Dr. Grayson were in the little sitting room off our staterooms. I was amused by the Secret Service who said they always watched for the President's shoes to be taken in from outside his door so they would know just when to prepare to get ready to leave. Finally they were taken in and he came out looking rather badly, I thought, from his severe cold. We pulled in slowly down to the docks in Hoboken and finally reached our stopping place opposite the pier. There a detachment of soldiers was drawn up, with General McManus in command, to escort the President. Behind them were the emergency canteen workers, the only women who were allowed on the docks in war times, and who stood at the gangplank as the men embarked and gave them postcards and words of good cheer.

Arrived on board, we took a look at our rooms. President and Mrs. Wilson have a very fine suite: dining room, sitting room and bedroom, all newly done by Wanamaker, as was mine. Mrs. Wilson wants me to take luncheon and dinner with them. Breakfast we get in our rooms. I have a big room beside theirs, very comfortable and very luxurious, with everything one could want and a fine big bath. Nothing could be better.

Of course there was much enthusiasm as we started. The piers lined and everything with a whistle tooting. Mr. Wilson, Mrs. Wilson and I went on the bridge, Dr. Grayson and Mr. Creel coming too. Perhaps tomorrow with a larger perspective I can get my impressions together. It was stupendous, the noise of whistles, the aeroplanes sweeping about and doing all sorts of stunts overhead, and that very lonely figure on the upper bridge, with his face set toward the old world, with his great ideals of the world to be. Can he carry them out? Will he be disappointed? He is so lovable, so human to us who are around him, and it seems almost hard to realize he is setting out with this great purpose of his, absolutely single-minded. He is no austere person in his own home—just human and lovable.

December 5, 1918

I am amused by my stewardess, who cares for Mrs. Wilson and me. She is a dour-looking person—Irish, skinny, with spectacles, and has followed the sea nearly as many years as I have. This ship is a funny conglomeration of Navy and merchant service. Yesterday I couldn't get a stewardess and rang and a bluejacket came into my room in real old Navy style without knocking, but I didn't mind him even though I was a little disheveled. My friend, the stewardess, said the Commanding Officer sent for her and she being a young thing of fifty and worn around the Adam's apple, said: "And I didn't like to go to a gentleman's room at that hour."

The stewardess seems to know royalties and says doubtfully, "I don't know what the Queen will think of Mrs. Wilson for she is very old-fashioned." As a ray of hope for us she added, "But she is very democratic."

December 9, 1918

Last night we went down to the crew's Old Salt Theater, below decks. The crew had a "sing" to which all the rest of us were invited and the first to arrive was the President for he is always on the minute of time. The place was packed and the words of the songs were thrown on the screen, and we all sang, the President with great gusto, for he has a good voice, and Mrs. Wilson and I piping along merrily. Some poet had composed a verse lauding the President and the crew all took kindly to that and whooped it out with great glee. A fearsome movie followed with ladies losing their clothes and gentlemen likewise—but not in unison as it were.

Mr. Wilson made a ten-strike with the crew by asking Captain McCauley if he might shake hands with the men. You never saw such a lot of happy faces as those waiting to be greeted.

December 10, 1918

The more I am with the Wilsons the more I am struck by their unrivaled home life. I have never dreamed such sweetness and love could be. One never hears anything between them but just love and understanding, and it is very beautiful to see his face light up and brighten at the very sight of her and to see her turn to him for everything, though she is a woman of a lot of spirit. Then they are so lovely to me I hate to be away from them, for they are so nice, and always make me feel they want me around. I told Mrs. Wilson my only regret was that I hadn't a nice thick setter's tail to thump on the deck to show how happy I am.

The President has become a movie fan. He was so tired out at first that he slept nearly all the time, but now he is rested and from despising the movies he clamored to go last night.

He is suffering terribly under the elaborate French cooking. Everything, of course, comes with a sauce and he says he can't "see any sense in wrapping up food in pajamas." He loves ice cream and can't get even that without a sauce. Mrs. Wilson and I love it, of course, all women do. He is having growing forebodings of the food to be served at the Murat Palace where we are to stay in Paris, but blackest of all is the thought of the cold in that princely residence.

December 11, 1918

Dr. Grayson came in for luncheon and said Swen, Mr. Wilson's stenographer, who knows some French, is conducting a class which Ike Hoover and the Secret Servicemen are attending. They were going over phrases from some sort of a primer and Mr. Hoover said "no grammar for me—only a few little handy phrases." One of the men asked what would be "I am in the President's party" and Mr. I. H. promptly said, "Just hand that out to me." In another place are phrases for a restaurant. Mr. Hoover said, "Just give me the words for 'I want a cup of coffee, a beefsteak and some bread' and you fellows can have all the rest." He also observed that if we visited any of the battlefields he wouldn't pick up any "scrapnel."

I have taken in a detective story Mrs. Knight gave me before leaving for the President to read. He is very fond of them and I hope this will prove to be a good one. He has another trait peculiar to great thinkers. He likes to play solitaire and plays nearly every night before going to bed. At the White House he is very apt to come in at noon when he has no appointments, and play for an hour before luncheon. I think Mrs. Wilson taught him to play, and that he never did it much until lately. He does away with the theory that great people do not sleep much for he always sleeps a lot. Mrs. Wilson is a night hawk and he says they are going on the vaudeville stage as "Midnight Mary" and "Dopey Dick."

December 13, 1918—Plount, Brittany

I didn't write much last night. Today, of course, was the great day. We were told the fleet would meet us between three and four this morning, but I didn't get up to see it, fortunately, for they were late and there would only have been searchlights and ships' lights. When I got up I could see them from my window. The *Arizona, Oklahoma, Utah* and *Wyoming*. There were also all the destroyers over here, and I was shown one of four which might have been the *Benham* as she was in the group. As we neared the harbor, a squadron of French ships came out from the land on our left, made a fine sweep and came into the harbor behind us. I don't know if you have ever been in at Brest, but it is a very lovely harbor with high land, cliffs nearly falling steep to the water, and a narrow passage to pass through. As we approached this the President went on the bridge, and as we passed the battleships the bands played "The Star-Spangled Banner," and the crews lined up on the decks and cheered. As soon as we dropped anchor Admirals Mayo, Sims, Rodman and Henry Wilson came over in the launch. Margaret Wilson had come down with Mr. and Mrs. Ross David, with whom she is traveling and giving concerts. She said an odd-looking individual, who looked like an undertaker (for the French always get themselves up like that for visits of ceremony), asked if he might present some flowers to her and turned up with two trunks of chrysanthemums, borne by five men apiece. All of them bowed solemnly and deposited their dear remains on the floor, and only on opening the trunks did she find the flowers.

We stood around and stood around, waiting for it to be time to go. Finally four o'clock came and we started on the funny little tender moored alongside.

Brest is a socialistic port, very turbulent at best I believe, and the

Mayor is very Bolshevik. Jusserand had cautioned Mr. Wilson about him. Having arrived at a stand-still on this raft, more black-coated gentlemen, some with broad sashes of tricolor, stepped up to Mr. Wilson and one ponderous person who turned out to be the Mayor started an eloquent address, to which Mr. Wilson listened with polite attention and made a reply, neither one understanding the other. Then the Mayor's little daughter, about five, a cunning little thing with a Breton cap, came up to Mrs. Wilson and gave her a bunch of flowers. Some American Red Cross workers followed suit.

Then came the great moment, after Mr. Wilson had been thus duly welcomed, for him to step on French soil. It was a great moment for a people who are intensely dramatic and very alive to the great historical value of such scenes. We could only see him go out, and then the cheers.

Brest is built on a steep cliff and it was a steady climb with lovely views of the beautiful harbor. The crowds were held back by lines of men in khaki, and bluejackets, and a very few French, and the men in the motors were pathetic the way they spoke of America and pointed out with pride these fresh-looking lads policing the town they had made over to us. A little way up the street were crowds and crowds of school children, shrieking and calling, and my motor friends asked if I had "remarked" how good our soldiers were to them and indeed there seemed a good comradeship as the little heads stuck even between the legs of the soldiers, and the men held back the eager little bodies very tenderly. Arrived at the crest of the hill were lines of peasant women dressed in the Breton costume, every little community having its own headdress. They were very beautiful and even though the motors were going slowly it was hard to take it all in. I saw a group of hardfisted Breton fishermen in velvet coats and velvet sailor hats. The President said that on the drive up, the first banner he saw read a welcome to him in English as the founder of the League of Nations, which he laughingly said was a little premature.

The station was at the top of the hill, very prettily decorated, and the movie men took us all as we got out of our motors. The President's car is the French President's and gives us a lesson in comfort.

It is very ornately decorated in rose, with huge armchairs, but the best part is that there are wide doors which open on both sides of the car and he can address a crowd. Then the entire side walls are plate glass windows and one has an unobstructed view. It has this one large sitting room and a smaller one off. Next came the sleeping quarters, very comfortable.

Gathered on the platform were all the people, just beaming good will at us. The Mayor's little daughter came aboard again with another huge bunch of flowers. The President, thinking they were for Mrs. Wilson, was about to hand them to her, but the little thing, very shy, held them firmly and said, *"Pour Mademoiselle Wilson,"* and she was kissed by Margaret, who adores the country and makes friends very sweetly with everyone.

The pathetic desire of these people to show honor to the President and the United States is just heartbreaking. Nowhere are such lovely lilacs grown as in the French hothouses, but they must be very dear now. Nevertheless, the employees of the road had a wonderful basket for Mrs. Wilson and one for Margaret. We made two stops before dinner and at each one deputations of the military and civil authorities came aboard with wonderful bunches of flowers. They look upon the President as almost divine and are always so deeply moved. Twice the French Ambassador was away and I stood beside the President and translated his speeches, and when he brought the visitors back to introduce them to Mrs. Wilson, translated again. Rather moving it was to do it, for Mr. Wilson is very human and seemed to feel it all deeply.

At the station in Paris, Mrs. Wilson and the President were met by the President of France and Mme. Poincaré. He is a small, rather insignificant-looking man and she is rather handsome in a kind of way, with very painted lips. I think she must have been shy or embarrassed, for Mrs. Wilson said she scarcely spoke to her as they drove along. In the first carriage were the two presidents; in the second Mrs. Wilson, Mme. Poincaré, Mme. Jusserand and Margaret.

A young aide tried to say I was to come directly to the Murat Palace, and I said I wouldn't, and Mrs. Lansing said I shouldn't, and my Boss, later, said I had done well not to be shunted off, and

I knew I had, too. She says to fight for my rights, which I am doing. Anyway, I got my own way.

We had to make a tremendous detour from the station, crossing and recrossing the river, and finally bringing up at the Ministry of Marine, just as the first carriage appeared on the Place de la Concorde, on which the Ministry stands. It was a wonderful sight, a clear blue sky, the French soldiers in their blue, lining the way and keeping a broad path open for the President, and the rest of the immense square packed and jammed with people. We had been told not to expect as much noise from this crowd as from a New York one, but I have never heard anything like it. They all went mad. The only people who were allowed inside the lines were the wounded, who were wheeled along in chairs. Unlike ours, the procession was just a small guard of the city police and the carriages. No military escort or large procession.

The house is really superb. There is always a detachment of city police outside and the street is kept clear. Every mansion of this size in Paris has a little house at the entrance gate for the *concierge*. Ours is filled with military police and soldiers. Passing two magnificent footmen in scarlet and white stockings, I fell into the arms of Hoover and the Secret Service and felt at home, and ran up the marble staircase over Aubusson carpets, past priceless paintings, into the room of my Boss who is equally overcome by the glory of it all. She has a sitting room, bedroom, dressing room and bath, and he has the same, all very magnificent, but no good bathing facilities like ours.

I crept up to my own estate, piloted by one of the Secret Service, who doesn't think highly of the unmodern improvements. I also am in a delirium of rooms. My frame is stretched upon a wondrous bed, but I had no place—bureau—to do my hair. My worldly goods in the small line lie in wonderful satin-lined drawers. I have a dressing room, a sort of corner behind my bedroom, and various weird washing articles repose there. There are three baths on this floor and I have one. The little maid who cares for me will get my hot water in the morning. A bath in France is a holy rite. My little maid is doing all the necessary sewing and pressing on my clothes.

Hoover doesn't think highly of the other two footmen, equally resplendent, who live in the upper hall and sit like Great Danes outside the President's door and Mrs. Wilson's, and stalk solemnly down in front of us when we go out. "Now you know, Miss Benham," said he plaintively, "the President doesn't want none of that." He doesn't either, fine, simple soul.

We had scarcely arrived in the house when we had to get ready for a grand luncheon at the Élysée, the French President's palace. We started in great state, the footmen in scarlet stalking grandly down the stairs ahead of us. There is a detachment of the Civil Guard at our gates and when the President is due they sound interminable ruffles on their horns.

The big gates swung open, the police motor went ahead, and a lot of bicycle policemen alongside. Margaret and I and our General in the next car. The streets were packed with shrieking, yelling people, just delirious, shouting *"Vive Wilson"* and then crying to Margaret in her car *"Vive Miss Wilson."* One American soldier called "Hurrah for Margaret." We finally reached the Elysée and were welcomed by nine black-coated minor French officials and then by the Poincarés.

During the reception the Poincarés stood first and then our President and Mrs. Wilson. Margaret and I were told by an official to sit on a sofa while our little party of aides stood behind the Presidents. Facing the Presidents were a Master of Ceremonies and more officials. The doors opened and people filed in. They didn't seem to come, save at first, in any particular order of precedence. We are always careful about precedence at the White House dinners, for the people there are formed in a circle at dinner and the President and Mrs. Wilson walk around and greet them. Maybe the luncheon was too large for there were 250, and I imagine some of the diplomats came late. None save the military were in uniform, and I was glad to see dear old Joffre to whom I spoke after luncheon. I also saw the famous Clemenceau, who is very little, very old and no hair. Colonel House says Clemenceau has quite a keen sense of humor, speaking English perfectly, and said in discussing the Armistice terms, "Well, we have taken everything away from the Kaiser but his breeches."

Mrs. Wilson, Margaret and I went for a drive in the afternoon, for the President had endless interviews. The pathos of the poverty of France is so apparent in the little things. The motors we have are very poor but they are the best they can give us, for all the good ones have been used for the Army since the war. We went without attendants, and no one recognized us until we got to the Place de la Concorde, as Margaret wanted to be left at the Hotel Crillon and there an American soldier recognized Mrs. Wilson. When the President goes out, we go in state, and have soldiers to drive and a soldier as an orderly footman.

December 18, 1918

This afternoon Foch came to call on the President, and Mrs. Wilson and I hid behind a door to watch him come in. One of the impeccable French aides caught us. The President said he found Foch as he expected, simple, direct and fine.

Mrs. Wilson and I went this afternoon to do some shopping, hoping we could do a lot of tooting around when we were less busy. It was all right in the first place, a glove shop, but in the other, a department store, where I was buying a pair of gloves, some witch recognized us and a crowd began to form. I think the girl who waited on us passed on the word. Anyway, we were nearly mobbed. I caught hold of a French officer, pulled him to us and told him he must make a way for Mrs. Wilson, or we would have been there still. He and his son pushed ahead and I closed up behind. It was better, politer than an American crowd, and they were all so happy to see her and began to call, *"Vive Madame Wilson,"* but I can tell you I was glad to get back to the car. We were so mad, for we wanted to do lots. We did decide to walk along the Rue de Rivoli, and one woman with a French officer spied her, but they were not quite sure so they hit on the clever scheme of walking by and the man said, "Madame Wilson, Madame Wilson," but she never turned a hair and I think they are guessing still if they were right.

December 21, 1918

Mr. I. Hoover is installed in the palace antechamber. He sits in a wonderful brocaded chair, an artistic French portfolio beside him, an Empire table to write upon, and a portrait of the Princess Murat, a wonderful thing of a typical French aristocrat—dark and scornful—floats above him.

The President told quite a good story about Mrs. House on one of her trips to London, with Colonel House. An invitation came via the American Embassy for both him and her to dine at Buckingham Palace. When they arrived there was some commotion. He thought something was wrong and it turned out it was a men's dinner and the Embassy had made a mistake. While the officials were fussing around he turned to her and said: "Lulie, scoot" and "Lulie" scooted.

Chapter 7

PATH OF GLORY

December 26, 1918—London

Here I am at the Court of St. James, lying in an abnormally large bed, with a British fire of coals burning in the fireplace and a steady air of respectability around. I have "abluted" with a British can of hot water, my page has left me at the door of my suite, and I am alone to dream American dreams. It all seems so unreal, I shall probably waken to find myself back in 918 Eighteenth Street again.

We reached Calais promptly on schedule time, 10:15, were met at the wharf by some British officers, having previously passed some German prisoners who were working around the docks. The President is so kindhearted he said he didn't like to humiliate them by staring at them, but I did not mind, after hearing all we have heard about what they had done in France. They are certainly a healthy-looking lot and they crowded around quite curiously to see us go by.

We had the usual guard of honor drawn up at the dock. The British are great at that, and the President always goes with the commanding general to review them. A nice jolly English officer,

Sir Charles Cust, a great friend of the King's, who had him sent over to meet us, and a cheery Admiral, Sir Roger Keyes, who had been at Rio with Father, and asked me if I was related to him, were along. Sir Roger Cust is aide to the President and is an old lamb. An English destroyer let us out of the inner harbor and six French destroyers took us halfway across and there were some airplanes flying in beautiful formation. At the halfway station six British destroyers raced down to us, separated, made a dashing side sweep and lined up three to a side. You have never seen a more beautiful maneuver.

There was the usual guard of honor to meet the President, and to be inspected, and they were surely—the British soldiers and sailors—a smart-looking lot. We walked along a beautifully decorated covered way and little girls strewed flowers in our paths, and then reached the station platform where the Mayor of Dover received us, and dressy-looking gentry in gray jute wigs were also there. One of the gray wigs read a speech for the Mayor, who had an imposing person with a mace beside him. The President replied very happily and then we got on the train and pulled out. The train —a Pullman—was one of the royal coaches and very handsome. The President had a conference going up with Lord Reading, and Mrs. Wilson and the Duke of Connaught, who is a nice-looking old man, chatted alone. She said he was the typical Army man and she couldn't find much to talk to him about, though he is nice.

Arrived at Charing Cross station. The King and Queen and Princess Mary were there to welcome our royalty, and the Queen is surely a much-maligned woman by the photographs, for she is very handsome, very tall, and has a superb carriage, but I noticed both she and her lady-in-waiting had the busty small-waist figure of 1890. In fact, the only modern figure I saw was the Duchess of Sutherland, but she came in later. The Princess Mary is a pretty girl with lovely coloring. After the President and Mrs. Wilson met the notables, among whom was a fine-looking maharajah, he went off to inspect our Guard as usual and we scurried to our carriage. "We" were Lord Reading, the famous Mrs. Asquith, the woman whom Kipling wrote about as the "woman with the serpent's tongue," General John Biddle, Dr. Grayson and me. Mrs. Asquith is a curious, haggard-looking woman and most interesting and nervous. Mrs. Wilson said she was enthralled by her but was afraid she would go away and say Mrs. Wilson had said certain things. I saw her later at the American Embassy and flew over to her. She said, "Awful bore, this sort of thing." I meekly said, "I like to look at the faces." "Silly things, not one face I would like to look at again, now would you?" "Yes," I said, "I would—yours—for you are considered by us to be the cleverest woman in England."

In the court were drawn up the royal carriages, four of the most superb horses to each landau, with a postilion—a man riding on a rear horse—and an outrider. There was also the guard for this. The horses' manes were outlined in red silk and the harness was red. The carriages were beautiful things, with nice little ladder steps to climb into them. We were in No. 4 carriage and we started off behind the royalties (I seemed to rank next to the Queen's lady-in-waiting), to the booming of a great deep-toned bell, or bells, and the cheering of an enormous crowd. It was a holiday and the streets were packed and jammed. I think it was quite equal to the Paris ovation in size, but nothing could equal that in love.

As we turned into St. James Park, there is an arch through the middle of which only royalty and royal carriages can go—others go to either side entering Buckingham—and of course we drove through the center into the square, literally packed with people, through a lane of people bordered in part by some little children in red, and up to the palace. Here guards of honor received the President and near the house, of course, were sailors, as they have precedence here. We descended and went inside into the hall where a line of gentlemen were presented to the Wilsons. They were the master of the household and such, and one a master of the horse, whom Dr. Grayson said he was about to congratulate on the looks of his stable with those magnificent horses which drew us. Then a fearsome period of waiting began. We stood around and waited while the royalties had gone to show themselves to the crowd. When a crowd forms in front of the palace and calls the king, a visiting royalty must show himself, and Mrs. Wilson said the Queen told her it was most inconvenient at the time the Armistice was signed, for they were "called for" at all hours and had to race from dinner.

General Biddle, whom the English seem to like, for he is as careless of ceremony or pose as they, hauled me gaily up to the Duchess of Sutherland, the mistress of the robes, and proceeded to tease her about her duties, of which *she* knew nothing. She is a lovely woman. Again we stood and stood. People would be solicitous about my fatigue from "the crossing," but no one offered to show me a room to rest my face. At intervals of waiting the King and Queen would appear. He is just like his pictures and seems very simple and nice. When they appear, three or four gentlemen with billiard cues—or what looks like that—trot ahead of them and as the royalties seem to be always changing their minds and walking very fast, billiard cues and royalties all get terribly mixed.

This place is so enormous a page was assigned to me. I always think of a page as young and tender. They aren't! Mine is long and bony and many teeth are missing, but he looks on me with a benevolent eye and pilots me through miles and miles of corridors, all so cold one's teeth chatter. I said I would go to my Boss and we penetrated through miles of little corridors.

I found her dressing to call on some royalties, Queen Alexandra and others. General Biddle had asked me to his house for tea, if I wasn't wanted, so, accompanied by my Ganymede, I went through miles of corridors to the wing in which we are all quartered. I own a magnificent suite, pink brocade furniture and very lovely. My bedroom adjoins and I have a room for my maid and a bath miles away. Cleanliness is not made easy here with these long distances.

I find my gentlemen friends come to the door. Ganymede acts as a watchdog and I think from the decorations he bears on his chest—they look like a row of pennies—he must have bitten many a suitor. Anyway, when I emerged from my room dressed, fortunately there were Biddle and his aide and I went off with the General, Ganymede behind, and had tea with him and his three aides in his pretty house.

I went to see my dear people when I came in and found Mrs. Wilson in a gale from her round of visits. They called first on the Dowager Queen Alexandra who is deaf. Mrs. Wilson said they entered and there was this little old lady, the most popular woman in England, surrounded by her daughters. One was the Queen of

Denmark, but Mrs. Wilson said she would say, this is Alice, this is Alexandra, and they would fall back into line. Then the brisk Sir Charles Cust took them in hand and they went around leaving cards on other personages, and if the door was not answered at once he would say, "All right, they can have a card," and drive on. The English bother little with conventions. Mr. Wilson came in looking tired. He has had a hard day and has dreaded the trip. He is shy and has to be met more than half way, and the English are shy, too, but there is no doubt but that the English people met him more than half way. He sat by the fire and laughed at our chatter, always a little alarmed someone would hear us. We have all been consumed by curiosity over tiny little wash basins on our wash stands. We want to use everything but we don't know what on earth to do with them, and so cannot show our high state of civilization.

The President and Mrs. Wilson dined with the royal family in a cozy little dining room near the royal apartments. The ladies-in-waiting and the gentlemen of the household have their own dining room, and my sweet little Lady Katharine Coke came for me, accompanied by a French woman, Mlle. Dessau, who I think is some sort of a companion to the Princess Mary, the daughter of the King and Queen. General Harts and Dr. Grayson were there, too. I sat beside Sir Derek Keppel, who is the Master of the Household, going out ahead with him for dinner.

Mrs. Wilson said their dinner was very nice and both the King and Queen are very pleasant. She said the King seemed very nervous, so nervous that when he talked his voice grew louder and he tapped all the time on some sort of a mustard box in front of him. In fact, he seemed quite overwrought, which was the same criticism the President made of the King of Italy. Mrs. Wilson said this one couldn't seem to get off the subject of the war and its horrors.

Apparently the Americans are very popular here, for the King seemed much amused at them. He told one story about visiting the American trenches and one soldier said, "Who's that bug?" and was told it was the King of England, to which he replied tersely, "He a king! Hell, where's his crown!" Another story was about going to the Y.M.C.A. Eagle Hut and one soldier asked to shake hands (one doesn't shake hands with royalty—one bows) and of course he did, and another one came up and stuck out his hand, and said, "Put it there."

Tonight was the great event of my life over here, the state banquet. It is the first time in four years and the first one, of course, that a President of the United States had ever attended, and the English seemed to feel the historic importance as much as we did. When I came to dress I found a wonderful little blue enamel and diamond pin which the King had presented to me. Lord Herschell, one of his household, General Harts and Dr. Grayson had cuff buttons given to them. Isn't it wonderful?

At 8:10 old Ganymede came to fetch me. He was all done up in scarlet with white stockings and a black rosette at the back. He conducted me down to the hall where people were coming in and Sir Derek Keppel took me into a room where we were placed in a half circle. There are very few women as this visit is considered primarily for the President to meet the men. The women were the Princesses Louise and Victoria, aunts of the King, covered with diamonds and orders—real dowagers; the Princess Patricia, daughter of the Duke of Connaught; the Duchess of Sutherland, very beautiful in a daring gown of silver tissue with a wonderfully becoming tiara and a diamond necklace and ropes of pearls; Princess Mary, of course; Lady Reading; Mrs. Davis; the Italian Ambassador's wife literally upholstered in claret velvet; Baroness Chinda, wife of the Japanese Ambassador, and Countess Airlie, lady-in-waiting. The men who were to take us out were placed beside us and I drew Lord Curzon.

The princesses were all near the doorway. The King and Queen and President and Mrs. Wilson appeared in the next room. The Queen is surely a royal figure and wears her crown and diadem or whatever it is called, her orders and ribbons, splendidly. They walked around and spoke to us and all the women had to curtsy. As they made the tour, the billiard-cue gentlemen went ahead. Then they all went to the center of the room and the men all filed in and were presented.

I asked Lord Curzon to tell me who they were and he did as they went along. Everyone looked like his picture save Winston

Churchill, who is blond and quite insignificant-looking (I have the printed list of the dinner guests so I won't go on with them here). There were 119 in all. Admiral Jellicoe is smaller and younger than his pictures. It was a thrilling sight to see all these famous men of the Empire, and those who have held it together, file in.

Then the procession led by the King and Mrs. Wilson started off. At intervals in the hall were picturesque Beefeaters from the Tower in red uniforms, stiff coats full around the bottom, with ruffs and red hats on. They stood against the wall.

The dinner was in the ballroom with a gallery at the end for the musicians. In glass cases against the wall is gold plate, though we had on the table an entire gold service, the most superb thing you ever saw. Not only were the table ornaments of gold but we ate off gold plates. That and scarlet poinsettias and red anemones made the most superb blaze of color and all the room is in red and the thrones behind made a fine background with the dais in red over them.

The King made a very happy speech to which Mr. Wilson replied. I don't think it was as good as some of his speeches in delivery, for he was very tired. Lord Curzon, I had always heard, is awfully disagreeable, but I pitched in at the beginning and he was very nice. He was rather critical of the President's speech, though he said it was spoken with obvious sincerity and deep feeling. His only criticism was that the President didn't say anything of England's four years of suffering.

The speeches over, came salad and dessert, and the healths of the President and Mrs. Wilson and the King and Queen were drunk. After the speeches we filed out by another door. Then the real ordeal of the evening came. The lady-in-waiting notified different persons when the Queen wanted to speak to them. My time came. I was hauled over—made my curtsy—and was engaged in conversation. "Was I comfortable?" "I was," some ecstasies over my state of beautitude here. Catching sight of the pin she spoke of it and I was duly thankful to her. We spoke of furniture, for she has rearranged the furniture and ornaments here and they are very well done. She said the King collected stamps, but she thought one had so much to show if one did furniture. Then another person was led up.

After everyone finished in this room the men who had remained in another one to smoke were brought in—not all—just some chosen sheep like Haig, Jellicoe, Ambassadors and the like. Keppel would take them up and a man would know his time was over by seeing another approach.

We stood and stood. Lady Reading said no other Queen has ever stood like this one. She is very strong and never seems to think of the feet of her court. We finished coffee, and after supper they served orangeade and lemonade. That was done and still we stood and stood. The Readings were moaning audibly. The beautiful Duchess said she had new shoes and was suffering agonies. The only two who sat were the old aunts. We stood until nearly twelve. I really thought I would faint. Finally Her Majesty started. They all passed around and curtsied.

Today my little old Lady Katharine Coke, lady-in-waiting to Her Majesty, took me through the Queen's private rooms, and the Queen, hearing I was there, showed me around herself. She is really quite a wonder, for she has made a study of furniture and has arranged the beautiful things so they really show. I was truly interested, and I suppose she saw it, for the King sent for her and she went off and I went down below. Then she sent for me to come back and again went around telling me about all the beautiful things. She is a great and gracious woman.

The person who has made the great impression is Susie Booth, Mrs. Wilson's colored maid. Miss Booth went to view the banquet last night from behind a grill in the balcony. She also told me she had seen that "thorn room and the room where Queen Victory was crowned." The Queen gave her a little pin, also one to Brooks, and this morning Her Majesty sent for Miss Booth, whom the servants had taught to make a curtsy. The English have a lively interest in colored people, and this must have been the first time they had seen one at Buckingham.

Mrs. Wilson was much amused last night. Some woman came up to her and asked if she was a Quakeress. Mrs. Wilson, surprised, said "No" and the woman said, "Oh, I thought you were because you wore no tiara." Mrs. Wilson said, "I would wear one, but, you see, my husband can't afford to give me one."

Jan. 3, 1919—Rome

This has been another terrific day. I think the most full of incidents of any since we came. We arrived here promptly at 10:30 escorted by a large Caproni biplane and a dirigible. At the station to meet the President and Mrs. Wilson were the King and Queen and the Duchess d'Aosta. The King a tiny little man, very simple and democratic, dressed in a simple service uniform, no decorations. The Duchess d'Aosta they consider very beautiful here. She seems to like to accentuate her height by wearing the tallest tiara I have ever clapped my eyes on, at dinner tonight. After the usual greetings at the station we got into the state carriages, the same high-swung landaus with four little steps which let down, fine horses, not as beautiful as the English ones, and two footmen in red who ride on a seat behind and a coachman and footman also in red.

I nearly forgot to describe the Queen. She is, you know, a Montenegran, tall and dark and better-looking at a distance, for her skin is not good. She looks good and kind—just what she is.

The King and Queen are no longer living at the Quirinal Palace. All of it is given over to be a hospital save the apartments they have reserved for state visitors like ourselves. Their Majesties live at the Villa Savoia. Of course, there were crowds of people to welcome the President and Mrs. Wilson. We all piled into our carriages, the King and the President, Mrs. Wilson and the Queen, the Duchess d'Aosta, Margaret and the Countess Bruschi, a lady-in-waiting, who has been assigned with her husband to Mrs. Wilson. The procession started and we halted when some state carriages were drawn up before a very dressy guard in red.

Of all the crowds this was the greatest and most enthusiastic. Not only were the streets along which our cortege passed packed, but up the side streets for a block and more the people were wedged together and I don't think they could have seen the President, even on the roofs. Before the royal carriages went a detachment of the guard, splendid things with shields and long black plumes, and after the four royal carriages, Margaret's and the Duchess's, there came another detachment and then the other carriages. I think it was the greatest ovation the President has had and some of the court set let drop the fact that it was the biggest demonstration Rome has seen. I mean that people can remember.

The Quirinal is huge and there the usual standing around began. Finally royalties started on a tour of the hospital part, and the rest of us raced along after them. The men in the wards were so serious-looking as we passed, very different from our men, who are so good-natured-looking and always smiling. There were pitiful enough cases among them. At one place the King, Queen, President and Mrs. Wilson went on a balcony and showed themselves to the immense crowd below. Over this balcony was draped red brocade and over the line of march they had strips of this same wonderful red brocade hanging from windows. It is certainly very remarkable and fits here, but I don't imagine it decorating a skyscraper! The royalties made another tour of more rooms and then returned to the balcony, of course the President getting always an immense ovation. The red brocade was taken in to show the people that the royalties would not appear again. Finally we all got back to the same big anteroom hung with glorious tapestries, which I later discovered was separated in half by a huge curtain, because it was to be the room in which we were to dine as well as a reception room. Finally we were taken to our rooms all along a long narrow corridor and by far the best we have had. The President and Mrs. Wilson have a wilderness of rooms which are most comfortable and beautifully finished. The President has one charming little room all paneled in Japanese lacquer. It is all very well lighted, with electric light and heat, which latter seems very generally used here.

Mrs. Wilson has a high priest in black with a chain and two acolytes in red guarding the entrance to her door and living anteroom. The President has the same and he is always so funny about his royal state. He waves his hand comprehensively toward them and says, "Will you be so kind as to indicate to one of these gentlemen that I should like a glass of water?"

My regal apartment consists of a most comfortable sitting room, very large with quantities of fine old furniture, and beside it a large bedroom, again most comfortably furnished. My troubles began in a third room, a large fine white mausoleum for trunks and clothes. I wanted to wash. I needed it as never woman did. I made signs;

Italy led me to a washroom; I made for it and began to wash and he gazed at me, making miserable signs all the time, but I had him, for he saw he had to get me a towel to get me out. The strain was telling on me, for he had shown me a fine bathroom opposite my bedroom and he had shaken his head vigorously when I wanted to wash there, so I went along until I found an English-speaking officer. He did some heel-clicking, some rapid-fire Italian, and I found the big bathroom was mine alone. What the other was I don't know. Anyway, I shall always be grateful for it.

After changing clothes we started out for the Villa Savoia. I won't bore you with descriptions of places. I can only say I think Rome is the most fascinating city in the world to look at and the Villa is the sunniest, prettiest house. It is really a house set in a large garden, not a palace. The King met us on the steps, just a few of his household around, and we went directly from the entrance vestibule into a large living room like an inner court covered with glass. It was the sunniest place you can imagine and the Queen stood waiting for us with all her family around her. They are such nice children. The eldest, Princess Yolande, is dark and pretty like her mother, the next with a shock of blond hair. Princess Mafalda is like the King and ugly. Between comes the Crown Prince, also dark and nice-looking. The name of the fourth girl, a dear little witch about thirteen who explained some archaeological finds to General Harts, I have forgotten. The youngest girl is about four or five, Princess Marie, and the sweetest little child you ever saw, with great brown eyes, perfectly natural and unaffected and so well brought up. She chatted to us and came and went perfectly self-possessed but never the least bit forward.

There were just his household, plus an Admiral, and Commander Moreno, who came to meet us at Turin. I sat next to the young Prince, a handsome dark boy with charming manners and, like all the other children, speaking English perfectly. Because he had been sick the day before and was dieting, Commander Moreno teased him and said it was because he had eaten too many chocolates. Luncheon was rather a trying meal I imagine for the higher up, the King; though he speaks English very well he has a habit of biting off his sentences and she speaks only French, but she has such a sweet face it doesn't make so much difference. I think she can understand some English.

After luncheon we went into the same sunny room, filled with photographs; just a lovely light place to live in, and she took Mrs. Wilson over to a table where there were three exquisite pieces of silver modeled in some Pompeiian designs and exact reproductions of the old; one for Mrs. Wilson, one for Margaret, and most touching of all, a little one for me. Isn't it wonderful to have these things? There was a statuette of Victory, last but not least, for the President. We talked there for a little while and then the King showed us a little room he had turned into a museum of the war, with relics different people had sent him from time to time. Two of the worst weapons were a short stick heavily loaded with lead at one end for killing off prisoners and wounded, and the other stick had spikes growing from it for the same purpose. I was interpreting for the Queen part of the time and she told us of the weapons with poisoned bullets and the awful wounds they had made. The King took off. Mrs. Wilson and I had a little talk with the Queen.

She is the sweetest easiest person you can imagine. I spoke of the hospital and she told me she had worked there, assisting at operations and letting these poor lads go through the valley of the shadow of pain holding her hand, and of their courage and how they told her it helped them to have her. How she couldn't think of her own children about whom she had always worried so much because she felt she had to be the mother of Italy now, and so when the hospital was bombed she hurried to these sick boys. When someone asked her how she could leave her children she said they had their little legs to run away but these lads hadn't.

After finishing with this little room we went into the large one again, said good-by. As I was leaving the Queen put in my hand a little box containing a ring set with a ruby, a diamond and an emerald—the colors of the House of Savoy. We drove back to the Quirinal by the Borghese gardens, under such a lovely blue sky and sunshine, almost the first we have seen since we left home. The Quirinal is so huge that there are lots of different entrances. The President's has a detachment of the guards at the entrance, then one goes up a long flight of stairs, turns, and another lot of guards are stationed there. They are picturesque in their long boots, white trousers, silver cuirasses and helmets with long plumes, and they were evidently picked men and very tall.

No sooner had we returned than we went to call on the Queen mother. Her servants were in black livery. Arrived at the top of the usual high flight of stairs, we found her waiting for the President. She is a very handsome old lady, a little bent, but one can easily see what a great beauty she must have been. She has a very sweet manner, but I didn't have more than the usual royal few gracious words when I made my curtsy. The President, Mrs. Wilson and Margaret went in an inside room with her and I stayed out with the Countess Bruschi and the old ladies of her court, who are tremendously nice.

January 6, 1919

The dinner the night of our arrival at the Quirinal was quite ceremonious, of course. The President, Mrs. Wilson, Margaret and I all assembled in the rooms and we thought we would sit there all night. The President asked me to look out and all I could see peeping through was a collection of tiaras, so he asked if I would inquire outside so I had to race all the way through their apartments, out into the outer passage into the big reception room where all the men were, the tiaras blocking the way. My skirt was awfully narrow, the way was long, there was nothing to do but pick up my skirt, which I did—to my knees—and down I flew like a bunny rabbit, got General Harts, who conferred with the master of ceremonies and got the welcome word that the same master of ceremonies would notify us, as we had to wait for the King and Queen, who are always late, to come in from the Villa Savoia. I could have no stately walk back for I had to get there before my royalties started out. I got there and found them just starting. They had made the tour of the tiaras and were going to the outer reception room to wait for the King and Queen, Duchess d'Aosta, Duke of Genoa and Prince Udini.

After dinner we were due at the Capitol where the President was formally to be made a citizen of Rome. There I had my first experience of Italian crowds and I can only say in excuse for the rudeness, the pushing and jostling, that they were all beside themselves to get near him.

Finally we got to a little room after surging through miles of territory. We were let through what seemed to me all the population of Rome clamoring at our heels and diplomats wildly shouting to the custodian of the gate the names of their embassies as a passport. Arrived inside, there was a table where various drinkables were spread out. Prince Colonna asked me if I didn't want to see the Forum illuminated and took me to a little window in an outer room and then I looked down on the most inspiring sight of my life. The whole Forum was lighted with green and red lights and among all the old ruins and the Arch of Diocletian, in the foreground, they looked like a myriad of sacrificial fires burning to this new god who had come from the West to help these war-tortured countries. Even Prince Colonna, who had seen it so often, seemed moved by it and said, "Twenty centuries look down on you, Mademoiselle."

January 8, 1919

At Modane, the border town in the Alps, a cable was brought in announcing [Theodore] Roosevelt's death. The President sat quiet for a moment, then asked Close to take his dictation and sent the message, which I think was this: "May I offer my deep sympathy in the loss of your distinguished husband, the news of whose death has just reached and deeply grieved me." He thought for a moment and changed it to "shocked." Speaking later of Colonel Roosevelt and his life he said he had no constructive policy to his record. He saw the evils of the trusts and enacted certain laws, but he left the constructive part to later legislation.

Chapter 8

THE LEAGUE IS BORN

January 10, 1919

IT SEEMED TOO GOOD TO BE TRUE to get back to Paris again and have a little rest, for the mail is much less and I have my office force really established now and things go smoothly. Mrs. Wilson and I had to go out the afternoon of our arrival to hunt up presents. These dear people are suffering for the gifts royalty makes and this traveling like a king is a very expensive business. Dr. Grayson inquired and found at Buckingham that Poincaré, who had been there with the same number of people the Wilsons had, gave $800 in tips. That was the usual amount. Besides the Wilsons had to send their pictures framed in silver to King and Queen and Dowager Queen, one in leather of the President to Lloyd George, of both to Lady Katharine Coke, Countess of Airlie and Lord Mayor, and I can tell you the large frames for their big pictures are by no means cheap. Besides these, there had to be gold cigarette cases to Sir Charles Cust and Lord Herschell. I think the President will send a handsome set of his books to the King, as he sent a book to the President about Windsor.

We really had to hurry to get the things off for Italy, for the Duc de Lanti was going back last night. It is hard buying for royalties but Mrs. Wilson said the maid and everyone else were much impressed by the wardrobe trunk which Mrs. Wilson had. Several people came and took measurements of it, so she decided to get one for the Queen of Italy. You can imagine the prices over here now. Mrs. Wilson's cost $35, when she was married. I suppose now at home it would be $40. This was $95.

Yesterday at luncheon the President spoke of the delays the English are putting in the way of the conference and trying to discredit it in the eyes of everyone by making it appear that it is not of much importance. I judge Clemenceau is being annoying for siding with the English, but the President said he could put the screws on in the matter of the loan. He also dropped a fearful bombshell to the effect of a surprise he intended springing on them by coming back. So far as I can judge they hope to delay things as long as possible for him, and as soon as he gets away make combines and arrange things as they choose. That is, Lloyd George and Clemenceau and I imagine Orlando. That he hoped to defeat by coming back.

The President said he had been reading a memorandum prepared by André Tardieu whom he cordially dislikes. The article in question was full of obscurities and very long, and he remarked that all went fairly well in Washington until Tardieu learned English, for before that he had been able to talk to him, through de Billy, also on the High Commission in Washington. Mr. Henry White (American member of the Peace Commission) said that Tardieu always represented himself as high in the counsels of the President and had said he saw him almost daily in Washington and had constituted himself almost the President's mouthpiece in France. The President, I don't think trusts him at all. Mr. White said he first knew him at the Algeciras Conference and then he was only a clever journalist but had climbed up and on. The President and he also touched on delays being thrown around the meeting of the Commission. Mr. White has been in diplomacy for years and told us an amusing story of a presentation he made at one of Queen Victoria's drawing rooms where all the old dowagers used to turn out in low neck and paint in the afternoon, looking simply ghastly. To him had been given a Bishop from somewhere to introduce. The Queen had her hair and a crown surmounting it, making a rather towering erection. His last view as he stooped to bow was this. When he raised his head there was a little old head perfectly bald, only two or three wisps of hair standing up on end. It was still the Queen but one of her ladies-in-waiting, the Duchess of Buccleugh, had pulled off crown and wig as she reached for a curtain. He said he stared into her face which was purple with rage, then she began to laugh and one of her attendants led her away. She returned in a few moments bewigged and quite calm as though nothing had happened.

January 14, 1919

Today Mrs. Wilson told me something I didn't know—that the Duke of Connaught had told her that it was the first time he could remember that any women have been at the big state dinners. Usually they are simply stag affairs. She could scarcely believe it, but Lord Sandhurst, the King's Chamberlain, said the same—that never in his memory had any women been at the state banquets. That I suppose accounts for the few there were, but I didn't realize at the time I was assisting at a precedent-making affair. Mr. White last night at dinner told Mrs. Wilson French society was all agog over this, and also over the fact that she had been invited to Buckingham. Mme. Poincaré, he said, and the wives of the other French Presidents, were never invited to Buckingham, and to royalties it was often intimated their wives were not wanted and they were left at home.

This evening is one of the first times I have had a really long talk with the President about really vital things, for conversation is usually more or less general. Tonight Dr. Grayson was out, and Mrs. Wilson, the President and I were alone. He had been speaking of the Conference, how annoying Pichon, the Minister of Foreign Affairs, is as a presiding officer. He never seems to get any of the proceedings correct and his summaries are invariably wrong.

The Conference too is very much wrought up over the leakage of news to the press.

They have tried to give it out through a central news bureau or committee, but very important things are constantly filtering, with constant bad feeling with the reporters. The leakage is entirely with the French, the President feels.

Mrs. Wilson spoke of what Mr. Henry White has said to her this afternoon with regard to the inadvisability of the President's returning to America. He thought from what people told him that it would be in the nature of an anticlimax if the President came back again and that it would be better if he could settle most of the great questions before he left.

The President said he agreed with the anticlimax part and he could see much against it, but he felt Mr. White took the viewpoint of the newspapers and he could not consider them representative of the American feeling as they were controlled by large moneyed interests and not in touch with the people. The President said that he always found out if you told the people the truth and pointed out the ideals to be followed, they invariably backed you up.

He dwelt on the fact that there is a latent consciousness of world ideals, new ones, which may have come about without the whole body of the people being conscious of them and yet when they were presented to the American public they were supported. When they had heard expression given to them they knew they heard what they had always thought. He said he had never spoken at any time to the American people about anything which, if a new process of thought was involved, had not been enthusiastically supported.

I asked how he got his impressions, if not from the papers, of what the new national ideals are and what truths are to be presented to the people. He said he would get them from different sources and piece them together as one would a mosaic; that I must remember he had been a student of American political history for years and had saturated himself in it.

I said, "But these are deductions only, aren't they; helpful, but don't you go deeper than that? Don't you feel as though you are dipping into ether—getting from some source which holds all things

—the consciousness of the new ideals of America and making them articulate?" He said he thought so but he felt so filled with the American spirit that when new ideals came to him, he was able to express them to his countrymen. All this he said very humbly and very simply as he does everything.

January 16, 1919

This afternoon Mrs. Wilson and I went to one of the hospitals here with Mrs. Franklin Roosevelt and Mrs. Geoffrey Parsons of New York. It is under the direct charge of Dr. Blake, the famous New York surgeon. His wife, who used to be a very handsome woman, has turned into a person with perfectly wild hair and generally eccentric-looking. Mrs. Wilson was literally pushed into a room with young Colonel Roosevelt. She made what objections she could, for she didn't think he would care to see her, but the people were all very firm. The President received the stiffest kind of a message acknowledging his cable to Mrs. Roosevelt, signed "Quentin Roosevelt, Major, U.S.A.," a trifle unnecessary it seems to me.

The Murats were expected to tea but didn't turn up, probably my note going astray. Mr. White had been asked to help entertain them so we had him alone to entertain us. He was much amused at Mrs. Wilson's account of how the Dowager Queen Alexandra received them in London. She said all the ladies wore long brown suede gloves and the Queen would say, "This is Maud, this is Victoria; here, Maud, you introduce the children"—Maud being the Queen of Norway. They all gathered around her—Mrs. Wilson—when she signed the inevitable autograph book and were much surprised when she signed "Edith Bolling Wilson." Evidently, as Mr. White said, they had expected her to sign "Edith" as they had probably never met a President's wife before.

January 18, 1919

Yesterday was rather a lost day for there wasn't anything interesting said or done at luncheon, and in the evening the President and Mrs. Wilson went to a dinner at the Italian Embassy. Mrs. Wilson says all these Embassy dinners are rather terrible, for the host and hostess come down to the front door to meet them, and she never has a chance to see if any powder is missing from her nose. And the President says he has to divest himself of hat, muffler and coat while his hostess has her arm all crooked waiting for him to start upstairs.

Today at luncheon the President described the way the United States was seated first in the Peace Conference. The French suggested that they use the French nomenclature *Etats-Unis d'Amerique,* then Lloyd George said jokingly, if that were so they should give Great Britain her title, *Empire de la Grande Bretagne,* but Mr. Lansing capped it all by saying that the United States was designated, *L'Amerique, les Etats-Unis de,* and so we finally came first. He spoke of the difficulties with the newspaper men and told Dr. Grayson, who gives the interviews to the newspaper men and is the general goat to whom all people come with their complaints, that he hoped they would not put much stress on Yugoslavia having a navy. It will be a turbulent nation as they are a turbulent people, and they ought not to have a navy to run amok with.

At dinner the President asked Dr. Grayson to carry down to General Smuts a copy of his draft of the Constitution of the League of Nations. It was, of course, such an important document and still so secret that Grayson had to deliver it into the hands of Smuts himself. Smuts had written what the President considers one of the best expositions of the aims of the League of Nations and its practical application and constitution. Someone asked the President if he hadn't written most of this present draft himself, and he said no, that the original was made by an English Society. He had made certain additions and changes to that, then Smuts had presented certain other features and a very statesmanlike addition and he (the President) had made another draft of his own which he had sent down to Smuts for criticism and change. The reporters, I imagine, would have given a great deal to have waylaid the little Doctor and taken the document from him. (I think a copy went to Lloyd George, too.)

January 22, 1919

This day Mrs. Wilson and I have devoted to shopping done with great execution. Now that the conferences are on she is much more alone. The President hates to walk and is like a bad child in trying to find excuses not to walk to the Quai d'Orsay, where the Conferences are held, or to walk at other times. She insisted he had the newspaper men trained to stop him at a certain point on the deck of the *George Washington* and stop his walk. Usually he is too busy for he is seeing people nearly all day when he isn't at the Foreign Office. She always drives or walks over with him, and sometimes I go, but usually go there to pick her up and go on some shopping excursion.

Mrs. Wilson is unusually self-contained, admits scarcely anyone to her friendship, though always wonderfully gracious. Her smile and charm are proverbial. I do not believe there has been any other woman who has occupied the position she has who has her beauty and charm and is so good. The first two qualities fit a number of sovereigns, but the last usually seems to have been left out and given to the stodgy and amiable Victorias. She is very quiet about her dislikes, but a very intense and very loyal friend. There never was anyone with a keener sense of humor. He has the same, but she is a born mimic. I have never seen anyone enjoy anything more than he does one of her stories or experiences after she has been somewhere without him, for she always sees something funny.

Lots of the Faubourg St.-Germain aristocracy have called on Mrs. Wilson. The Serbian Minister told Mrs. Wilson at dinner at the Lansings last night that a Princess de Rohan had said she had heard Mrs. Wilson was quite democratic—meaning, she supposed, common—but he said he had heard Mrs. Wilson was descended from one of the first princesses of the original natives of America, the Princess Pocahontas, and now she would come to call. Mrs. Wilson said that when I met her I must tell her that Mrs. Bolling lives at the Castle of Powhatan (Hotel Powhatan in Washington). This afternoon one of the French women said she was part American for her grandmother was American. She added impressively, "My grandmother was the wife of my grandfather." The President commented that such statements are at times necessary.

January 24, 1919

Today has really been the great ball of the season—the tea the President and Mrs. Wilson had for the guard here around the house, the French guard, chauffeurs, and messengers, the Navy yeomen and enlisted men who have been working here for me and for Mr. Close. I also asked for an invitation for Corporal Allen of the Marine Corps and his friend, Private Harris. It was a real party. They all filed in, the first sergeant of the soldiers making the presentations to Mrs. Wilson in General Harts' usual place. They all began to line up but the telephone girls and I managed to break it up and we got it to looking more like a tea.

The President was detained at the Conference but got there in time to shake hands with the French guard and then Americans filed around him and shook hands. The crowning joy was a flashlight of the President and Mrs. Wilson flanked by a French and American soldier and behind them the French first sergeant, the American first sergeant, Yeoman Schindler of my establishment, Corporal Allen and a first-class seaman who is doing duty in Close's office.

Fine trencher work was done with the hot chocolate and cakes and it looked as though a devastating flood had swept over things. The President had a big crowd around him to whom he talked and told stories. Mrs. Wilson had another about her. This after all the handshaking, eating and photography was past.

January 29, 1919

The long-expected clouds are growing around the Conference, for the President had a very bad day today. These smaller meetings are called conversations and are necessarily behind closed doors. I think the press criticisim of closed sessions is not well founded, for the President said he never believed in all public meetings, for every premier of the big and particularly little countries would be talking for the benefit of their people at home and much time would be wasted in fruitless orating. He believes the results of all discussions —I mean resolutions adopted and all treaties made—should be absolutely public and that there should be no more secret treaties ot understandings such as the Bolsheviks discovered in Russian archives.

The "conversation" today was a most exhausting one. There are a few men who take down the skeleton of the discussion. Mr. Frazier of our Embassy is doing it for the President, but no stenographers are allowed and the press, of course, gets none of it.

I think this has been one of the hardest he has had, and I fear there will be many more. There is no doubt the people of every country are solidly behind him. The politicians know this and are afraid, and I imagine the Governments, knowing this, while outwardly friendly are putting every spoke they can in the wheels. He said this is the test of the League of Nations and if the majority of the nations of the world didn't want it he might just as well give up and go home. The longer I am over here, the more I hear, the more I am convinced that the old order of things has gone and the masses will have a change. It was Bolshevism in Russia and we can't have that at home, and the only way seems making changes in our social and economic fabric. I don't advocate this as a disciple of socialism. It is to apply remedies before the Bolshevist plague spreads around the world.

February 1, 1919

Sundays are always quiet for us. Mr. George Creel came to luncheon and gave an account of a trip he has just completed through Poland, Czechoslovakia, and those other mysterious old-new countries. He brought back some posters and the inscriptions translated read, "We want a Wilson Peace." He went among the poor people, who regard the President as a new popular Saint. His pictures hung in many windows and the people told Mr. Creel that they wanted Wilson to reign over them. The President says that such expressions make him very nervous, for he fears the revulsion which is bound to come when they find he can't do all they hope. Such revulsions of popular feelings are dangerous to a degree.

February 7, 1919

Yesterday was a great day for me socially. For some time there had been a lot of suppressed excitement about my office, and telephone conversations abruptly ended when I came into the room. This invitation tells the story:

Tuesday
February 4, 1919
The undersigned U.S. Navy men
request the honor of the presence of
Miss Edith Benham
and friend to the dance to be given by the
Enlisted Men of the United States Navy
at the Palais des Fetes, Paris, on
Thursday Evening, February 6th
1919

Francis A. Kennedy
N. P. Schindler

(The two signers, of course, were the men on my staff.)

My acceptance went at once. There are fewer letters now, and two of my stenographers have gone back to the Crillon, leaving Chief Petty Officer Schindler and Seaman Kennedy. They explained that they wanted to have this a small dance and most exclusive—only fifty couples and all hand picked. Admiral Grayson was invited, too, but he had made arrangements to go to Verdun. One of our Army Signal Corps telephone girls was asked, so I said I would take her with me, and "Should we meet them at the hall?" "No, they wanted to do everything well and would meet us here and escort us down." Both gentlemen asked if they might absent themselves early in the afternoon. Mr. Schindler was much preoccupied over the fit of a uniform, and both he and Kennedy were evidently bound for the barber, as they appeared in the evening very shiny as to countenance, hair closely shaved on side and pompadour effect in front. The nice telephone girl came up to my room to primp, and there we found bunches of violets awaiting us.

The President had been so much interested in the party he asked for bulletins about it from time to time, and the hair-cutting details appealed to him particularly. We all piled into a motor and the

Army chauffeur outside whistled all the way—just to indicate his indifference to things Naval. Then we got lost. Kennedy, it turned out, was the only one who had ever been to the Palais des Fêtes, and he only once, but a small boy came to the rescue and directed us to *le Bal American*. "Joe" met us on the sidewalk. "Joe" is a soldier and is Miss Telephones' "dancing partner." At the head of a long flight of stairs we were met by the Floor Committee, and a soldier band of four pieces did great execution in the jazz line. Taken by itself, it is a dreary little hall, but everyone had such a good time dancing that environment meant nothing. I started off into the mazes of the dance with Schindler, Joe and Miss Telephone following, and Kennedy found a girl and was off, too. One of the bandsmen announced that soldiers could take off their coats, and my escort hastily explained that it was because the coats are so warm. The drum sounded and the bandsman announced Admiral and Mrs. Benson and aides, and we all stood at attention against the wall until they were duly received and opened the ball formally. The Admiral grasped his wife firmly and led off in a waltz, the rest of us following.

Ladies were in the minority, and nearly all in uniform—Red Cross, Y.W.C.A. and a few French. One of my young partners cheered my declining years by telling me that I was "still light on my feet."

February 10, 1919

As the President said tonight, it was very difficult to continue to treat France sympathetically even with the kindliest feelings toward her, when she persisted in regarding him with suspicion. At the conference today Klotz (Minister of Finance, I think) read a long paper in which it was stated as something new that Germany had destroyed ultimately all the French industries and that this was an economic war. As the President said, he had known and everyone had known this all along and it didn't need a final note from Balfour "This is for you" to let him see it was directed against him. In summing up the situation he spoke of the selfishness of the French, who feel they are the only nation which has suffered, forgetting Belgium, with all the machinery gone from her factories, no economic life left, Serbia and Poland. Because he had said in one of his speeches that those countries must be treated justly, the French had the idea he had come over as the partisan of Germany and were suspicious of him.

February 15, 1919—On board the *George Washington*

My first appearance on the scene of action after several days in bed with a touch of the "flu." It is very annoying to have been so ill these last few days in France, particularly as I had to miss the one thing which I would have given worlds to have seen—the plenary session of the Peace Conference at which the League of Nations was adopted. My first day downstairs was that very day, and I was incredibly weak, but my spirit was willing to go on. As I have written you, women are not allowed at these sessions save women reporters and those stenographers, etc., attached to the different delegations. Just after luncheon Mrs. Wilson told me that she was to be smuggled in through a side door, and I was to go with her. It was the chance of a lifetime. Everyone has been clamoring to go to these conferences, which are infrequent, and the room in which they are held is small and could not accommodate an audience. It is better anyway. The serious business is being transacted, and these sessions should not be turned into side shows. Here was this great opportunity and I had to let it go by. Dr. Grayson sorrowfully said that he couldn't answer for consequences if I went out, and into that poorly ventilated room.

Early that afternoon before Mrs. Wilson went to the conference, Mme. Poincaré and Mme. Pichon, wife of the French Minister of Foreign Affairs, came to present her with an exquisite table set as a testimonial from the women of France. It consists of cloth, doilies and napkins, all heavily embroidered. The two ladies did not remain very long for we were to leave that night for home, and the President and Mrs. Wilson were due at the Élysée Palace at six o'clock to make their farewell call on the Poincarés. We left the house shortly after dinner. Downstairs were a number of people like Prince Murat and the French aides and their wives to say good-by. It was really hard to say good-by to the servants who had waited on us all very well, but the old maitre d'hotel said he hoped they would return to "serve the President" when he comes back.

It all depends on the question of the house. While accepting the hospitality of the French Government in the home on loan from Prince Murat the President did not feel he could entertain much, or at all. It would be easier if the President could rent a house and be free when he returns to Paris.

Chapter 9

THE LONELY FIGURE

WE WERE BACK IN WASHINGTON less than a month before we again set sail for France, this time to complete the negotiations for the Peace Treaties. Once more my letters to Admiral Helm take up the tale.

March 14, 1919

This is the beginning of the second installment of "dere Dairy." We reached Brest at night, a heavenly moonlight one after a rainy day. Shortly after we came to anchor the same old crowd of people came aboard on the little Navy tender. On leaving Brest Admiral Halstead explained the French had insisted on their own arrangements and took one of their own boats, but this time they were less proud about having the President set his foot on French soil or French wood first and allowed our Navy to send a very comfortable little boat to take us. We are to have the same aides and the same old crowd, the Jusserands, the Minister of the Navy, M. Leygues, with his dejected walrussy mustache, the old Admiral of the Port with his long beard, General Harts and aides and Halstead and aides.

Going ashore it was different. We landed at the place the President disembarked the first time. Two huts—Red Cross—are there, one a canteen which the engineers at Brest had helped build and made a perfectly charming little place of it. One part was a kitchen where they fried the most delectable doughnuts and, of course, the soldiers swarm there. The pretty part was the little sitting room with a huge fireplace at one end and cheery little paintings, done by native soldiery talent, around the walls. Later we sampled the doughnuts for the canteen was boiling with them, and as one of the workers said, they could see no reason why the President shouldn't have some when Generals and Admirals were eating them.

After this we went to the other hut, rather a sad little place where one thought of all the pain which had gone through it. The trains with the troops are brought now right to the wharf and the wounded are taken off and the stretcher cases laid on racks until the poor pain-racked bodies are put on the boat and their faces turned to their own country. Poor homesick things. I don't wonder it gives them a new lease on life to go aboard the ships.

Our train was waiting just outside and we got aboard and looked out on a mass of French and American uniforms of all sorts, and to make the picture a little more kaleidoscopic, some officers from a Japanese ship were there. Some colored troops went by on a caisson and to really fill out the picture some Chinese from a Chinese Y.M.C.A. came along with a Y.M.C.A. banner. Someone said the Y.M.C.A. has a large following in China on account of the excellent medical work it has done there. Our train finally pulled out, we kissed the Mayor and Prefect of Brest good-by and went along through several miles of American sentries stationed along the tracks, and one splendid-looking boy on a coal pile with his musket and figure silhouetted against the moon might have made a picture of the ideals of America standing guard over the destinies of Europe in the little old Breton town.

March 15, 1919

I didn't finish yesterday, but really there was not so much for our arrival was quiet. The Poincarés were there, all the Embassy and Peace Commission. My old friend, Mr. White, seized me by the arm and we sailed along, for Mr. White, though an elderly man, has the peculiar art of steaming through a foreign crowd at full speed. Getting through any of these crowds is no light job for people push in from all directions.

We were terribly curious to see the new house, of course. It is in a newer part of town and on a cunning little square. It is a curiously arranged affair. A man named Bischoffsheim built it. He was a great collector of Renaissance furniture and old paintings and the home is filled with wonderfully valuable things, paintings by Van Dyck, Watteau and Romney and fine old carved furniture, but all very badly arranged and the whole place overdecorated. Contrary to the French custom and the custom everywhere for that matter, the bedroom suites for the President and Mrs. Wilson are on the ground floor which opens at the back on a pretty little garden. The President was convulsed by the bathing arrangements in his room. A large green tub partly in the room and partly built into the wall. Over this is a mezzanine gallery where he could have musicians to play while he scrubbed, but I think Major Brooks will probably press clothes there.

The second story has a ballroom, small parlor, large library and dining room. The library is a very comfortable room with nice big chairs in it. It is there the large paintings hang. Upstairs is my room which is sweet and clean and bright and so different from the gloomy grandeur of the bedroom I had at the Murats'. I had converted a little bedroom I had beside it for my office force who turned up in the afternoon very shiny and very clean and very glad to see me, and we all fell on each other's necks. We started in housekeeping, running down at once to the big ballroom which has had to be used for an office and picking out the best typewriters and coming up merrily with them before Mr. Close's office force began their deadly work. I think, though, they have swiped some of our big envelopes from us. Kennedy, Yeoman, 1st Class, U.S.N., had saved up for months and was given leave and went off on an extended tour through the Riviera, in Italy and in England and all for $200. When Kennedy departs from Uncle Sam's service he is a wool salesman and he says very wisely that he can never take a trip like this again and so he took advantage of it now. Schindler went up to visit his brother, another chief petty officer, at Cambrai and has returned with two shell cases which he is having polished up for me. They are two nice boys and I love their prattle and the fact that they come to me to have all questions of etiquette settled.

March 21, 1919

All today I have been thinking of something Mr. Bernard Baruch said yesterday about Russia: that the civilized world has been letting this monstrous oppression of one hundred and eighty million people go on for years, and has never raised a finger to prevent it and now Bolshevism is spreading over and tainting all the world.

March 22, 1919

Last night the President came in tired out. He said he had been so much with his colleagues—"The Big Four"—that he knew just what they were going to say before they opened their mouths. The French are behaving badly and he says he really thinks they want to begin the war again. They want to do just what Germany did in '70, annex some of Germany and then stir up the same bad feeling there was after the annexation of Alsace and Lorraine.

A curious thing came up. The Germans had been asked to allow the passage of Allied troops to Poland to establish order among the Poles. Foch stated he had been refused, so a meeting was called yesterday afternoon to determine what should be done, for it was a queer situation and looked as though a resumption of the fighting would be necessary if Germany refused. They considered all afternoon methods of procedure. Finally nearing the end of the meeting the President asked for the written statement from Germany. They replied there was none and all that had been asked was the elucidation of certain points about carrying out the transportation of the troops and absolutely no refusal. The French are always trying to make such situations. They are in a perfect panic and yet one can't blame them after these four years and the treachery of the Germans.

April 11, 1919

I am rather putting the cart before the horse, for I didn't write yesterday, and while today's memories are fresh I thought I would put them down. The great event, of course, was the Queen of Roumania's coming for luncheon. After saying she would bring four from her own household, yesterday morning when the President and Mrs. Wilson went to call, she said she would like to bring her sister, the Infanta Eulalia. Great consternation for we thought it was the disreputable Eulalia who toured America several years ago, at the World's Fair time I think, and has had many husbands and near husbands. However, we found that it was her sister or sister-in-law who turned out to be a very attractive person—not as good-looking as the Queen but far more genuine and clever. I think the Queen is rather a spectacular person. She enjoys being at the head of her troops and standing in every way in the limelight.

She was invited at one and the President arranged to meet her upstairs. Harts and Grayson met her at the door and conducted her and her party upstairs. Of course, the President and Mrs. Wilson were ready promptly, and we all went upstairs to wait, looking out of the windows of the drawing room so the President and Mrs. Wilson would have time to go out to the head of the stairs to meet her. Nothing infuriates the President like waiting or being late. The Queen had come to establish a propaganda for Roumania, a Greater Roumania, and she did the worst thing she could in being nearly twenty-five minutes late. Every moment we waited I could see from the cut of the President's jaw that a slice of the Dobruja, or Roumania, was being lopped off. At one time he threatened to go on and begin luncheon without her, and asked me to telephone the Ritz to find out if she was coming. By the time she did arrive he would scarcely go out into the hall to meet her and it required all Mrs. Wilson's powers to persuade him. We sat like this.

	President
Queen Marie	Infanta Eulalia
General Harts	Mrs. Wilson
Princess Marie	Princess Elizabeth
	Dr. Grayson
Madame X	General Biffal
	Me

I never did know the name of the lady-in-waiting, for they said one would come and quite another person appeared. We had been told that the Princesses, as daughters of a reigning King, would have precedence over the Infanta, but the Queen when she reached the dining room and saw where we were putting her eldest daughter, took matters into her own hands and put the Infanta next to Mrs. Wilson. The Princesses are two fat lumps who take no pains to make themselves pleasant or interesting. I was in luck for General Biffal, who speaks no English, is a very nice person. Also the lady-in-waiting. After luncheon we sat around and the President and the two sisters talked over the political situation, but I must say the Queen was more interested in expounding her views than listening to what the President had to say. She begged him when she left to do what he could for her country, but I fear the worst with that twenty-five wasted minutes!

April 15, 1919

Colonel and Mrs. House's dinner to the Paderewskis was quite a grand affair. I got there promptly and found Mrs. Whitelaw Reid and Mr. Venizelos already there. She is a handsome old lady encrusted in diamonds, but genuine—her character, not the jewels—for she has given a big house for a Red Cross hospital for officers, one which Mrs. Wilson and I visited in the winter.

I sat next to Mr. Thomas Lamont, who is one of the American specialists on the question of reparations and indemnities. Curiously enough, he said he couldn't keep books if he were set at the task. All sorts of celebrities were there, beginning with the Paderewskis, for whom the dinner was given and who were half an hour late. Madame Paderewski told me that her husband has quite given up his music, has not touched a piano for two years now.

April 21, 1919

These are very trying days for the President with the continual wrangling over the Italian question. Lloyd George and Clemenceau had agreed day before yesterday to stand by him and refuse Fiume to the Italians. This morning—no, yesterday morning—they came and said they had been considering it over night and had decided they must stand by the pact of London. Today the President said that Orlando, for whom he says he has not only a liking but a real affection—and I haven't often heard him say that—made a very moving speech at the Big Four Conference. He read this speech, which was really Italy's ultimatum of what she must have or withdraw, and then when the end came he gave a little gulp, went to the window and sobbed piteously.

April 24, 1919

I wonder if I have made clear the stages of our negotiations as I have gathered them from what the President and Mrs. Wilson have said. Orlando has wanted to withdraw for some time, in fact has practically withdrawn since he delivered his ultimatum when he went to the window and sobbed. Saturday Mr. Wilson went down to the Crillon and consulted with the other members of our Peace Commission to see if they could suggest anything else, and none of them could. The *Echo de Paris* had the nastiest article in it about Americans and the President.

The house is just as tense today as it was the day before war was declared at home. At luncheon Hoover came in to say Mr. Kerr, Mr. Balfour's secretary, was there and he wanted to know if the President would come to Mr. Lloyd George's apartment, as they looked on that as neutral territory and would prefer going there to coming here. The President said, "What children!"

May 1, 1919

Today has been stupid for we stayed in all day. The Government was terribly afraid of socialist demonstrations and stopped all the street railways and underground. We did drive down with the President when he went to the Quai d'Orsay (Foreign Office) to a conference, and it looked quite warlike to see the bridge leading to the Place de la Concorde guarded by soldiers, and a little field kitchen nearby where their meals were prepared during the day's bivouac. On the other bank of the river on the Place de la Concorde the people wanted to have a demonstration but that had been forbidden, and some regiments of cavalry were there and we could see them and their long sabers guarding that end of the bridge and the avenues which debouch there. All the American soldiers were ordered off the streets, to their great disgust, but I imagine some of them will slip out and be found in some of the disturbances which may take place tonight.

May 5, 1919

Mrs. Wilson and I were two disappointed women yesterday. The President, Mr. Clemenceau and Mr. Lloyd George had decided they would go out and examine personally the room in which the Germans are to receive their credentials when they appear to hear the terms of the peace treaty, so as to see if the newspaper men could get in.

It was all very secret, for they were to go by different ways and meet out there so as not to have the press at their heels. Mrs. Wilson and I were very eager to go, naturally. Also Dr. Grayson, and we all sat around and used our best endeavors to get the President to let us go. He even withstood Mrs. Wilson's pleadings, and when he can do that his mind has to be fully made up.

For tea Mr. Charles Crane brought Miss Alice Masaryk, the daughter of the President of Czechoslovakia. The Austrians put her in prison for six months. Part of the time it was in a small place with seven other people and sanitary conditions were very bad. She said she did a little surreptitious needle work and for several months after she was released she found herself hiding her work under anything when someone was in the room, as she had grown so accustomed to hiding it from the guards who watched the prisoners, fearing they might attempt to commit suicide. She was ill, too, and from undernourishment her finger nails dropped off. She is a woman with a quiet exterior, but one feels the fires of enthusiasm burning behind. Mr. Crane spoke of her popularity and said recently she had gone to some miners who were on strike and induced them to go back to work.

May 7, 1919

Just now at 2:20 the "Office" and I have been hanging out of the windows to watch the President leave. The English cars from across the street had started and the doors of our hotel were thrown open, and the big black car with Slum driving—the sergeant who always drives the President—Murphy of the secret service beside Slum, the President's flag fluttering and the President all alone inside. Of course it is a terrible disappointment not to be able to go, but they are allowing no women. Mr. Lloyd George's daughter is here and wanted to go, but they decided better to have no one.

At luncheon the President said how he hates to meet any of the Germans. He wouldn't mind the old crew so much, but not these nondescripts. A New York *Times* correspondent asked him what he thought about the peace, if he felt it was all right, and he said, "Yes, as far as it was possible and the Germans would be the only ones to object," but he didn't feel it was unduly severe for them.

May 8, 1919

The President said the Germans made an unfortunate impression on everyone. In the first place, the President, Lloyd George and Clemenceau went out to see about the arrangement of the rooms and if the table could be placed so the Germans wouldn't have the appearance of prisoners at the dock, but they could not arrange it differently.

Then they had arranged that they should stand when the Germans came into the room. Of course, as you have seen by the papers, Von Brockdorff-Rantzau (I hope I have spelled it straight) sat when he made his speech. Mr. White told me that when he went up to meet the Germans when they came, Von Brockdorff-Rantzau looked like a ghost and his knees shook so he could hardly stand, so he may not have been able to stand. But he certainly, as the President said, should have given some explanation.

The President said the sight of the Germans, for they were arrogant still, aroused all the old animosities and hatreds which had been dormant in part, in the desire to bring Germany to a realization of the part she would have to play to be admitted into the society of decent nations.

May 12, 1919

Probably no one will realize fully if the President's work does come to anything, how much Mrs. Wilson has done to make it possible. She is the most wonderful wife in the world, to a man who needs love and care more than any I have ever seen. Without it I don't believe he could live—certainly his work would be greatly crippled. She never leaves the house now, in these days when he is so busy, if she thinks there is the slightest chance of his going for a walk. It is her constant care which keeps him so well.

Chapter 10

THE PRICE OF GLORY

May 19, 1919

GENERAL PERSHING came to luncheon today. Conversation turned on Italy and he said he is getting advices from his Intelligence Bureau that the Italians consider the German peace terms too heavy and feel that the French are very heartless in welcoming the Austrians as they have, or not hating them as the Italians want them to.

Censoring the German mail in the part we are occupying brings rather strange information, the gist being that the Germans say the terms are hard but only what they would have made the Allies pay, and no more. The President said it is hard for the German people to realize now that they must suffer for the sins of their government. It is always hard, he said, for people to realize that. He went on to speak of the Italians and how they had always had a raw deal in every distribution of territory after a war and in a way they could hardly be blamed for being as tricky as they are.

May 21, 1919

Before going out to dinner last night I stopped in to see the

President and Mrs. Wilson and to say goodnight. As usual they were playing solitaire. The President laughed at his panacea for rest to his mind and said, "I am afraid you will always think of me as an amiable old gentleman playing solitaire."

We are all interested in the acceptance or rejection by the Germans of the peace terms. Monday, as I wrote you, the President had General Pershing here to luncheon and discussed with him in another room what was to be done in case of certain eventualities.

Before he left the room the General said he understood that the peace terms gave to the military power over the German courts and civil processes, and the President considered this inadvisable, particularly as it would be the French who would be in command of the joint forces. The President said he thought this should not be, and the French and other Allies should understand at once that it could not be.

May 22, 1919

Mrs. Wilson told me yesterday that Mr. Baruch telephoned the President that the French are scared to death for fear the Germans won't sign and will begin the war over again. The financial experts say now they are willing to reduce their claims for indemnities, but of course they want the President to present this, for the Government here is afraid of its own people and it has led them to believe the indemnities will be immense, and lots of the population is not working, simply waiting for peace and the money to come from the Germans, and if they are disappointed there will be a revolution. They want the President to draw their chestnut out of the fire.

Yesterday the President had a sick headache and he really does look very thin and bad. Mrs. Wilson hoped he could go for a game of golf, but he had an appointment at four.

May 30, 1919

Today seemed the ending of the week, though it isn't Sunday but Memorial Day. The President was too busy to go to the church services. I went and sat with the Wallaces in their pew at the big American Church. It was a very impressive service, a military band, and when the clergyman and choir came in they were preceded by one soldier carrying the Cross and another carrying the Flag, and followed by four soldiers, four sailors and four marines. A little French Protestant clergyman read one of the most beautiful prayers I have ever heard for those who had fallen in the war. It was quite an international affair, with the national hymns of France, Great Britain and the United States, and a priest of the Greek Church in gorgeous cloth of gold robes to assist.

This afternoon the services were at the American cemetery at Suresnes where the men who died here after the Château-Thierry drive, when the city was a shambles, are buried.

Going out to the cemetery, the President was preoccupied and nervous, as he always is before a speech. The cemetery is so new and bare and brown, but very well kept, and the women of Suresnes have kept flowers on the graves, and it will be lovely in time.

We could not get out on account of Mrs. Wilson's infected foot, so we sat in the car and watched the President walk up to the stand; then we drove up behind him and waited and listened, while he made one of the greatest speeches I have ever heard him make. There is no doubt that he is the idol of the little people.

I sent out the two boys who work with me. They wanted to go and I wanted them to have some ideals to take home and make a part of their lives. I didn't think they would care for the speech at all, but that just shows the big truths aren't meant just for the educated—they belong to the world. One of my two boys told me it was the great day of his life and he was going to cut out a clipping of the President's speech and keep it just to inspire him. He said the "little rough-neck motorcycle driver" next to him was crying, and all around the men were too much moved to know if they ought to sit still or applaud.

June 4, 1919

I am ashamed of the brevity of my notes. The house twice a day —at eleven and four—is usually full of people for the conferences, consideration of the German proposals, and finishing of the Austrian treaty. At those times I usually go down to Mrs. Wilson's room and sit with her, sometimes read with her, sometimes sew.

June 7, 1919

After luncheon today we adjourned to the President's little study downstairs where he showed us how the "Big Four" and their advisers always sit before the fireplace:

```
                    Table
    The President       Mantoux (Interpreter)
                            Sir Maurice Hankey
    Clemenceau          Orlando
    Lloyd George        Vacant Chair
                    Open Fire
```

The conversation is always in English, and Mantoux whispers the translation in French to Orlando as it goes along.

This afternoon the President went out to Picpus Cemetery to replace the flower wreath which he had left on Lafayette's grave in December by a very beautiful bronze one. The artist had copied his handwriting perfectly: "To Lafayette from a Fellow Servant of Liberty, Woodrow Wilson."

June 15, 1919

Our great excitement is finally settled, our trip to Brussels, and now the next will be when we go tripping home. Someone was speaking today at luncheon about being homesick and the President said no one could be more so than he. He is certainly an unadulterated American when it comes to that and if he were not so busy I think he would be utterly miserable with homesickness. Mr. I. Hoover comes a close second and then the rest of the entourage. The President said he thought he knew a good deal of the seamy side of American politics, but they were as nothing compared to the deviousness of the French.

June 16, 1919

Mrs. Wilson and I went to the Baroness Wedel's (Norwegian Minister's wife) to tea. She has a beautiful house which belonged to Lafayette before he sold his property to help America in the

Revolutionary War. It is built as houses were in the time of Louis XIV, with two rows of drawing rooms around the sides of a square. They have beautiful paintings and the house is ideal, with very little furniture, very little decoration.

Baroness Wedel was a rich widow and her husband a widower, and the story goes among the antique dealers that she married him to get some wonderful old French silver table pieces he had. Such pieces are rare, for they were nearly all melted up during the Revolution.

June 18, 1919—Brussels

Here I am in the tallest and stateliest royal bed I have been in yet. When I really publish my memoirs I think they will all begin and end with beds. At Buckingham I was really in the vasty deeps. I think it was one from the Victorian era, with sheets of slickness unparalleled. It was cold and dank there and I skated from one spot to another until I finally made a little hole for myself and dug myself in. At the Quirinal it was vast but less slippery. Here I am in an erection of brass, modern but fearsome high, and tall as I am, I had to make a running leap to get into it. The suite itself is lovely—an antechamber, a large cheerful sitting room and a lovely fresh-looking chintz room. It hasn't the beautiful things in it as at the Quirinal or Buckingham, but is really prettier. Curiously enough there is no bath, only a portable tub, but perfectly fitted with modern plumbing otherwise. It is curious to understand the reason for these inconveniences when the place is partly fitted with modern plumbing. There are two rooms, one with a huge wash stand, and the other with other articles.

The Palace is quite imposing on the outside though, of course, not as huge as Buckingham or the Quirinal. We arrived promptly at 9.15 and it was still light. The streets were lined with people and it was a pity they had closed motors, for the crowd couldn't see the President. The station was beautifully decorated with palms and flowers and looked quite unlike a station. The inevitable red carpet of honor was down.

The crowd was very thick around the Palace and enthusiastic. We drove into a side entrance. A row of flunkies at one end in scarlet livery made a nice touch of color against the white marble at the end of the corridor. The royalties went along ahead and we followed discreetly behind, going up a lovely and perfectly symmetrical staircase, which Baron Moncheur very truly said is the best part of the building, for we got into an ugly reception room and ugly drawing room, where the Cabinet, a lady-in-waiting for the palace, Cardinal Mercier, and Army men, simply covered with decorations, were lined up against the wall. The President went first and the King followed, mentioning each man by name as the President shook hands with him, and right behind came Mrs. Wilson with the Queen doing the same for her. We all waited in a little group by the door. One of the King's equerries came up and asked if Margaret and I would go over to where the President and Mrs. Wilson and the King and Queen were standing, after the presentations, and so we went there and stood until another move was made. This time it was around to a balcony where the huge crowd called for the President and he showed himself to them in the window. We stopped for a moment in what I imagine was the Royal Apartment, the King and Queen said goodnight to us, and the two ladies-in-waiting and the Equerry showed the President and Mrs. Wilson to their rooms. They are miles apart. Mrs. Wilson's lady-in-waiting got her orders for tomorrow, which amounted to leaving Mrs. Wilson and me alone, and I went out with Margaret. I am glad enough to get into bed for we have had a fearsome day. We got near Nieuport at nine, after an uneventful trip, in the same French train which the Belgian Government took for the occasion. The King and Queen met us, coming on board the train when it stopped. The usual guard was drawn up, tooting away hard over "The Star-Spangled Banner," as another did tonight at Brussels. We piled into motors. I was in No. 3 and feel tonight I might be married to Baron Moncheur after passing so much of the last twenty-four hours with him.

It was certainly a pitiless chase they led us, and I think before the President gets away he will see every devastated corner of Belgium. I always think of what Mrs. Sharp, the Ambassadress, said: that the French are like children with a sore foot. They want everyone to see and sympathize with them. Of course, it is perfectly natural and everyone does want to see the places where the world's agony took place.

Of all the regions I have seen Flanders is by far the worst. It can't compare, of course, with the length and extent of that done in France, but the ruin seems more awful in Flanders. We went to Nieuport where the dyke which holds five canals was opened at high tide and the country flooded. The town was all shot to pieces, but an enterprising soul had opened a new café in some bit of ruin. We went on through village after village, through what had been beautiful grazing land, now turned into what looks like our burnt-over swamp lands, pools of water in the shell holes, and in places huge craters filled with water still. We drove finally to Houtholst Wood, and as we watched the motors come up I thought I had never seen such a trail: the financial experts Baruch, Norman Davis and McCormick; Hoover and a naval aide, assistant to the Food Commission; endless newspaper men and camera fiends and movie men. The little signal corps man, Jackson, who has been on both trips with the President, was everywhere. Motors stop at a village and the next thing Jackson is clinging onto a telegraph pole or climbing up a ruin to a balcony and taking pictures from there.

(That was the day when we started at 8 A.M. and ended up at 7:30 P.M. with no opportunity to "freshen up." The lady-in-waiting told me the Queen had trained herself to spend a day in public appearances without benefit of rest room. I explained patiently that we had not had similar training.)

I intended to put in my impressions of the royalty last night when I stopped to sleep, and will add it here. He was the first to come aboard and is always so charming, very handsome, very slow of speech, rather a silent person, but nice. Much to my surprise she is small, very plain, done up in a white wash dress, white canvas shoes and cotton stockings. I don't wonder when silk stockings are the price they are over here. I think it must be a court fashion, for the Countess d'Oultrement had them on, too. The latter did not come on the train. After royal greetings were exchanged Margaret and I were introduced. Then we all got out of the train and Star-Spangle Bannered along the platform. The Queen has hay fever terribly, and Mrs. Wilson said she told her the particular thing she could not stand was roses, and at the first village they passed into the motor two huge bunches of flowers for Mrs. Wilson which she wanted to put outside, but the Queen said no, that feelings would be hurt, and that they must be kept in until they got outside the village, and then the poor lady nearly sneezed her head off, and continued to sneeze at intervals all day.

Our party was Close, the President's secretary, General Harts and Lieutenant Irving, who is at the house. Then there were a lot of aides to the King. Houtholst Wood must have been a lovely place. Now most of the trees are shot away, and a scraggly vegetation is coming up. We walked up a little road and found a camion with the luncheon, and a little tent covering the luncheon table. There we all sat down informally, save the royalties. The King and President, the Queen beside the President, and Mrs. Wilson beside the King, evidently an inflexible ruling. It was a simple enough affair; cold chicken, lettuce salad, sandwiches, and strawberries. The photographers had a merry time with us at the end of luncheon, getting lots of pictures, and the Queen, who is a camera fiend too, went out and took some pictures. At the cars we lingered for some time, and finally Lieutenant Irving came to me and said they were waiting for the President and Mrs. Wilson to make the move. So I approached Mrs. Wilson and made known to her that the destinies of the thirty motor cars and their occupants hung on her, and so off we went merrily, eating anew of the dust of Flanders, which process kept on for miles. We passed ruin after ruin, with patches of fairly good country between. During the morning we had run at the beginning between the old Belgian and German lines, and then into the German.

The country grew worse and we got into that awful desolation around Ypres, and finally we were near enough to see the outline of a ruined town, and then swung into what had been the lovely Gothic Square, the pride of Flanders, and the peaceful little town of 30,000 before the war. As Verdun is to the French, Château-Thierry to us, so is Ypres to the British, and it seemed very fitting to find the place full of English soldiers, working in the ruins and making their German prisoners undo a little of the harm they had committed. The British Empire is going to make of Ypres a shrine,

Miss Edith Benham launching the *Benham*, Philadelphia, March 22, 1913. *Left to right:* Rear Admiral W. H. Brownson, Rear Admiral C. C. Clark, Miss Edith Benham, Master Harry Benham, Mrs. H. K. Benham, Miss Emily Benham, Mrs. W. Kilduff and Miss Katharine Kilduff, cousins.

The author with her mother, father and brother in front of the Commandant's house, Mare Island, California. At upper left are their friends, Mrs. Harrington and her daughters.

President Wilson with President Poincaré of France on his arrival in Paris, December 1918. *Courtesy National Archives*

Palais Murat, where the Wilsons stayed while in Paris. *Courtesy National Archives*

Left to right: Queen Elizabeth of Belgium, President Wilson, Mrs. Wilson, King Albert. Royal Palace, Brussels, June 19, 1919. *Courtesy National Archives*

Miss Benham with her staff (N. P. Schindler, Chief Yeoman, U.S.N., and Francis Kennedy, stenographer) in her office in the Palais Murat, Paris, 1919. *Courtesy National Archives*

Arrival of President and Mrs. Wilson in Rome. King Victor Emmanuel III and Queen Elena in center.

President Wilson's Christmas dinner in U.S. headquarters at Chaumont, 1918. General Pershing between President and Mrs. Wilson, Miss Benham at right. *Courtesy National Archives*

Arrival in London, 1918. *Left to right:* Mrs. Wilson, Queen Mary, President Wilson, King George V and the Princess Royal. *United Press Photo*

Mrs. Roosevelt holding one of her first press conferences, in the Monroe Room in the White House, 1933. *Courtesy Franklin D. Roosevelt Library*

Picnic at Grayville, Illinois. Mrs. Roosevelt seated between Mrs. Helm (*left*) and Miss Thompson.

President Roosevelt with his secretaries, Marguerite LeHand, Marvin McIntyre, and Grace Tully, in his study at Hyde Park, November 4, 1938. *Courtesy Franklin D. Roosevelt Library*

Mrs. Roosevelt with Mrs. Helm and Miss Thompson in the White House, April 1941. *Photo by Jackie Martin, courtesy Franklin D. Roosevelt Library*

Queen Elizabeth at the British Embassy Garden Party, Washington, June 8, 1939. *Courtesy Franklin D. Roosevelt Library*

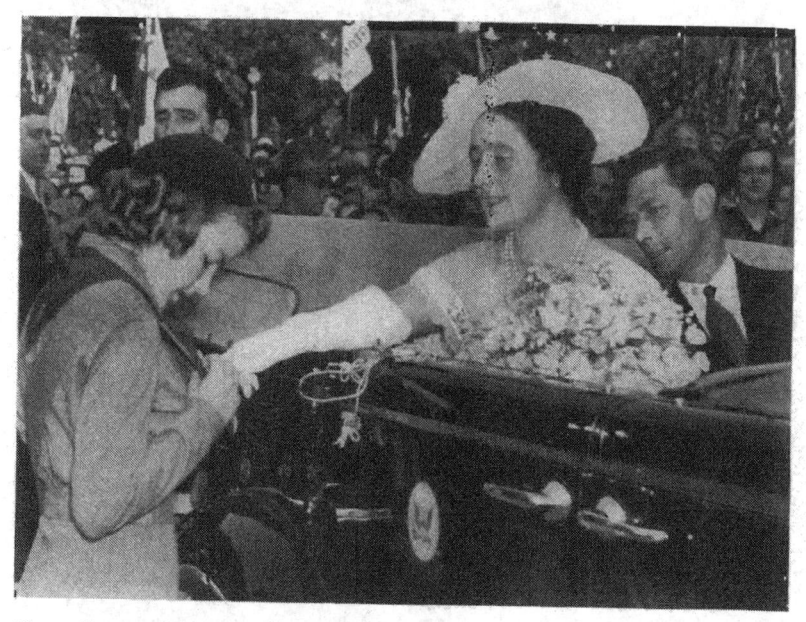

King George VI and Queen Elizabeth greeting a girl scout while touring Washington. *Harris & Ewing Photo*

The Roosevelts and Their Britannic Majesties after morning services at St. James Church, Hyde Park, June 11, 1939. *Courtesy Franklin D. Roosevelt Library*

(Left) Author and artist Hendrik Willem van Loon asks the Social Secretary of the White House for explicit information on an important point: "The man from whom I rent such things would like to know for December 19th whether it is to be This or This? Will you kindly indicate the desired garment and thank you."

(Right) Although press photographers were barred, a guest managed to snap this picture of a picnic lunch at Hill-Top Cottage, Hyde Park, for Their Britannic Majesties, June 11, 1939. Guests being introduced to the King, standing next to Mrs. Roosevelt, and Queen Elizabeth, sitting next to the President. *Courtesy Franklin D. Roosevelt Library*

The President and Mrs. Roosevelt with Queen Wilhelmina at the White House, August 5, 1942. *Courtesy Franklin D. Roosevelt Library*

President Roosevelt at extreme right with Crown Prince Olaf and Princess Martha of Norway, on the porch of the White House, June 29, 1939. *Courtesy Franklin D. Roosevelt Library*

Mrs. Roosevelt at the annual egg rolling on the White House lawn, March 25, 1940. *Courtesy Franklin D. Roosevelt Library*

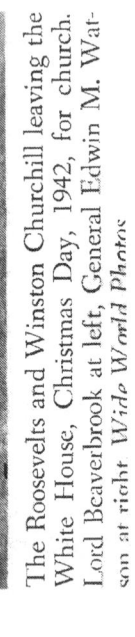

Madame Chiang Kai-shek and Mrs. Roosevelt on the White House lawn, March 1, 1943. *Acme Photo*

The Roosevelts and Winston Churchill leaving the White House, Christmas Day, 1942, for church. Lord Beaverbrook at left, General Edwin M. Watson at right. *Wide World Photos*

Christmas in the White House, December 1939. *Courtesy Franklin D. Roosevelt Library*

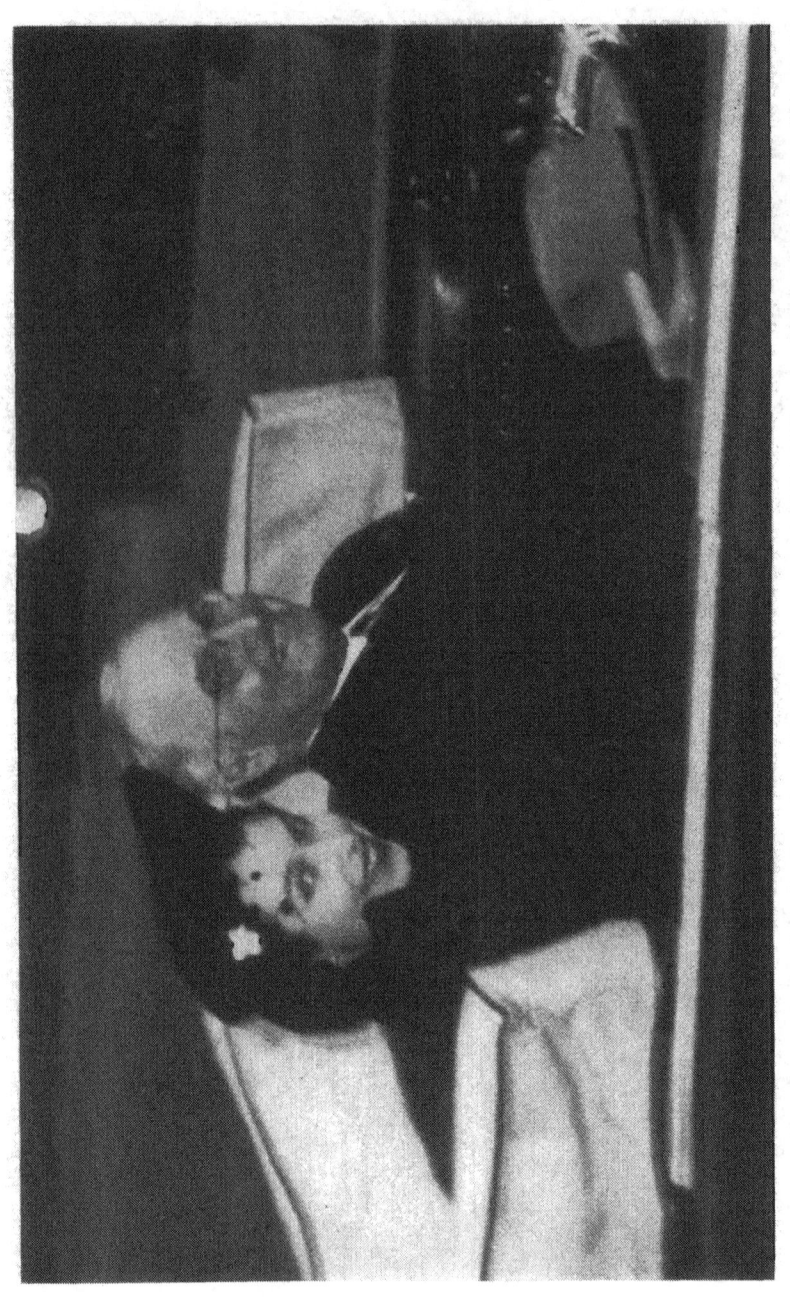

Princess Elizabeth of England with President Truman en route to Blair House, October 31, 1951. *Harris & Ewing Photo*

Princess Elizabeth and Prince Philip playing host to President Truman and his family at a state dinner in the Canadian Embassy, Washington, November 1, 1951. *Acme Photo*

"The Briars," Mrs. Helm's home in Boyce, Virginia.

Living room of "The Briars."

and very fittingly when one thinks of the quarter of a million lives she gave there. With our common heritage of language Ypres seemed closer to me than Verdun. A pleasant Canadian colonel was in command and walked around the little square with us, and thinking of him and what Canada had done in those battles of Ypres it seemed very fitting to see a part of the old town ramparts set aside for Canada's holy ground.

Driving in and driving out we passed other war relics, tanks shot to pieces, and the usual miles of barbed wire still unsalvaged. Swinging out again to the north we climbed up one ridge and saw the little hills like Passchendaele which had been drenched in blood, and you could only wonder anything ever lived and held on in that town below. At Roulers and the other little towns the children were turned out in the streets and the Mayors made addresses, and at Ostend we got out and went into the town hall where the President and Mrs. Wilson had to sign their names in the usual book. They are mad over signatures here.

The next stop was, with Ypres, the most interesting of the whole day—Zeebrugge. There the Commander of the *Invincible*—Carpenter—met us and Commander Evans, who has been in the Arctic and nearly everything else, judging by his medals. We got out of the motors at the beginning of the historic mole, saw the big hole in it where the British submarine charged with explosives was run against it and sunk, then walked along and on the very spot where Carpenter and his men landed. He told us very quietly and modestly his share in it. How his men ever got down the wall under fire I don't see, and how they got 200 of the wounded 289 up again is still more remarkable. The sky was so blue and the whole scene so peaceful, and Carpenter himself so young and untried-looking, it was hard to think the mole had seen such scenes, but we only had to look toward the land and the entrance to the Bruges canal and see the sunken ships to know it is all true. Carpenter would point a finger here and there to show how the ships came up, and he spoke of the great difficulty of getting upon the mole, for there is a high parapet on the ocean side.

At Zeebrugge the train was waiting for us, and after a good clean-up we had an excellent dinner in the train. There were two compartments in the dining car, and twelve dined in the one with royalty, and the others had an overflow meeting in the next one. At Zeebrugge we picked up Mme. de Wouters, an attractive woman who had been assigned to Mrs. Wilson as lady-in-waiting. They are a sort of liaison officer for visiting royalties. This one was a very sweet woman (a friend of Mme. Havenith—Helen Ffoulke's, who had spoken of me to her) and was really some help—unlike the one in Rome.

Dinner went off very well. The King and Queen are very quiet but very nice, but quietness does not make for gaiety at a dinner. I had Mr. Whitlock, our Minister, beside me. He is a charming man and a delightful person to talk to. The Queen had changed her gown of white linen to white silk—I believe she wears white nearly always—and looked very well, though she is very plain. I have never seen anything like the way the people adore them. It was everywhere shrieks of *"Vive la Reine!"*

June 20, 1919—Paris

I had to finish this up when I came home, for we went so hard all day and didn't get to the train until 10:30, when I was more than ready for bed. The ladies didn't go on the excursion to Charleroi, where the President went to see one of the factories quite dismantled by the Germans. He said he had never seen a more thorough job in his life. I went out to see Helen Havenith, who has had a slight operation, and was in a hospital. I think all the royal motors must have been out on the road or getting ready for the afternoon jaunt, for I went in the most disreputable little Ford limousine, with a gum-chewing chauffeur, and the royal insignia (S.M.) on the outside.

Our cars had gone up from Paris, to be sure, but the other Americans of the party were using them, and of course we couldn't use them, being at the Palace. Things are rather disorganized at the Palace anyway, for the King and Queen are living in the country and only came for the President's visit. Some of us were in one part of it and others in another part; the President, Mrs. Wilson, Margaret and I in the original palace, and Dr. Grayson, Close and Irving in the extension added by taking a hotel which had stood beside the palace and connecting it by a corridor to the original building. I never did have a chance to go over the Palace, for we were so constantly on the run.

June 24, 1919

The great excitement of the day was the Treaty signing. About six Mrs. Wilson saw a French officer jump out of a motor before it came to a stop, and dash up the street pavement into the house. Then the President came down a few minutes after, from the Conference, to tell her the Germans had agreed to sign. After a little while pandemonium broke loose, sirens moaning and guns being fired and the church bells ringing. Before dinner my office force said the maids had kissed all of them in the hall. This didn't seem a complaint. The garage had been making merry in the back yard, making a fiendish noise with motor engines and horns. At dinner we had champagne glasses at our plates, and when the President started to drink I asked if he would let us drink to "The greatest man in the world and the greatest peace made by him." He is so modest he never seems to think much of himself, but the rest all drank heartily to it. Then he raised his glass and drank, "To the Peace, an enduring Peace, a Peace under the League of Nations." Mrs. Wilson and he drove down to the Crillon after dinner, where he had quite an ovation. The people waited for some time for him to come and then formed a lane for him to drive through. Everyone was going down to the Boulevards, so about ten H.S.K. telephoned to know if I did not want to go, and so he and Kiely came for me. As we were leaving the house, a camion filled with doughboys and Red Cross and Y. girls came by the house, having broken through the police cordon to pick us up. We were all ready in cars outside the door, and with a rush the President's motor passed, and we fell in behind. His flag was flying from the front, for all the delegates to the Peace Conference carry the flags of their countries, and the President carries his own. The road to Versailles was spaced at intervals by policemen, and there seemed an endless procession of cars. Arrived at Versailles we turned into the broad Avenue de Paris, a splendid wide avenue, imposing always, and doubly so then, with a double line of cavalry, each blue-coated poilu with a banner on his lance. The effect was a lovely one of misty horizon blue and the colors of the banners. In the courtyard was a company of the Garde Républicaine, stunning figures in white trousers, cuirasses, and helmets with a long horse tail. They lined the staircase we went up. The setting was certainly all that could be desired for impressiveness. The demand for seats was so great that a number of people had to be put in a room adjoining the long Galerie des Glaces, and consequently saw none of the signing. The Galerie des Glaces is a long room running along the front of the Palace. We entered at one end, where more of the Garde Républicaine were stationed to keep people from crowding in from the other room. The chairs, benches, were placed on either side of the aisle, and the French, with characteristic politeness, had given Viviani and another Frenchman armchairs across the aisle, while Mrs. Wilson sat on one of these tapestry-covered backless benches! She had the front seats, and beside her Mrs. Lansing and Mrs. House; next came some foreigners, I don't know from which country. Behind came Margaret, Mrs. Wallace and me, and so on with other Americans. Someone did finally bring Mrs. Wilson a chair. The French had really arranged the room very badly. Instead of raising the seats and letting us look down on the delegates to see the signing, we were all on the level and the delegates were on a raised platform covered with a carpet and rugs. There was a lot of running around with autograph albums and programs to be signed, and I thought the occasion was robbed in that way of lots of solemnity.

Then there were secretaries flying around, so the delegates' part looked bustling and busy. This did stop when we heard the bugles for the Germans. An officer spoke to the two big guards at the head of the line at salute, and told them to sheathe their swords, and then he came again and withdrew the guards against the wall. A ripple of suppressed interest passed over the place, for we knew the Germans were near and, attended by an officer from each of the Allied nations, they came in. They were certainly a contrast to the men of blood and iron who had signed in '71 in that room, or stood around when the Empire of Germany was made there, and very different from the Hindenburgs and Von Tirpitzes who succeeded them. There were two miserable-looking, ill, shaking men. They looked like druggists—second-rate ones—tall and thin, not even scholarly-looking. They did carry themselves with a certain dignity and, because they were so wretched physically, I couldn't hate them. They were taken to their seats directly in front of us, with their backs to us, and their legs shook when they sat down, though when they came to sign they walked with perfect composure, and seemed quite at ease later, and when they went out. Of the signing itself I could see nothing. When the President went to sign with the Americans we stood to see, but I could only see the top of his head. He said he realized he was very excited, because after signing "Woodrow" with perfect ease he had difficulty signing "Wilson." As the delegates walked around to their seats he looked at Mrs. Wilson and smiled. Mr. White, who is the soul of courtesy, stopped and faced her, and made a little bow, and passed on. After the Germans left there was some scrambling and confusion. The delegates started to walk out, but I can't say there was any order or dignity about it. The cannon booming when the last signature went on the treaty did make a solemn sound.

Mr. Clemenceau invited all the ladies to take tea in the Senate room in another part of the grounds. The President said afterward that the old man was so excited he really didn't think he knew where he was going, for he walked out rather aimlessly and led the President into a thick crowd, who just went mad around them. Mrs. Wilson had decided not to go to the tea, so we stayed in the same room, going to the window to watch the crowd below, and we could see them fairly seethe around the President and Clemenceau. There were a lot of American cars parked at one side, and I am sure they were the ones that started their horns going with the guns. It was a beautiful sight, for the fountains had started and the day was wonderful. We left the President out there, for he had a final meeting. I drove later on the Boulevards, and the crowds were beside themselves. After a quiet dinner Mr. Lloyd George came in to say good-by, and said to the President that he could not only congratulate himself on the Treaty, but on drawing England and America closer together than they had ever been before. There was an enormous crowd around the station, and very enthusiastic, and in leaving France I think the President has regained all the popularity he may have lost for a time. On the platform everyone in the world was crowded to say good-by, and I felt quite badly to see the last, in those surroundings, of all those people who had been so sweet. Shortly before we left, the Poincarés came and bade a fond farewell. We had the usual French officials to go down with us, and the usual ones at Brest, and the same puffing little tug to get us aboard the old packet.

July 2, 1919

The trip has been just about as usual, though the weather has been great, and I haven't been as bored as usual. The people I like, so far, best on board are Mr. and Mrs. Thomas Lamont. He has a keen quizzical face and a very alert mind, not just a business mind, but one interested in lots of other things. They asked me up to dine in the Peace Conference dining room last night, for Mrs. Lamont had a birthday party. She is a clever woman, too. The President is busy writing his message to Congress, and getting some rest. Mrs. Wilson hauls him out every day to walk, which he despises but does meekly. He spoke today with real regret of leaving old Clemenceau, of whom he is very fond despite his shiftiness, which he feels is more due to his advisers, for he says the old man's ideas are all straight, and if left alone he would be honest.

Two of the newspaper correspondents came to luncheon today. Conversation turned on the violent attacks made on the President by Americans living abroad during the war, and the fact that we didn't go into the war sooner. The President said he didn't go into the war until he was sure he had the country behind him; that he felt he could not have gone one minute sooner, for the American people were not ready. He said he used to ask the members of his Cabinet at meetings every week what they heard, and they said the Americans would follow him, but he said: "I couldn't have them follow. They had to go into it with a whoop."

I will be with you in Washington almost as soon as this letter reaches you.

So ended my diary, written as personal letters to Admiral Helm. And so began the tragic finale of the Wilson administration—an oft-told tale that I shall not here repeat. Suffice it to say that President Wilson was not able to take the American people into the League of Nations "with a whoop" and he would not settle for less. At Wichita, Kansas, on his return trip from his September, 1919, transcontinental campaign in behalf of the ratification by this country of the League Covenant, President Wilson collapsed. The White House revolved around a very sick man for many months. There were a number of people—and I was one of them—who thought they saw courses of action which might save the League, and who made efforts to have them followed. But Woodrow Wilson was no longer physically able to put over his program.

Mrs. Wilson's devotion to her husband, in the days of his illness, was superb. She never spared herself in her loving care of him.

There were a few lighter memories among those dark days at the White House. The King and Queen of the Belgians visited this country the last part of October and saw the President in his room. The official entertaining for them was done by Vice-President and Mrs. Marshall. One day Mrs. Wilson took the Queen of Belgium for a drive, and the lady-in-waiting, the Countess de Caraman-Chimay, and I followed in another car.

In November the young Prince of Wales came, saw President Wilson briefly, and was feted around the town. I recall going to the old British Embassy, where I had once served as social secretary, to a reception in his honor. The Prince went to the Congressional Library to another reception on this same visit—an enormous affair, but lacking the dignity of the Embassy party.

Nothing could have been more memorable than seeing the heir to the British throne standing beside Viscount Grey of Falloden, then the British Ambassador.

The Minister at the Embassy during that period was Sir William Tyrrell, a delightful person who later became Ambassador to France. He was the typical career diplomat of British novels. The Ambassador was nearly blind, a widower, and Sir William acted, as he once said, "as eyes" for the Ambassador, and in every way was a great help at the Embassy.

Sir William joined me after I spoke to the Ambassador and the Prince, and stood looking at His Royal Highness. "He is very like his grandfather," said the diplomat; and as an afterthought: "In more ways than one." History bore out this appraisal.

Sir William made another comment I have always remembered in connection with the old British Embassy on Connecticut Avenue. I said something to him about the Victorian solidity of the Embassy staircase, which was an impressive example of the "black walnut period." It climbed solidly from the entrance hallway, divided at a landing midway to the second floor, and over the landing hung a charming portrait of Queen Victoria in her youth.

"Do not regret that example of the Victorian period, Miss Benham," said Sir William. "It was a period in British history which will never return."

In the course of the two Wilson trips overseas, I had been completely won to Wilsonian Democracy by the President himself. He made no effort to convince me of the worth of his ideas for America and the world. I simply saw the validity of his arguments. Certainly, coming from a conservative family, and ingrained besides with Navy nonpartisanship, I would seem to be an unlikely person to become a Democrat. But that is what happened to me, and I found it hard to watch the thwarting of President Wilson's aims by a small group on Capitol Hill.

This may possibly have contributed to the case of nervous exhaustion which I suffered after our return from France. But certainly I had overworked while there. Our party was so small that all in it had to take over many roles. For instance, the day of our arrival in Paris, I was the only one in it who could speak French, and I had to translate all incoming telephone calls. Again, I took over for Mrs. Wilson the ordering of food—the President could eat no pork nor veal and it was necessary to rule items not on his diet out of the menu. Other special duties kept arising. I also felt the heavy responsibility of checking invitation lists, particularly after Jefferson Caffery, later to be Ambassador to France, then just starting his career at our Embassy in Paris, had pointed out how one of the suggested guest lists I had received from a French protocol officer had been weighted with his personal friends. Of course we quickly corrected that situation. All this in addition to my secretarial duties for Mrs. Wilson.

Whatever the cause, I was so thoroughly tired that my physician advised that I give up my position and take a long rest. This worked in well with my personal plans. Admiral Helm and I, drawn even closer by our correspondence, had decided we had waited quite long enough.

We were married in my apartment in April of 1920. It was the quietest kind of wedding. Our only guests were Mrs. Wilson and a Washington friend of mine of many years, Miss Jane Hunt, daughter of the Army officer for whom Fort Hunt was named, and a young officer friend of Admiral Helm.

Chapter 11

A WASHINGTONIAN OF THE MINORITY

AFTER MY MARRIAGE, I naturally saw very little of the White House or official life in the Warren G. Harding, Calvin Coolidge and Herbert Hoover administrations. I had been so much a part of the Democratic scene that I was indeed among the minority in a Republican regime.

However, my husband and I led a very comfortable and satisfying life—seeing old friends, going to luncheons and dinners, giving luncheons and dinners, going to the theater.

I also became an active member of the Woman's National Democratic Club, a favorite gathering place for the few hardy Democrats who survived the Republican change-over. Having always been afraid of debt, I was frightened by a project to buy a clubhouse. Some of those women talked of $100,000 as though it were a mere nothing. But when the time came to vote on this matter, I helped to take the debt on—and I also worked to pay it off.

For a short while Admiral Helm and I lived in my apartment close to the White House.

Quite often on our walks to the market we ran into John Mayes, the tall and courtly White House doorman. Always we stopped to chat with him.

Later we moved to an apartment house on California Street.

My old friend Miss Laura Harlan was Mrs. Harding's secretary, and it was through her, I am sure, that I was invited twice to the White House. The first time, in May of 1921, was the occasion when Madame Marie Curie, the discoverer of radium, was presented with $100,000 worth of radium, gift of the women of America, locked in a little ribbon-draped casket. Her whole triumphal trip to this country from France, during which she was weighted down with honors, had been organized by Mrs. William Brown Meloney, an exceptionally able New York newspaper woman. President Harding made the presentation of the radium at an East Room ceremony. My old friend and fellow traveler to Europe, Ambassador Jules Jusserand, introduced this frail little wizard of a woman who seemed even tinier beside the handsome figure of President Harding.

My other White House visit in the Harding Administration was when both my husband and I were invited to sit in the stands behind the President and Mrs. Harding to watch a Shrine parade. I found Mrs. Harding to be a pleasant hostess.

Our summers we spent, at my insistence, as farmers at Grayville, Illinois, which had been founded by my husband's maternal grandfather. My husband had thought I was a too indoctrinated Easterner to enjoy the life there. But I loved it. The weather which grew the corn was indeed hot, as he had warned me. But the warmth of friendship in Grayville and the neighboring town of Carmi compensated for the horror of the heat. In the early morning when my husband and I used to ride over the farms he owned there, I got instructions in farms and farming, which has stood me in good stead since.

In the fall, we returned to Washington and its social rounds. The Supreme Court circle offered good neutral territory. Often I poured tea for the Monday "At Homes" of my friend Mrs. Louis Brandeis, wife of the famous liberal Justice who was appointed to the bench by President Wilson.

I first met the Justice and Mrs. Brandeis through Mr. and Mrs.

Charles Hamlin, whom I had known when I was a young girl in Paris. Mr. Hamlin had returned to Washington as a member of the Federal Reserve Board, and I had resumed my friendship with his wife, who is still my friend today.

My recollection is that the Hamlins were living in a rented house on New Hampshire Avenue and had given a large and pleasant dinner party in honor of the new Justice and his wife. I felt very much like a Cinderella when the Justice sat down beside me and talked to me after the dinner. From then on, Justice and Mrs. Brandeis took me to their hearts, with a friendship and love that will always stand out as one of the brightest spots in my life.

People said of the Justice and Mrs. Brandeis that when a distinguished foreigner, particularly in the intellectual world, came to Washington, he paid his respects first to the President and then called on the Brandeises.

There was no pretension about this distinguished pair. They lived as modestly as possible and their apartment was plain to a degree. One of my friends, who herself was far from well off, said of them: "When I have been to their apartment and go home and look around I feel that I am living in sinful luxury."

Their furniture was adequate. Their apartment was large and very comfortable and it contained all the necessary things, but nothing was valuable. Evidently they had had their furnishings for a long time. Their guest room, as I remember it, had an iron bed.

The Justice, who always got up about four o'clock in the morning, had his "chambers" in another apartment where he could write in the early morning hours when his mind was clear and he was undisturbed.

It was part of their social belief that one should live simply and not surround oneself with costly objects. They gave small dinners, never more than eight or ten guests. The food was always delicious, simple, and the dining table usually had table mats and no cloth. Mrs. Brandeis always carved the fowl or the roast.

I can see the Justice now, directing the conversation so that every guest at the table would have some part in it. The dinner guests always included widely differing personalities in political and religious spheres.

Both the Justice and Mrs. Brandeis liked to have young people with them. At their numerous days "At Home" one of the Justice's secretaries was present to help in taking care of the guests. The secretaries, whom he selected from the leading graduates of Harvard Law School, brought in many other young people.

A man who has always stood out in my mind as one of the most brilliant of the Justice's secretaries was Dean Acheson. It was at one of the Brandeis' "At Homes" that I first met him and his handsome wife.

In the main, however, thinking back on the Harding period makes me feel as though I had been through the Babylonian captivity with the golden calf on the altar stone. The proudest boast of a Cabinet dinner then was that the aggregate wealth of the happy guests was a billion dollars.

I remember going with my husband to a luncheon where all other guests were staunch Administration supporters. The Teapot Dome scandal was at its peak and we had bought a newspaper "extra" on the way, telling of the sentence of former Interior Department Secretary Albert B. Fall, who was convicted of accepting a bribe involved with the transfer of naval oil reserves to private interests. The only comment at the luncheon was that Senator Thomas J. Walsh, Montana Democrat who conducted hearings on this celebrated case, had been unfair to Fall, Harry Sinclair, Edward B. McLean and others involved! Harry Sinclair was the oil operator charged with paying the bribe and Mr. McLean was a wealthy Washington newspaper publisher and close friend of President Harding.

At a dinner a few nights before, Senator Walsh had told us that he had tried to obtain indictments against others involved in the Teapot Dome case of whose guilt he was morally certain, but he could not get hold of all the facts in the mass of lies and evasions.

My first introduction to the Calvin Coolidges was when he was Governor of Massachusetts. He and Mrs. Coolidge greeted the President and Mrs. Wilson when they landed in Boston on the return from their first trip to Europe. As First Lady, Mrs. Coolidge was a charming and gracious person. I remember once when I had a long illness she sent me flowers—a kindly remembrance for which I am sure her secretary, Miss Mary Randolph, was partly responsible.

My husband and I were invited to one of the Coolidge musicales. The occasion lingers in my mind because of an amusing experience. As I was moving along the receiving line, a relative of the then social secretary happened to notice that I had on no gloves. I was like a great many other people who saw no reason to buy long, expensive gloves just to go to the White House. This lady, who was exceedingly formal, said, "Oh, Mrs. Helm, have you left your gloves in the dressing room?" "No," I replied, "I did not wear any." "Wouldn't you like to borrow one of mine to carry?" she asked. I thanked her but said I would go "as is."

Of the many Calvin Coolidge stories circulating around Washington during his administration, none is more amusing than that which Miss Mary Patten used to tell on herself. The Patten sisters had one of the most famous social salons in all the history of Washington. It was frequented by diplomats, high State Department officials, Senators. The saying was that it sometimes cost a man his official neck not to be there. And there was a quip that official Washington had three means of communication, telephone, telegraph and tell-a-Patten.

Miss Mary Patten was invited to dinner and was told that she would be seated next to Mr. Coolidge. She made a bet with one of her friends that she could make him talk, so when she sat down at the table she turned and said brightly: "Mr. President, I have made a bet with one of my friends that you would talk to me during dinner." President Coolidge turned and drawled in his nasal New England twang: "Madam, you have lost," and never said another word during the entire meal.

Standing out as a tragic memory of the Coolidge administration —a memory which will always be with me—is the burial of Woodrow Wilson on February 6, 1924. When a man who has been President dies, custom decrees that his political foes as well as his closest friends pay him homage. Those of high rank, whether friend or foe, take their places beside the bier and in the forefront of the procession. It is, in a way, comforting, as a symbol of national unity.

Woodrow Wilson, when a mere shadow of his former self, went through the strain of riding in the funeral procession of President Warren G. Harding. Similarly, President and Mrs. Calvin Coolidge attended the services at the Wilson home, and rode in the slow procession to the burial service in the Bethlehem Chapel of Washington's National Cathedral.

It was a deeply impressive ceremony. The chapel seats about three hundred, which brought into sharp focus many faces that linked present with past. In one section reserved for them sat the members of President Coolidge's Cabinet; in another, men who had been in President Wilson's Cabinet.

There is a memorial sarcophagus to Woodrow Wilson in the Cathedral's Bethlehem Chapel, and it is the general belief that he is buried there. That is not the case. After the service was over and all officials of the government had gone, the members of the family and a few intimate friends were asked to go to a nave adjoining the Bethlehem Chapel. After a stone in the middle aisle had been raised by machinery brought in for that purpose, we came back to the Chapel. The casket was lowered into the crypt and was placed in a catacomb there with the usual committal services of the Episcopal Church. As the casket descended, a bugler sounded "Taps" outside in the Cathedral grounds. The newspapers next day said this was the same bugler who had sounded "Taps" for the Burial of the Unknown Soldier, and that his bugle was inscribed in commemoration of that event.

I never knew President Hoover when he was in the White House. But I met him, and was witness to the great acclaim given him in Europe as the result of his food relief work in Belgium following the Armistice of 1918.

I am afraid that Mr. Hoover always blamed me for a prank played on him, at the time of President Wilson's visit to Belgium, by Bernard Baruch, then as now friend and confidant of Presidents, and Dr. Cary Grayson, who was very close indeed to President Theodore Roosevelt as well as President Woodrow Wilson.

We were making an all-day trip and each car had its place assigned in the procession after President and Mrs. Wilson and the

Belgian King and Queen. I was riding with Dr. Grayson and Mr. Baruch, and our car was fifth or sixth. Mr. Hoover's car was the one immediately ahead of ours.

We went along at what seemed like breakneck speed—motors did not run smoothly as they do now. As we were dashing along, Mr. Baruch leaned over to the chauffeur, showed him a hundred-franc note and said, "If you can get ahead of that next car and stay ahead, you will have this."

Of course that was enough. We dashed ahead, nearly demolishing a dog on the way, and we stayed ahead. And for some strange reason, Mr. Hoover apparently thought I was responsible, because after the state dinner that night he came up and asked me my official rank. I replied that I had none—I had only a clerical position with Mrs. Wilson. He said nothing more, but I got the distinct impression that he felt I was trying to show that I was more important than he and that it was I who had ordered the chauffeur to get ahead of his car.

During the Hoover administration I do not remember being asked to the White House, save to those purely official affairs like Army and Navy receptions, to which, because of my husband's rank, he was invited automatically. When Mr. Hoover was in the Coolidge Cabinet, however, Mrs. Hoover asked me to receive with her on some of her "At Home" days. That was when the Hoovers lived in their house on S Street. Mrs. Hoover had considerable flair for interior decorating, and was responsible for some innovations in the S Street House which at that time were considered novel and daring.

Her large and lovely living room was striking indeed in its use of black and gold. The window curtains were of sheer black marquisette. Two sofas, done in black satin enlivened by a gold conventionalized flower motif, were set out from the walls so as to form centers for conversational groups. This was at a time when by custom furniture ran an orderly course against the four walls. For her fall teas, bouquets of huge golden chrysanthemums stood on end tables beside these sofas, heightening the dramatic effect. In front of the sofas were very solid low tables of beautiful redwood on which, as chairs became scarce, people were encouraged to sit to talk to those on the sofas. Over the high mantelpiece, on which sat matching alabaster lamps, were large matching copper plaques from China where the Hoovers had lived.

In the dining room, papered to the wainscot in bold forest design, very new then, Mrs. Hoover had a table which went clear across front windows framed in gold. There her centerpieces and other table decorations were often combinations of fruits and vegetables, including chestnut burs, eggplant shined to a fine sheen, green and red peppers, and pomegranates.

I am not sure about the Hardings, but the Coolidges and Hoovers were remembered in Washington for serving only water at their receptions. I had this fact impressed on my mind when Mrs. Roosevelt revived the custom of serving modest refreshments at receptions. A Washington newspaper man who was an habitué at these affairs assumed an air of utter amazement when he failed to find the pitchers of water and the paper "lily cups" which had adorned the console table at the north end of the State Dining Room in those years when only water was provided to quench the thirst of the multitude.

To the Hoover administration goes the credit for finishing off the old tradition of the New Year's Reception. These annual observances, no doubt pleasant when the city was smaller, were long the bane of the White House staff. All who cared to come were admitted, wearying the President and First Lady with an incredible amount of hand-shaking, and tracking winter slush through the mansion. The last New Year's reception was held on January 1, 1932. After his November defeat by Franklin Roosevelt, Herbert Hoover went South for the Christmas holidays, and the White House New Year's reception has never been resumed.

Chapter 12

AFTER MANY YEARS—
AGAIN THE WHITE HOUSE

I WAS VERY MUCH AT LOOSE ENDS following my husband's death in 1927. After many years of work before my marriage, and the loss of many interests that had come into my life through my husband, I could find very little to occupy my time other than certain charities in which I was interested.

The election of my long-time friend, Franklin Roosevelt, as President, bringing his wife, who had been my friend even longer, into her position as First Lady, resulted in my facing up to this personal problem. I knew the White House well. I was fond of the Roosevelts and agreed with their political principles.

My first recollections of Eleanor Roosevelt—she was born a Roosevelt, a niece of President Theodore Roosevelt—were of a long-legged girl coming to the little country club at Tivoli-on-Hudson while I was visiting some old friends, the de Peysters. But my real friendship with her had started when Franklin Roosevelt was Assistant Secretary of the Navy under President Wilson.

Others were amazed at the energy and the varied enterprises of Mrs. Roosevelt when she first entered the White House. I was not, for I had seen her in action years before. She was the dynamo behind the canteen service for the troop trains going through the Washington railroad yards in the First World War. While we were in Europe at the peace negotiations, she had swept Mrs. Wilson up into her project of visiting the war-wounded in the hospitals.

Franklin Roosevelt, as Assistant Secretary of the Navy, had gone over to France on official business. Mrs. Roosevelt had accompanied him and they had come home on the *George Washington* with President Wilson when he returned before Congress adjourned on March 4, 1919, in order to be able to sign bills that had been passed and demanded his signature.

It was a long and slow trip, but President Wilson wanted to be at sea as long as possible, because he needed rest after his strenuous months in Paris. Every afternoon I had tea with the Roosevelts in their cabin.

It is a truism that the peculiar intimacy of shipboard enables one to know a person much better than casual meetings on land. Thus I really came to know the Franklin Roosevelts on that voyage.

During the winter before the Roosevelt inauguration I was in New York. I called up Mrs. Roosevelt and said that if she had time to see me, nothing would give me more pleasure. She suggested that I lunch with her. At that luncheon I first met Mrs. Roosevelt's personal secretary, Malvina Thompson, with whom I was to be associated most happily for all the years of the Roosevelt administration. Of course, I had no idea of it at the time. I told Mrs. Roosevelt then to let me know if there was anything I could do for her. She suggested that I lunch at the White House a few days after the inauguration.

So to the White House I went, right after the Roosevelts moved in. At that luncheon I asked if Mrs. Roosevelt and Malvina would like to have me come down and help in any way. Both seemed glad of my suggestion. Malvina later used to laugh about my Red Cross sewing. She said I had brought it down with me to the White House but that they had put me to work and I never had a chance to finish it. At any rate, I stayed for twenty years—more than twelve with Mrs. Roosevelt and more than seven with Mrs. Truman.

Until President Roosevelt came to the White House in 1933, I had seen him but once after the attack of poliomyelitis which paralyzed his legs. That was very shortly after the attack. I was staying with Mr. and Mrs. Charles Hamlin at Mattapoisett, Massachusetts, and he came into the harbor with some friends on a yacht. He could not come ashore, so Mrs. Hamlin and I went out to see him.

The next time I saw him was when he came to Washington at his inauguration. I have never seen a greater change in any face. He had always been a handsome man, handsome and gay and carefree; but this was a different head, a magnificent one; splendid shoulders and large, strong hands, stronger for having to hold his weight when he lifted himself up from a chair. Nothing was more tragic to me than to see that superb-looking man walk with the greatest difficulty the length of the White House hall from the elevator to the East Room, which was about as far as he could manage, even leaning on the arm of one of his aides. Usually, of course, he went about the White House in a wheel chair. Ramps were built where necessary, as, for instance, over a short flight of stairs up to the suites over the East Room. This was a part of White House living for many years.

I shall never forget my startled feeling one day shortly after President Roosvelt's death when I was working in the little office close to the elevator on the family floor. I was standing with my back to the door when I heard a voice. I turned quickly and saw that it was President Truman. It had been so long since I had seen a President who could walk into a room that the sight unnerved me. I must have given a terrible start for President Truman exclaimed and asked if he had frightened me.

One of the earliest social functions which I helped engineer in the Roosevelt administration was the Diplomatic Circle of March 11, 1933. This formal function, about which the public knows little, is in a class by itself, in that invitations come from the Secretary of State. After the inauguration of a new President, or of a re-elected President, the Chiefs of Mission of the Diplomatic Corps are presented to the President and his wife. The 1933 invitation was worded as follows:

> The Secretary of State presents his compliments to Their Excellencies and Messieurs the Chiefs of Mission and has the

honor to inform them that the President and Mrs. Roosevelt will be pleased to receive them and their wives at The White House on Saturday afternoon, the eleventh of March, at five o'clock.

Their Excellencies the Ambassadors, Ministers and Chargés d'Affaires and their wives are requested to arrive at The White House by the North Entrance and to assemble in the East Room not later than half after four o'clock in order that their presentation may be made to the President and Mrs. Roosevelt at the hour above named.

That spring of 1933 I did all I could at the White House before going, as usual, to spend the summer in Grayville, Illinois. I am afraid I was not of much help, for there was at that time a curious set-up by which any number of people seemed to do the work of the social secretary. This was a hangover, one might say, from the Hoover administration.

There is practically no social work at the White House in summer, and Malvina Thompson was well able to cope with all there was, though of course she was unfamiliar with Washington and its ways. When I returned to Washington early in the autumn, Mrs. Roosevelt asked me if I would care to come to work at the White House on a salary basis. I accepted gladly, and I was given a very modest salary and the title of social secretary, Malvina being the personal secretary.

At that time there was a system at the White House by which the regular White House employees were comparatively few in number and additional clerks were "loaned" to the White House staff from various government departments. This has all been changed; the White House now has its own staff, and all the people who were "loaned" have been "blanketed in" on the White House payroll.

In those days there was a White House position as secretary which carried a larger salary than the government paid to a clerk. That went to Malvina, who did so much more work than I. She had been with Mrs. Roosevelt before she came to the White House and certainly deserved the larger pay. But I was a "loan" to the White House, from whatever government agency might have some financial margin. Finally I landed with a very sensitive agency, which investigated its employees carefully.

When I went out to Grayville that summer, the editor of the local paper met me and in a shocked voice revealed that a Secret Service man had been down there to investigate me. I wondered why I was being investigated and hoped that whatever the reason my friends in the little town had not been acquainted with this fact. The editor assured me that so far my reputation was intact. My secret was safe with him; no one else in Grayville knew of the investigation.

In due course I found it was only a routine check-up and when the Secret Service agent returned to his Springfield office, he reported the town said I was "a very nice lady."

Mrs. Roosevelt heard about this and told the President, who later had a field day at dinner, teasing the Cabinet member whose department is in charge of Secret Service matters about this. I remember it started when the President fixed me with a glassy eye and said, "Edith, what have you been up to in Illinois? So you have had to be investigated?"

I was taken aback to hear he knew about the investigation, and perhaps my voice quaked a little. He said, "It must have been pretty bad." Then he turned to the Cabinet officer and started to tease him; said the investigation of a member of his household had vexed him deeply. The Cabinet officer squirmed. The President in this mood could be great fun.

Little did I think that I would ever live to see the day when no man, however impeccable in personal life and brilliant in public record, could take over an appointive office in government without first having been thoroughly investigated, not only for his honesty and reputation, but even for his loyalty to the country he is to serve.

I recall another characteristic instance of the President's sense of humor. Mrs. Roosevelt was interested in so many things that she made many White House innovations. As one instance, she started having many conferences in the East Room of the White House. One semi-pacifist organization met there—the Conference on the Cause and Cure of War, over which Mrs. Carrie Chapman Catt, noted suffragist leader, presided for many years. Mrs. Catt and Mrs. Roosevelt were old friends.

The Cause and Cure of War organization didn't exactly advocate beating swords into plowshares or scuttling all our battleships, but it did firmly believe in the possibility of a peaceable solution of recurring international problems. The President addressed this earnest, eager group one afternoon and told them very frankly his opinion that it would be suicidal policy for us to leave ourselves without any protection. He pointed out that having weapons for defense did not mean we were going to plunge into war the next day. From the expressions on the faces of his audience, I judged that his remarks were not what they had hoped to hear.

The East Room was crowded and I was standing at the door of the Green Room listening to his speech. As he passed by he gave me a fiendish wink, knowing very well that I would agree with every word he had said.

Except for a few such incidents, always entertaining, I saw little of Franklin Roosevelt in the White House, as compared, for instance, with my much closer contact, when White House life was simpler, with President Woodrow Wilson. In fact, I really saw more of Franklin Roosevelt on that return trip from France in 1919, after accompanying the Wilsons to Paris for the Peace Conference, than I did in the White House as social secretary to Mrs. Roosevelt. It has sometimes seemed to me that President Roosevelt and his secretaries and Mrs. Roosevelt and her secretaries operated in two separate worlds, although we had the friendliest relations with each other.

It is always difficult to explain the White House set-up to outsiders, because it is such a very large establishment. Starting at the top, each section has its own duties to fulfill and each works more or less to itself. There could be little contact between the Social Office and secretary of the President's wife, and the West Executive office which is headquarters for the President and his immediate staff, on account of physical difficulties. You have to walk through the entire lower floor of the White House—a distance of much more than a city block—to go from the West Executive office to the East Executive office wing, where of late years the Social Office and military, naval and air force aides to the President have been established.

The President's two secretaries were Miss Marguerite LeHand and Miss Grace Tully. The former, commonly known in the Roosevelt clan as "Missy," lived on the third floor in the White House. Though I met Missy occasionally, going up and down on the elevator or on the second floor with Mrs. Roosevelt, I did not see her after my working hours. She was a very handsome woman and had a great many friends in Washington. Her illness and untimely death late in the Roosevelt administration shocked and grieved us all.

Miss Tully, like Miss LeHand, came to Washington with the Roosevelts from New York. I saw her occasionally, too, but only during working hours.

My own work brought me in much more frequent contact with Mrs. Henrietta Nesbitt, Mrs. Roosevelt's former Hyde Park neighbor who was housekeeper at the White House during all the years of the Roosevelt administration. There were details about arrangements for parties which I had to clarify for her. I liked Mrs. Nesbitt very much and always was glad to stop by her little office on the ground floor, for the warm welcome I knew would be waiting for me.

The capable group of White House ushers also were favorites of mine during my White House service. Mr. Ike Hoover, who was in our party when I went to Europe with President and Mrs. Woodrow Wilson, still was chief usher when I returned to serve as Mrs. Roosevelt's social secretary. When he died of a heart attack in the fall of 1933, just as we were getting under way for the first winter, Mr. Raymond Muir, second in line in the office, was advanced to the position of chief usher. And when Mr. Muir was again promoted to the Protocol Division of the State Department, Mr. Howell G. Crim became chief usher and still occupies that position.

On the ushers devolves responsibility for the entire White House timetable. They keep the engagement list of callers who come to the White House proper to see the President, some downstairs and some in his study. These are personal friends or persons whom the

President prefers, for one reason or another, to see more privately than in his office.

The ushers also keep the engagement list of the President's wife, and of course the timing of all these engagements must be absolutely correct. As a rule the ushers know by sight the persons admitted for private interviews.

The chief usher also is superintendent of the White House, a position formerly occupied by an engineer officer of the Army. Mr. Crim has three assistants—Wilson Searles, Charles Claunch and J. B. West. All four combine friendliness with efficiency and do an outstanding job.

During the winter of 1933-1934, Mrs. Roosevelt began giving teas for people who were known to her or to someone among the White House personnel. A great many misconceptions have existed about those who were invited to such parties, due to an erroneous impression, given by some newspaper correspondent, I think, that anyone who left a card at the White House would automatically be invited to a tea.

This obviously could not be the case, because something must be known about people who are invited to the White House. I think it can be readily seen that every person who leaves a card might not be an appropriate guest for the President's wife to invite even to somewhat informal parties, as the teas were called.

There also are many groups who ask to be received at the White House, notably the Daughters of the American Revolution, for whom an enormous reception is given every year.

Mrs. Roosevelt often received alone, even at these huge D. A. R. receptions. She was able to shake hands indefinitely, never seemed to tire or to need any help in a receiving line. One letter to Mrs. Roosevelt will explain the feelings of a guest who watched her shake one hand after another:

MY DEAR MRS. ROOSEVELT:

About this time last month I attended a conference in Washington on the Cause and Cure of War.

I was one of that long line of delegates that filed past you and shook your hand. After I had visited the state dining room I stood for a few minutes looking through from the front hall and watched as the delegates behind me came through. What a strong hand, mercy how many more people in this line, etc. In short do you shake and think or do you just shake?

Cordially and Sincerely

It is only a very strong woman who could stand the strain of shaking several thousand hands.

During that first winter in the White House, so many of the Roosevelt family were in residence that Malvina and I had to share the tiny second-floor office by the elevator. This inspired Mr. Richard Southgate, our Chief of Protocol and friend, to dub us "The Girls of the Second Floor Front," which had a lively connotation that we did not live up to. That our friendship survived that winter, with two telephones in the tiny room and often two conversations going on at the same time—and with Mrs. Roosevelt occasionally breaking in with a third—speaks for itself. The next winter there were fewer family and house guests, so I was given one of the small bedrooms on the third floor as an office. Later, when the East Executive office was built, my office was moved there.

In a short time it was possible to get things running as they had been when I was there during the Wilson regime, with the social secretary entirely responsible for social affairs. That was the reason why Malvina and I functioned together so marvelously; she had all of Mrs. Roosevelt's tremendous personal work to do, and I only Mrs. Roosevelt's social engagements in Washington. Those in other cities were taken care of by Malvina.

I have said many times, and I am happy to repeat it here, that in all the twelve years Malvina and I were together we had only one quarrel even when we were cooped up in the little two-by-four office. And if any two women had cramped space and the facilities for quarreling, we certainly had them.

One thing we always did—at about four o'clock in the afternoon we always agreed that it was time to have some tea and to talk of the various idiotic letters and requests that had come in, exploding with rage over some of the impossible things that people asked of Mrs. Roosevelt. There was, however, just one incident in all those years which might be called a disagreement.

This happened just before one of the Roosevelt inaugurations.

It had to do with what might be called an idiosyncrasy of the Roosevelt family for all sorts of nicknames. In that family you may have been christened Jane, but you are never called Jane. You are Lulie or Tootie or something like that.

Before this inauguration various little memoranda had come to me from Mrs. Roosevelt, saying, "See that Tootie—or Lulie—or so-and-so—has an invitation." By that time I was in my third-story office, so I would trek down the stairs and say to Malvina, "Who is Lulie?" and Malvina, who had been with the family for years, always knew the answer.

She had all these exasperating interruptions from me, in addition to the enormous amount of work she was doing for Mrs. Roosevelt all the time—taking care of Mrs. Roosevelt's column as well as so many personal letters that at times there were literally clothes-baskets full of them.

One of my last treks was in connection with some organization from Hyde Park that wanted to come down to deliver bunches of violets or what-have-you prior to the inauguration. I plowed down from the third floor and demanded, "Malvina, *who* are these?" By that time she was goaded to the breaking point and understandably she made this rather sharp answer: "What do you want now?" I looked at her and tears rolled down my cheeks. I am not given to tears, but that Malvina should turn on me was more than I could bear.

I turned and went sadly upstairs, drying the tears as I went along, and wondering if our friendship would ever be mended. But Malvina was apparently just as upset as I. She was about to leave with Mrs. Roosevelt on one of her numerous train trips, and as she told it, she says she spent nearly a month's salary in long distance calls saying how sorry she was, etc. I, of course, was sorry too, and so the one unhappy episode between us was soon brought to a close.

One of the great griefs of my life has been the loss of my friend Malvina Thompson while I was writing this book. She was so much younger than I that her going seemed to me especially premature. And I felt that her death was partly because she gave herself so unstintedly in service to others—including me. I recall a luncheon together, at which I told her my plans for this book. She offered to search out for me, in the Hyde Park archives, things about the Roosevelt social regime which I might need to make my narrative more interesting. It was the type of generous gesture, beyond any call of duty or friendship, which will make Malvina live on with us who knew her best. I shall always miss her.

The White House to which I returned with the Roosevelts had changed so much since the Wilson days that I had little sense of returning to an old familiar spot. Yet I felt at home when entering by the North Portico, for there at the front door was Mayes, bowing from the waist. From time to time he let me know he did not consider that all of the Roosevelt parties were all that they ought to be socially. The invitation list sometimes went too far afield from "the old set."

And in the chief usher's office Ike Hoover, who had been with us all through the Wilson days including the trip to France, still was supreme. I also found many of my old friends in the Social Office of the White House. Still at its head was William Rockwell, my good friend of many years' standing, and his assistant Adrian Tolley, who had come into the White House shortly after I did in the Wilson administration. Other faithful colleagues in the Social Office were Mr. Earl Leslie, Miss Edithe Rowley and Mr. John McCabe. And later my right arm, Miss Ida Andrews, came along, and was still with me in 1953 when my services ended with the advent of the Eisenhower administration. Words cannot too strongly express my great gratitude to all of them for their wonderful cooperation during all my years in the White House.

One thing I have found out about the hazardous occupation of social secretary—very few people know much about it. For purely educational reasons I want to quote something Mrs. Roosevelt once wrote about my duties, in an article called "Making the Wheels Go Round in the White House."

This is how she put it:

"The next person to be seen in the morning is Mrs. Helm, whose particular responsibility is the social correspondence and entertainments given during the official season from November to June. She makes up the lists of people who should be invited to different entertainments. She goes through the cards left at the White House and arranges for all those to be received on my day 'At Home.'

"She works with the people in what is called the Social Bureau [later the name was changed to Social Office] who get out all the invitations. She helps me at receptions and teas, goes over the seating of the official dinners and lunches with the State Department and myself. She brings me every morning the lists and the table seating if there is a party pending and also any questions or notes that have come in on entertainments or social functions of any kind.

"She sees that I have a list of these functions on my desk, kept up to date, and reminds me again at the last minute who are to be my nearest neighbors at entertainments, and last but not least she brings to my attention anything which she thinks would add to the pleasure and comfort of my guests.

"She is, of course, free at any time to bring me her suggestions. Mrs. Helm takes all the telephone calls, and they are legion, on these subjects and notifies the head usher of all people on the purely social lists to be received and the hours of their arrival.

"As nearly as human beings can run these things without mistakes, it is done by the White House Social Bureau and Mrs. Helm and the State Department. Considering the numbers that are constantly contacting the White House for some social reason, I feel it is most remarkable that Mrs. Helm has been able to do such an extremely satisfactory job and yet at all times to remain calm and unharassed, at least outwardly. I have known her for many years and felt I was particularly fortunate to find her willing to join my group of 'wheel turners.'"

Having established no claim to modesty in quoting these flattering words about myself, I should like to insert here a typical telephone conversation in my office at the White House to give some idea of the hazards of my job. I am at one end of the telephone and the conversation will show who is at the other.

I say, "Is this Representative Blank's office?"

The answer comes: "Yes. His secretary speaking."

"This is Mrs. Roosevelt's secretary. Did Mrs. Blank receive an invitation to luncheon on January 25th sent nearly three weeks ago?"

"Yes, she did and she got around to sending an answer yesterday. Mr. Blank is here and he would like to know whether that invitation includes Mrs. Blank's niece."

"No, I am sorry. This is not a reception. This is a luncheon."

"Oh, Mr. Blank didn't understand. He thought it might mean Mrs. Blank could bring her niece."

"No, I am sorry. The invitation is only for Mrs. Blank."

In the White House Social Office we always tried to send out invitations for White House luncheons and dinners three weeks in advance, to give the Mrs. Blanks ample time for "getting around to sending an answer." And the nieces of the Mrs. Blank were not included in White House invitations for luncheons and dinners, because tables have size limits—even at the White House—and guest lists are carefully planned.

Each social season at the White House was made dramatic by ten large official events—five State Dinners, alternating with five State Receptions. The schedule for the season was announced to the press in October, permitting Washington hostesses to dovetail their own parties into the official social scheme. The White House events usually started in December and continued, at intervals, until Lent. After Lent we had the "little season," musicales and teas, and the big garden parties which are to my way of thinking the most delightful of White House parties.

At the big receptions, the President and Mrs. Roosevelt stood by themselves under the Blue Room chandelier, with an aide to announce the names of incoming guests. The Wilsons had included Vice-President and Cabinet in the receiving line, which slowed the passing of guests. But it was difficult for President Roosevelt to stand on account of his lameness. And so the line had to be speeded up.

Other Presidents and their wives had marched down the Grand Staircase to the receptions. President Roosevelt met his Cabinet by the small Family Dining Room adjoining the State Dining Room on the main floor, after coming down from the second floor on the elevator, and walked in line through the Red Room, where the

Cabinet remained, to the Blue Room. Every now and then during the receiving period the line was stopped so that he could rest.

One can understand that this "levee" duty of the President and his wife is not an easy one, because of the number of guests who attend State Receptions. The total number of guests invited to the Diplomatic Reception in December, 1933, was 1592, for instance.

The Diplomatic Reception was always the most fashionable of the large White House functions, and the one to which invitations were most in demand.

Formerly it was the custom to invite various persons outside the diplomatic corps—ex-ambassadors and the like—to this reception. In fact, when we first came to Washington, rear admirals of the Navy and major generals of the Army were invited to all the White House receptions, but that custom had to be stopped many years ago. In recent administrations these officers were invited only to the Army and Navy receptions.

As the size of the diplomatic corps increased, Diplomatic Reception lists had to be cut down. It had grown to more than one thousand people in the Roosevelt administration, and the Reception was three times as large as it had been in earlier years.

For the season of 1934-1935 I sent over a tentative list of dates for receptions and dinners to the President for his approval. This was returned with the following notation in his handwriting:

> O.K. but no dinners or musicales in between these Thursday parties—sorry but it is impossible for me—F.D.R.

That season Franklin Roosevelt restricted the Diplomatic Reception to official guests. It is really far more comfortable for everyone, to have these state receptions smaller. The White House was not built for such large gatherings and overcrowding made the place very uncomfortable. But cutting down the list meant many heartaches—social heartaches, we might say.

One morning when I entered the office, Malvina said, "I think these two letters will be of interest to you." One of them was a four-page letter written to Mrs. Roosevelt by a lady in a frenzy of rage because she had been left out.

The lady had telephoned me and the conversation had gone on and on for half an hour. She felt strongly she should come to the Diplomatic Reception and she had refused to be mollified when I had told her that although she could not come, that no invitation would be sent her, possibly she could come to a later reception. What she also said in her four-page letter was that I had hung up the telephone while she was talking. I am sure I did not.

The reply Mrs. Roosevelt sent back was a model of icy courtesy. She called the lady's attention to the fact that lists were being cut down, that I was acting on a directive of the President who was a man overburdened with work, that it was felt the size of the reception must be reduced and that here was no choice but to do so.

Nearly everybody understood when given a sensible explanation of such a situation. It was only the other five percent who made life difficult for a White House social secretary. It was almost like a phonograph record to hear over many years the cry from this group, "But I have always been on the White House list for this reception!"

As a matter of fact, there was no White House "list" stretching over the years to cover those considered fit recipients of White House invitations. Widows of ambassadors and, as I have said, ex-ambassadors were invited, plus a few personal friends of the President and his wife. The invitation list varied from year to year and there could be no continuing "White House list."

The Army and Navy Reception also was drastically cut—under Franklin Roosevelt. When both branches of the service were much smaller, all the officers on duty in Washington were asked to this reception. With the growth of our responsibilities all over the world, naturally the military services in and around Washington have shared in that increase and over the years the number of officers invited had to be curtailed. This meant eliminating those of lower grades.

Invitations for the Judicial Reception were easy. To it were invited members of the various courts from the Supreme Court down through all the lower courts and including the Department of Justice.

But the question of so-called "independent" government agencies —where to fit them into evening receptions was increasingly serious. There was a Departmental Reception, for officials of the Treasury, Post Office, Interior, Agriculture, Commerce and Labor Departments, and the natural place for independent agencies would have been with the departments—except that there were too many of them, as functions of government expanded.

There were the older "independents," such as Federal Trade Commission, Interstate Commerce Commission, and Reconstruction Finance Corporation. To these were added a flock of New Deal agencies—Work Progress Administration, National Youth Administration, Public Works Administration, Civilian Conservation Corps, Tennessee Valley Authority—and so many others that their very names became too much of a mouthful. They were called by their initials and Washington was compared to "alphabet soup." To include them all would have made the Departmental Reception entirely too large.

The problem was solved by fitting some of the "independents" into other receptions, chiefly those with which they had some official connection.

The Congressional Reception, of course, was another large one. To help assemble the guest list for this event, at the beginning of each season a questionnaire was sent to all members of Congress— senators and representatives—as soon as Congress convened.

I quote here a sample of the questionnaire:

Married_____
       (yes or no)
Sons and daughters over eighteen years of age residing with you in Washington, (if married, please list as Mr. and Mrs.)
_____
_____
_____

Washington address_____

I also quote an amusing reply to this questionnaire:

Dear Mrs. Helm:
Enclosed is the blank which you sent me to fill out.
Indeed I appreciate your interest in me.
Very sincerely yours,

M.C. Elect

Name of Representative
Wife or hostess: No wife; no hostess; no son, no daughter; no relative; just a 25-year-old man
Washington address: No arrangements

Requests were continually coming in for house guests to be invited to the different receptions, and the most crowded of all was always the Congressional. Apparently as soon as many of the Members of Congress learned the date of the reception, they arranged to have "folks from home" visit them. To take care of this situation I issued a memorandum to the members of my staff for their information when requests came in by telephone to invite "just one more."

> The Congressional Reception has reached the limit definitely set by the President and acting on his instruction I am closing the lists and no further invitations will be issued.

Even before these instructions were issued by the President, when the limit of invitations had been reached it was irritating to hear this refrain: "Well, two more people will make no difference." I had to explain that if I allowed those two to come it would mean that everyone who had one, two or three guests should be allowed to bring them, too. In other words, I could not play favorites.

Since it was more difficult to refuse invitations to house guests, this offered frequent opportunities for subterfuge. Many a "house guest" happened to be a guest the evening of the reception and was not staying in the house, but of course, not being a member of the F.B.I., I could not investigate these cases.

Usually sixty percent attendance is average for a big White

House reception or spring garden party. An exception was the garden party which Mrs. Roosevelt originated for women who held administrative jobs in government departments and agencies, and which was very popular with those long-neglected feminine workers. Looking at one list for this annual party, I note that 2400 were invited and 2000 were present.

This innovation of Mrs. Roosevelt's attained great popularity. Many of the women invited—important in their various fields of government activity—never had had an opportunity to go to the White House socially or to see its beautiful grounds.

Women employees at the White House also came to this party, and to one of the large evening receptions in winter. They were shuttled from one reception list to another, whichever had the smallest number. Those who had husbands were invited to bring them, just as men employees were asked to bring their wives.

Another innovation made by Mrs. Roosevelt her first year in the White House was a children's party for Anna Eleanor Dall and Curtis Dall, small daughter and son of Anna Roosevelt. Every year as long as they were children, this party was given for them at the White House. There was always a program, sometimes an entertainer and sometimes Punch and Judy shows, which I think were rather more popular than any other form of entertainment.

Mrs. Roosevelt also thought of the work-filled lives of the Senate and House page boys, up on Capitol Hill, who had to carry their school studies along at night while they availed themselves of the rare opportunity of seeing at first hand how laws are made. She held an annual party for them.

Indeed, as I think back over the scope of the life of this capital city, I find myself hard put to think of any area in which Mrs. Roosevelt did not offer special White House hospitality. Certainly in twelve years as social secretary for her, I watched her change the pattern of White House entertaining by bringing there more varied groups of people than ever before were entertained in the Executive Mansion.

Most Presidents' wives have engaged in much more work of the type that has come to be known as public relations than the country at large has ever recognized. And Mrs. Roosevelt's interests were so all-encompassing that life in the White House was an ever-amazing mosaic to one in her immediate orbit, as I was.

A random sampling may illustrate my point. Any short span of time in a winter season picked at random would do as well. I shall take the first half of February, 1935. On the morning of the 5th, the East Room was filled with representatives of the National Youth Administration, in a conference on how to open up more jobs. That afternoon quite a different group assembled there—members of Washington society and official guests invited for a White House musicale. Next day—a large official luncheon, and that afternoon a tea for the National Democratic Committee. On the 9th, after making a speech in Boston, Mrs. Roosevelt dashed home for a large tea party for members of the Washington Music Teachers Association. And the next day she had invited a large Citizenship Conference to gather in the South Grounds to hear President Roosevelt speak from the South Portico. Three days later there was a tea for the members of my own organization, Sponsors of the U.S. Navy —women who have christened Navy ships.

I could go on with page after page of this type—White House parties practically chasing each other out the door, liberally interspersed with out-of-town speaking engagements for Mrs. Roosevelt. Her amazing activities became an American legend which was not exaggerated. Far from subtracting from it, I would add!

Chapter 13

STAGING STATE DINNERS, HIGH TEAS AND DEB DANCES

I REALLY THINK I have gone to more White House parties than anyone else living. In twenty-five years as social secretary to the wives of three Presidents, I had a hand in entertaining that brought at least a half million people to the White House. And I was almost always there.

Such an experience adds to one's pride in our country. Whether it is a State Dinner for visiting royalty or a simple tea for a few friends of the First Lady, White House parties must be perfect in their appointments. No book or magazine article on the White House that I have read has ever given credit to the White House Social Office for this high standard of hospitality. This Office not only oils the wheels of functions in the large, but also goes into the type of minute detail which makes each invited individual feel that he or she has been singled out for honor.

Until very recent times, this included the delivery by hand of the engraved White House invitations, which carried the addressee's name or names in engraver's script matching the engraving on the invitation.

Hand-delivery gradually went out during the Franklin Roosevelt administration as more than half of the officials whose names were on the invitation lists migrated to the suburbs. When more had to be sent by mail than could be carried by messenger, it was decided to mail all.

And, except for the dinner invitations, which are still done that way, engraver's script had to be abandoned because of the inexorable changes of time. The White House social staff once included ten penmen who could write in this script a thousand reception invitations in a few days. But when the reception list swelled to two thousand right after the second World War, during which the penmen had dwindled to two—the Bureau chief and his first assistant—the Social Office had to settle for a fine Spencerian script. It is no longer possible to hire men who can do engraver's script.

Since the Social Office was started under President Garfield in 1881 there have been but three men in charge of it—all of them gentlemen and scholars, all deeply interested in American history and social customs, all having great respect for the Presidential office. The first was Mr. Warren S. Young, who was still alive when Mr. Tolley, the third of the trio, went to the White House in 1915. Mr. Rockwell, who had long been understudy to Mr. Young, took over when Mr. Young died in 1917. Mr. Tolley took over when Mr. Rockwell died in 1940. It comes about as close to being a line of succession as this country offers. Others in the Social Office stay for a long, long time. John Lincoln McCabe started delivering White House invitations by bicycle in 1904 and was still working on the invitation list when he retired, at the age of seventy-six, in 1953.

The members of this small and highly specialized staff often work far into the night at the height of the social season. When work slackens off in the summer months, they compile the social records and start planning, far in advance, for the next season.

Although Mrs. Roosevelt broke precedents and did many things socially which were different from most First Ladies, she was most meticulous in maintaining the dignity of official entertaining. Her forebears in Old New York society would have had cause for great pride in her regal bearing as a White House hostess and the high dignity of the functions at which she presided.

To give an example of one typical season, here are the official social events on which we worked, in their sequence during the year 1933-1934—and subsequent years up to World War II repeated the pattern:

November 16, Thursday	Cabinet Dinner	8 P.M.
December 7, Thursday	Diplómatic Reception	9 P.M.
December 14, Thursday	Dinner to the Chief Justice and the Supreme Court	8 P.M.
January 4, Thursday	Judicial Reception	9 P.M.
January 11, Thursday	Diplomatic Dinner	8 P.M.
January 18, Thursday	Congressional Reception	9 P.M.
January 25, Thursday	Vice-President's Dinner	8 P.M.
February 1, Thursday	Reception to the Officials of Treasury, Post Office, Interior, Agriculture, Commerce and Labor Departments and Federal Agencies	9 P.M.
February 6, Tuesday	Speaker's Dinner	8 P.M.
February 8, Thursday	Army and Navy Reception	9 P.M.

We who worked together on White House entertaining liked to think of a state dinner as similar to a theatrical performance. The guests arrived before the appointed hour and were shown to the East Room, almost as in a theater. At eight o'clock the curtain went up, when the procession of dinner partners entered the dining room and dinner was served. And all this followed preparations at least as detailed as the planning that goes into a theatrical preformance.

Weeks before the night of the party, a list of "must" guests—men and women in official life who must be invited to that particular formal function—was prepared by me as social secretary. Then of course names of friends and others were added by the President and his wife. When the list, approved by the President and his wife, was finally settled, invitations were prepared and sent out three weeks before the date of the dinner.

Enclosed in the envelope with the dinner invitation were a

response card, an admit card and a gate card for the guest's automobile. Response cards formerly read, "Please reply to the Secretary to the President," but later this was changed to "Please send response to the Chief of Protocol, the White House, at your earliest convenience."

That was what we asked for, but here is what we got in reply to one invitation. The response-card envelope was addressed to "The Office of the Proletariat, The White House, Washington, D.C." Our instructions later were revised to read: "Please send response to the Social Secretary, The White House, at your earliest convenience."

A list of those invited was prepared in the correct order of precedence, and acceptances and regrets were promptly recorded as received. All acceptances and regrets also were listed in alphabetical order on a final dinner list for the evening of the party, because, in the rare event that any guest failed to arrive by precisely eight o'clock, the acceptance must be produced and an effort made to reach him by telephone to ascertain the cause of his absence.

Once when an acceptance had been received from a high-ranking official and his wife, to the horror of Mr. Tolley and his associate who always were on duty in the chief usher's office while guests were assembling, the official appeared alone. When asked about his wife's whereabouts, the gentleman said he thought everybody knew she was in Florida! Because the table seating had of course included his wife, his solo appearance made it necessary hastily to rearrange the entire table.

Some time before the day of the dinner, place cards were prepared for guests who had accepted. "Escort cards" also were prepared—a card for each lady, showing who was to take her in to dinner, and one for each gentleman, telling him who was to be his dinner partner. Each escort card included a diagram of the table to show just where the person was to sit at dinner.

In addition, a large table plat was prepared. It showed the entire dinner table and was displayed in the White House entrance lobby where guests were received by ushers and the junior military aides to the President. Each guest saw his or her name at the spot where he or she was to be seated.

In this way, guests would know whether they were to go to the left or to the right, on the President's side of the table or on the side of the President's wife, when they entered the state dining room.

As an aid in seating the dinners—which really could be quite confusing when a large group of guests were to be seated—cut-outs were kept on hand to illustrate different table sizes from smallest to largest.

It is a little difficult to explain just what I mean by cut-outs, but I shall try.

The names of guests who had accepted invitations were written on small, thin cardboard stickers. The stickers were red, white and blue, for our own convenience; red for the President and the wife of the President; blue for ladies and white for the gentleman. With these distinctive colors, we could get the picture of a table-seating at one glance.

On the morning of the day of a dinner, the red, white and blue stickers were inserted in a specially prepared "cut-out" which represented the table to be used that evening. There was a tiny slit for each sticker and the stickers were inserted in their correct order of precedence. From this the handsome final plat was painstakingly made by the Social Office.

Not all the guests were seated in strict order of precedence, of course, and the stickers could be moved here and there as it was decided where unofficial guests should be placed. With the advice and approval of the President's wife, these were seated wherever it was hoped they would find congenial neighbors. Often, however, they were not well known to the President or his wife or the social secretary, so the seating was more or less a gamble, and the results were not always happy. At one of the Roosevelts' numerous dinners, for example, the publisher of an important out-of-town paper was placed next to the wife of an official of one of the government agencies. This gentleman had had ample liquid refreshment and had a gay and roving eye for the ladies. Later I met him and he moaned that his dinner partner was a mousy little thing with no conversation except her local small-town activities, mostly religious.

At three o'clock on the day of a dinner, almost everything was ready. Then came the preparation of a "press list," to be released to reporters and out-of-town correspondents at four o'clock, through the office of the President's press secretary. A stencil was cut showing the list of guests in their correct order of precedence and approximately one hundred copies were printed for distribution to the press. The lists always were society news not only in Washington, but also in out-of-town papers, because they almost always included important out-of-town guests.

White House aides came into the picture later in the afternoon, with a senior aide in charge. Precedence and "pairing off" lists were given to him and he issued the necessary instructions to other aides. Each was assigned a certain number of guests to escort to their places in the East Room. He memorized their names from the list given him by the senior aide, and was ready to receive them when they arrived.

These White House aides are unmarried Army, Navy, Marine and Air Force officers on duty in Washington, who are assigned to this extra duty whenever their services are required at the White House. They are replaced when they marry or are transferred to another post out of Washington.

The President now has three senior aides and a group of junior aides. People often think the aides have nothing else to do save serve at White House functions, but this really is only a very minor part of their duty. They are young men who look very well in their dress uniforms with colorful cords or aiguillettes worn over one shoulder—the right shoulder for a President's aide, left shoulder for the aide of a Cabinet officer.

The aiguillettes, I have been told, served a useful purpose at one time. A pencil was attached to one end of the cord, and if a President or other official wished to write a message to be delivered by an aide, the pencil came in very handy. Now there is only a symbolic pencil at the end of the aiguillette.

Going back to our state dinners, seven-thirty was the deadline for all arrangements. By that time the place cards, embossed with the President's seal in gold and written by the Spencerian staff of the Social Office, must be on the table, and the table plat, guest lists, and escort cards in the hands of the chief usher.

The State Dinner table, when it is completed to the last detail, is always a beautiful picture. Along the U-shaped table, seating up to 104, lie the various pieces of the "Monroe Centerpiece," a *surtout de table,* an elaborate mirror plateau edged by little figurines of Bacchae and Bacchants. After the White House was burned by the British, President James Monroe sent to Paris for it, as part of the new furnishings for the reconstructed White House. That was in 1818 and it has been used for State Dinners ever since. There are matching candelabra, Empire tripod vases, and fruit baskets. The White House florist and his helpers always produce one of their masterpieces. The place settings are of the current best china, flanked at either side by the White House gold-plated flat silver, some of which also dates back to Monroe.

Upon arrival of the guests, each gentleman was given his proper envelope containing his escort card and the diagram of his place at the table. All guests were shown the table plat. Then, having instructed each gentleman how to reach his place at the table with his dinner partner, after entering the dining room, the usher directed the guests to the East Room. As they entered this room, where large groups always were gathered to wait for greetings which precede the dinner, their names were announced by an aide.

At eight the guests were formed in a circle—this shepherding was left in the tactful hands of the White House aides; each guest had to be in his correct order of precedence, each gentleman on the left of his wife. The President then was notified and with his wife came down on the elevator to greet the guests.

This White House elevator adjoins the usher's office on the first floor. Here the senior military and naval aides met the President and the wife of the President, to escort them to the East Room. They were announced by an aide when they were within a few steps of the East Room entrance; they entered and stopped just inside the door. Then the guests "made" the circle past the President and the wife of the President, standing side by side, and were presented by one of the aides.

At the conclusion of the circle, gentlemen found their dinner partners with the help of junior aides, and a column was formed. The Marine Band played a lively march as the procession moved to the dining room, down the length of the main hallway parallel with Pennsylvania Avenue (the East Room is at one end of the White House proper, the State Dining Room at the other).

The military, naval and air force aides walked two by two, two paces in front of the President and ranking lady, who were followed by the wife of the President and her dinner partner. Other couples arranged themselves according to the rank of the gentlemen, as far as possible. As soon as all guests were seated dinner was served.

When military, naval and air force aides were guests at a dinner, they were not always given partners; their time usually was too occupied with their official duties.

I recall an amusing incident in connection with the Diplomatic Dinner of 1934. Mrs. Roosevelt had some special place cards which had been painted for her by a friend who was more artistic than versed in diplomatic ways. Fortunately, we asked our friend Mr. Richard Southgate, then the State Department Chief of Protocol, over to look at them. He gave screams of pain when he saw some of the scenes symbolizing certain countries. One, showing a buzzard eating in the streets of a city, I remember, he said was quite accurate, but would hardly add to the pleasure of the diplomat representing that particular country. The good gold seal of the U.S.A. went back into its accustomed place on White House place cards.

After the State dinners, there was always music in the East Room. I cannot say that these were occasions of unmitigated joy, for some of the dinner guests were definitely not on the "music lover" list.

Small gold chairs were placed side by side—very small gold chairs, very close together. They were uncomfortable at best and one was definitely not at ease in them after a large dinner and with the pitiless glare from the huge crystal chandeliers shining down from overhead. However, it seemed to have been etiquette from years past to have arias sung and Beethoven played for this changing official audience, the majority of which, I think, was a suffering one.

Not only were there the regular state dinners and receptions, but there were a great many non-official dinners numbering seventy to eighty people—almost as large as the official dinners. These, with musicales following, and with Mrs. Roosevelt's luncheons, some

Lenten afternoon musicales she had one year, and her innumerable teas, made a formidable list for any social staff to cope with.

I feel I made one contribution to Mrs. Roosevelt's successful entertaining; I suggested to her the large luncheons she gave for fifty or more guests, which we called "get-together luncheons."

To understand these one must know something about the rigid system of protocol which hedges about all Presidential wives and their guests, like the laws of the Medes and Persians, changing not from administration to administration.

"Protocol" as I am using it is the code of international courtesy and part of it applies to order of rank or precedence. Over my desk in the White House social office I always kept the following quotation from a British diplomat: "Since the good God made us so that we can not all get through the same door at once, there must be precedence."

The State Department—also varying little from administration to administration—includes a Division of Protocol, with a Protocol Chief who knows all about the jealously guarded rank of foreign diplomats and U.S. officials. If the White House social secretary is in doubt on such Olympian matters, she goes to the Chief of Protocol and receives the dictum from above.

But since protocol rules that certain ladies always must be seated beside certain other ladies, because of their respective husbands' rank, this may become a little boring for the ladies and may also tend to keep them from getting acquainted with other feminine members of official society.

So I had the temerity to suggest—and Mrs. Roosevelt the greater courage to agree—that we should scramble important ladies at a luncheon series. We did. Mrs. Roosevelt herself wrote that these were the most successful luncheons she gave in the White House. Also, I might add with relief, as far as I ever heard there were no objections from foreign governments, the State Department or sensitive Capitol Hill.

For our "scrambled" luncheons we took the diplomatic corps—wives of ambassadors and ministers—and the wives of members of the Congress and others, official and unofficial, and divided them up, depending on the number of luncheons, two, three, four or whatever it might be. Some ladies would be invited for one day and others for another.

Then we did the same for wives of Cabinet members and other top-ranking U.S. officials. And we gave them a chance to get acquainted with those outside their own particular niche of official society, by the simple device of scrambled seating.

Of course, even here precedence applied at the very top. The wife of the Vice-President ranks next to the wife of the President; then wives of Chief Justice of the Supreme Court, retired Chief Justice or Justices, widows of former Presidents of the United States, wives of the Speaker of the House, Secretary of State and other Cabinet members in the order in which their respective departments were established. The ranking lady present sat opposite Mrs. Roosevelt.

Likewise, if there were wives of ambassadors or ministers present, the ranking one was seated next to Mrs. Roosevelt. Ladies of the diplomatic corps are ranked according to their husbands' length of service in Washington.

Subject to these limitations, we mixed our important guests. Instead of seating No. 2 ambassador's wife next to No. 1 ambassador's wife, we placed the wife of an American official next to No. 1. As these were very large luncheons, the plan actually was more complicated than it may sound.

For example, I find sixty-four ladies on the guest list for one of the "scrambled" parties in February, 1940. They included wives of eleven foreign ambassadors or ministers; two Cabinet members; Supreme Court Justice; seven senators and seventeen congressmen; the U.S. Solictor-General; two newly appointed assistant secretaries; assistant secretaries of five departments; and the chairman of the Securities and Exchange Commission. In addition, we had to seat one congresswoman; a lady government official; seven friends of Mrs. Roosevelt; the head resident of Hull House, famed Chicago settlement house; the wife of the chairman of the National Advisory Committee for Aeronautics; the head of the Women's Trade Union League, Washington branch; and the sculptress sister of one of the official ladies.

The only sour note inspired by these luncheons was injected by the wife of a senator who now is deceased. An invitation was sent to this lady and no reply was received. On inquiry at the senator's office we were told that Mrs. Senator accepted no invitations to places where her husband did not go.

Similar "scrambling," of course, occurred naturally at more informal White House teas, which were the most variable of White House functions. Teas might bring together fifteen guests or five hundred or one thousand.

Among the rooms at the White House, the Red Room is always associated in my mind with small groups that were entertained there for tea. Fifteen or twenty is really the limit that can be accommodated comfortably in that room, with the tea tables at one end, near the great crimson-hung windows and facing the doorway leading to the foyer.

At most of these teas, Mrs. Roosevelt was assisted by Malvina Thompson and me. We poured tea or coffee, seated at two small tables in the Red Room or in the State Dining Room. For very small groups I poured alone.

Having poured for so many of the great or near great, I was sometimes asked if I overheard snatches of conversation, perhaps state secrets, as I busied myself with the usual ritual of the tea-table.

I really never did hear anything worth mentioning. But Malvina heard a choice bit one afternoon, not very flattering, I fear, to the two of us, or to any ideas of social grandeur we may have possessed. A lady who had brought a friend was showing off all the glories of the White House, the State Dining Room, the beautifully appointed tea table in the center of the great room. Miss Thompson heard her say in a loud aside to the friend she was impressing: "Usually Mrs. Roosevelt has one of the Cabinet ladies pour. I don't understand why—today she just has her secretaries."

There was another amusing incident with tea-table implications in the Roosevelt administration. A flustered hostess telephoned to the State Department's Division of Protocol and asked for help. She said she had invited two friends to assist her at a party, one to pour tea and the other to pour coffee. She wanted to know whether tea or coffee had precedence, one over the other; she was anxious to have the more important lady pour the more important beverage!

The Protocol Division ended her anxiety. There is no precedence between a tea or coffee cup, they decided.

As to my own skill in the tea-pouring line, one of the most deeply appreciated compliments I have ever received came from the efficient butler who was brought to the White House by Mr. Hoover and who has seen many pourers come and go. He is "Fields" to everybody at the White House.

Fields said—and this was relayed to me, so I know it was inspired by a genuine feeling of admiration—"Mrs. Helm can pour more cups of tea in a given time than any lady I ever did see."

I can also say, after a long apprenticeship of serving either tea or coffee at the White House (usually tea), that I often wished I could prop up a little sign in front of me, reading: "Do you like your tea strong or weak?—Do you want lemon or cream?—How many lumps of sugar?" These were the questions I asked, how many thousands of times I shudder to think.

Too often an amiable lady would murmur in reply, "Yes, tea." And I would then turn politely and repeat, "Strong or weak?" But by that time a friend of the amiable lady would have come up and the two would have launched a conversation which it was difficult for me to interrupt. I still did not know whether the lady wanted lemon or cream, so again, another timid query. Finally the same process about sugar. Sometimes none, sometimes one, sometimes two, and we have gone as high as three or four lumps.

A little sign would have helped greatly, but it might not have added to the dignity of a White House tea.

I think the popular misunderstanding about invitations to the White House teas may have come from an old-fashioned Washington custom of leaving a card at the White House once a year out of respect for the President and his wife at the beginning of the official social season which ran from November to June. The shower of cards did not end with the beginning of the season, however. It continued through winter and spring; hundreds were left every week—several thousand in a season.

In the old days, when there was less need for guarding the President's family, people could walk up the curving driveway. Or drive to the front door and deposit their cards on the footman's silver salver, presented to them at the front door.

This freedom of the White House grounds may be gone forever. Today there are guards at the northwest entrance, and the northeast gate is closed. Cards now are left with the guard on duty at the northwest gate. I sometimes think more people used to leave cards when they could walk or drive to the front door.

It is a little difficult to explain the system of assembling guest lists from cards left at the White House and from other sources. I do not want to leave the impression that there is snobbishness in sending out White House invitations, or that only the great or wealthy or socially prominent were invited. But there was a very necessary routine for classifying the shower of cards and this was followed meticulously—like all other procedures of the Social Office and the social secretary.

The cards were collected regularly from the guard at the White House entrance—usually several hundred at a time. Names of callers were listed on a card index. Most of them were known to the social secretary, or if not, they were easily identifiable from social lists, the Congressional Directory or manuals of government officials.

If these sources of information failed to include names unknown to me, I had one last recourse. I would call on one or two of my friends in Washington who had a very wide acquaintance and were good enough to help me.

There was a large group of Washington people residing here permanently, who took the attitude that the reputation of the occupants of the White House depended only on whether or not these self-appointed social arbiters left their cards every season. Their attitude puzzled me until I read of the early days in Washington society when boycotting of the White House by this society group could really mar a Presidential reception. In my time the self-appointed arbiters were members of the so-called "cave dwellers" or old Washingtonians.

There were few officials of the government in the early days, and as the hordes of visitors who flock to Washington now were nonexistent in those times of limited traveling facilities, White House receptions depended upon local residential society. With airplanes and motors augmenting railroad traffic, this has changed, and an administration does not have to depend upon social Washington to make it—or to mar it.

Many persons having no connection with official life, and some others surviving from former administrations who have decided to make Washington their home, leave cards at the White House every year. These people may dislike the President and his wife both politically and personally, and yet they are on hand for every party to which they may be asked, and if they are left off a list, they register disapproval in no uncertain terms.

There is a curious differentiation in some minds between the office of the President and the man. When I have mentioned this to some of the more vitriolic critics of the administrations with which I have been associated, the reply has been that cards are left on the office, not on the man.

The distinction is too fine for my limited intelligence. There is no obligation on these people to call, as they are no longer connected with official life, and it is really a matter of personal predilection.

Occasionally I have heard another somewhat peculiar differentiation. "I dislike the President very much, but I like his wife. So I am going to call."

I have also occasionally encountered this question about White House invitations: "Do they mean more to women than they do to men?" I believe they do; it seems to me many men are dragged along to official or unofficial functions as unwilling victims.

Mrs. Roosevelt also gave a number of White House dances, some of them for her own young sons when they came visiting, and others for relatives and close friends.

Some cynic once said that the whirring noise one hears in Washington in the autumn is the sound of social axes being sharpened for the season. Another cynic—someone well acquainted with the pressure on the White House social secretary—said it would be better to face a man-eating tiger than a mother whose daughter had been omitted from a White House dance.

The first debutante dance Mrs. Roosevelt gave was for her niece,

Eleanor Roosevelt, on Saturday, December 30, 1933. This was a very large affair—nearly 700 invited and 515 attending. But it was not large enough to save me from the sharp tongue of one woman who was determined that her daughter should be invited.

Much later in the Roosevelt administration, Mrs. Roosevelt gave a debutante dance for Miss Joan Morgenthau, daughter of the Secretary of the Treasury and Mrs. Morgenthau. The newspapers at the time said this was the fifth debutante party at the White House in forty years, the others having been for Alice and Ethel Roosevelt, Helen Taft, and Eleanor Roosevelt, Mrs. Roosevelt's niece. The Roosevelt family thus tallied three out of five.

There was a small dinner before the dance for Miss Morgenthau. Six hundred young people were invited to the dance and nearly five hundred came. It was difficult to dance in the East Room, with such a crowd, but most of the guests seemed glad to be there and to have a good time.

Perhaps it is just as well that the young man who wrote me this letter did not arrive as the 501st guest:

December 23, 1940

DEAR SOCIAL SECRETARY,

Sorry I haven't written sooner. about that small dance at 10 P.M. Thursday. I won't be able to come.

No car, no money, no vacation and 3000 miles away.

I know it will be a success.

Yours,

_____Arizona

Another young people's party was a luncheon for Miss Margaret Houghteling, whose mother, Mrs. James Houghteling, is a cousin of Franklin Roosevelt. On my records for this party I find, in very black type, a notation that one of the guests was forty-five minutes late. I wonder how she ever dared to face the disapproving glances of the White House domestic staff! History does not record whether or not she was too late to get anything to eat. Of course, she may have been delayed in some unavoidable accident, but that very black type makes me fear this was not the case.

I am often asked if there are times when things go wrong at the White House. The incidents which I recall are few, but for that very reason the most ghastly. One stands out in dreadful memory.

So many people called at the White House that Mrs. Roosevelt started having two teas in the same afternoon, one group coming at four o'clock and another at five. On this particular day, she had asked some close friends in to see her for a few minutes after everyone from the four o'clock group had gone, and to stay on to tea with the five o'clock group.

After Mrs. Roosevelt had met her friends in the East Room, she said, "Now we will go and have some tea ahead of the crowd." As soon as they had reached the State Dining room, where the tea-table had been reset for the five o'clock group, Mrs. Roosevelt said to one of the ushers: "You can let everyone in now and I will go in the Blue Room to receive them."

He went to the East Room, where guests always were assembled before being received in the Blue Room, and came back in a few moments. "But Mrs. Roosevelt, there is no one there," he said.

And indeed there was no one there. The list of names for the five o'clock group had been all neatly stacked up on the desk of one of the employees in the Social Office (no longer a Social Office employee) but this list had never been given to the writers who made out the invitations.

So there were no guests; just the tables and the food and the Marine Corps Band orchestra playing to an empty room.

Mrs. Roosevelt was really remarkable about this. She laughed and said, "Well, we will send the food around to the different hospitals and let it go at that."

The employee who forgot the list of names was not discharged on account of this mistake, but everybody agreed in the Social Office that if it had been anyone but Mrs. Roosevelt that employee would have lost a job.

Chapter 14

I MEET THE PRESS—AND ENTER PICNIC POLITICS

I CONSIDER IT MY HISTORIC DUTY as well as my personal pleasure—not unmixed with a certain amount of reminiscent pain—to record something of the remarkable relations which Mrs. Franklin Roosevelt as First Lady had with the press. In her own book, *This I Remember,* she was all too modest about it. Her direct dealings with women of the press, which resulted in many lasting friendships for herself and for her "secretariat," Malvina Thompson and me, had broad scope, uninterrupted continuity, and deep significance. Mrs. Roosevelt was the only President's wife to hold regular press conferences, and she continued them the entire twelve years her husband was in office.

What delighted me about Mrs. Roosevelt and the press was the amazing way that one thing led to another. I can quite honestly say that I became a changed woman myself because of these press conferences. Mrs. Roosevelt got me into the habit of meeting the press and when Mrs. Truman came in and decided not to meet the press, that task fell to me. But that is another story.

From what I was able to gather, Mrs. Roosevelt had several objectives in starting press conferences. She wanted to raise the level of reporting done by women—many of whom were limited to social news, clubs and the like—and to interest them in some of the really vital affairs going on in the world and some of the important services rendered by government to the people. She was able to do this by her own activities and interest in such important things as child welfare, education, problems of youth, and social security. She called the women leaders in these fields into her conference to explain their projects.

She also wanted to increase chances of employment for women in newspaper work, at the time of the depression, when opportunities were limited. This she most certainly did accomplish. Men were not admitted to her press conferences, which made news widely printed throughout the country. So, because men were barred, many women were able to make and hold newspaper connections which otherwise they might not have done.

Then, too, Mrs. Roosevelt had had experience in Washington when her husband was Assistant Secretary of the Navy under Secretary Josephus Daniels in the Wilson administration. She knew the kind of ill-natured whisperings that could grow, from very small happenings at the White House, into disagreeable gossip. This she wanted to prevent by giving full publicity to what she was doing as the wife of the President.

Very often Mrs. Roosevelt had some interesting person from abroad at these meetings, which took place once a week when she was in Washington, over a period of more than twelve years.

Offhand I recall Ishbel MacDonald, daughter of the Prime Minister of England, telling about her work in the London County Council; and Eve Curie, of France, describing with the aid of a map an airplane trip to study Far Eastern conditions.

Madame Chiang Kai-shek, wife of the Nationalist Chinese leader, was one of the very distinguished public figures whom newspaper women were able to interview through Mrs. Roosevelt.

Queen Wilhelmina of the Netherlands also received the women of the press, with Mrs. Roosevelt, and answered questions which had been submitted to her in advance through the Dutch Embassy.

King George and Queen Elizabeth of Great Britain did not answer questions but did appear at Mrs. Roosevelt's press conference and shook hands with each of the women present. This in itself was an epoch-making event, something which British royalty never had done before.

Women house guests were welcome to sit in, and many of them did, discreetly taking seats at the rear of the room. The Grand Duchess of Luxembourg was one who came in this way, a patrician-looking woman indeed with pearls shimmering at her throat. Even more impressive was the President's aunt, Mrs. Dora Delano Forbes, visiting from Paris. She was very tall and stately for all her years, and walked with a stick of black ebony as tall as she.

As I recall it, Mrs. Forbes was accompanied on that occasion by her sister, Mrs. James Roosevelt, the President's mother. The elder Mrs. Roosevelt was beautiful. She and her brother, Mr. Frederic Delano, were two of the handsomest people I have ever seen, and also charming and gracious. Mrs. James Roosevelt, however, was a great lady who did not particularly relish the interest taken in herself and her family on account of the fame of her son. If the elder Mrs. Roosevelt did not like anyone she could show it very plainly; I am glad I saw only her kind, friendly side. She attended few of her daughter-in-law's meetings with the press.

Visiting newspaper women from other cities, from coast to coast, came to Mrs. Roosevelt's conferences. And when Mrs. Roosevelt later visited their cities, as was almost inevitable, they had the advantage of prior acquaintance in swinging into the interview of the day.

Malvina Thompson and I both attended Mrs. Roosevelt's weekly meetings, Malvina with a notebook to take down in shorthand what Mrs. Roosevelt said in response to questions on important or controversial subjects. My only part was to sit there and give Mrs. Roosevelt any corrections or explanations about the social engagements I had made for her or those taking place at the White House.

It was very interesting to sit with Mrs. Roosevelt and listen to the questions and answers, and also hear able women like Mary Anderson of the U.S. Women's Bureau, Grace Abbott of the U.S. Children's Bureau, and others speak of their own line of work.

For some time Mrs. Roosevelt received the newspaper women

informally in the West Hall on the second floor, which she had converted into a very pleasant sitting room. Later she moved to another room at the east end of the long central corridor, which was known as the Monroe Room because copies of portraits of President Monroe and his wife had been hung there by Mrs. Hoover. Also some pieces of the furniture were exact replicas which Mrs. Hoover had had made of furniture which President Monroe used in the White House, now in the Monroe law office at Fredericksburg, Virginia. Rows of chairs were placed for the newspaper women, who appeared in considerable numbers, usually almost filling the room.

It was during these conferences that my admiration for Malvina Thompson's extraordinary memory developed. Sometimes Mrs. Roosevelt would ask for some paper that had bearing on an engagement. Malvina had piles of material on her desk and she would say to me, "Look in the left-hand pile and you will find such and such a letter, the sixth from the top." And there it would always be.

Mrs. Roosevelt's contacts with newspaper women were in a way responsible for another innovation at the White House. And though Mrs. Roosevelt is one of the kindest women in the world, she never did realize the amount of suffering she inflicted by this second innovation—the Gridiron Widows' party.

Every year it was the custom of the Gridiron Club, an organization of newspaper men, to give a dinner for the President, followed by a program of skits for which the club has won national fame.

That left Mrs. President, and the wives of the Cabinet and other officials, sitting at home. So Mrs. Roosevelt started her Gridiron Widows' Party which she held the night of the Gridiron Dinner and to which she invited members of Washington's two newspaper women's clubs, wives of the Gridiron Club members and other feminine luminaries of the newspaper and official world, publishers' wives and the like, whose husbands would be dining with the President.

The very first Gridiron Widows' Party, in December, 1934, was a masquerade affair, and prizes were awarded for the best costumes. With invitations went this printed announcement:

> You are invited to come in costume with a mask. Prizes will be awarded for the three costumes judged best by a committee.

First prize went to a group depicting the Dionne quintuplets, one of the principal topics of conversation at that time.

That night, as part of the entertainment, Mrs. Roosevelt and her daughter Anna did a most amusing stunt. A motion picture called *Apple Annie,* in which an old woman selling apples was a lady for the day, was going the rounds. Mrs. Roosevelt came in dressed like an old apple woman, wearing shawl and decrepit bonnet. I think Mr. Louis Howe, who was living in the White House then, had helped to make her up and had coached her on this act. It was splendid. Her disguise was so complete her best friends didn't know her at first. Mumbling about her woes, she said, "the Divill, the Divill" and Anna appeared in a red devil suit to transform her into a First Lady for a day. In the end she decided her troubles were less as an apple woman and went back to selling apples. When Mrs. Roosevelt finished her apple woman skit, removed shawl and bonnet and took a bow, there was tremendous applause.

The pattern for the Gridiron Widows' Party was set that night. Always Mrs. Roosevelt with her staff or the Cabinet wives put on one skit. The Gridiron wives and press women alternated in putting on others.

It was all very well for Mrs. Roosevelt, who loved amateur theatricals. But some of her friends suffered horribly as actresses. I remember one perfectly ghastly occasion when Mrs. Cordell Hull, wife of the Secretary of State, and I had to do a stunt together. We writhed inwardly all through that whole act, and I know how far from a star I was. Malvina Thompson suffered, too, when it was her turn to turn actress. And we also suffered watching others suffer.

It was much pleasanter for Mrs. Roosevelt's friends when newspaper women and wives of Gridiron Club members put on the stunts, and really gave some very good performances. I quote from a program of December 11, 1937, after Mrs. Roosevelt's fine press relations had led to her daily column, widely syndicated, "My Day":

A recent literary event was the publication of a new volume of verse by Edna St. Vincent Millay. The Gridiron Widows present an even greater literary sensation, a preview of a forthcoming new volume by Eleanor St. Vitus MyDay. Its title is "Flighty."

PROLOGUE

Hi diddle diddle, the cat and the fiddle,
The cow jumped over the moon.
The moon laughed and laughed and said,
    "You're too late;
"Eleanor passed here at noon."

L'ENVOI

Little Boy Blue, come blow your horn,
The sheep's in the meadow, the cow's in the corn.
But thinking of fences, and speaking of sheep,
When, if ever, does Eleanor sleep?

After the various skits there was usually a sit-down supper and almost always Mrs. Roosevelt asked important women present to make brief talks at the end of the evening. These Gridiron Widows' parties were events in themselves, very popular and much talked about.

Gayest big party of the year at the White House was another innovation for the press originated by Mrs. Roosevelt, the annual Spring Dance for the accredited newspaper correspondents in Washington. Over the years these men and women had written about White House functions, but the first Spring Dance given by Mrs. Roosevelt was the first time they had been invited to the White House for a party of their own. It was called a dance, as there was supposed to be dancing in the East Room, and indeed many did manage to dance despite the crowded conditions. Mrs. Roosevelt even put on a Virginia Reel. But to one of long memory, like myself, this party was more of a Promenade. The great French doors to the terraces were thrown open for this springtime evening event, and couples walked and chatted on the roofs of the East and

West terraces, a lovely sight. The South Grounds also came alive, gay with voices and laughter.

The groups invited to these spring parties included the White House correspondents and news photographers, the press and radio galleries of House and Senate, and the active members of the men's and women's press clubs. The entire Cabinet was invited, and came.

This made an enormous number and it was decided that the women might bring an escort, wives could accompany their husbands, but bachelors were not permitted to bring their "girl friends." The last ruling was not very popular.

One man was stirred to the depths of his being by the restriction on girl friends, so stirred in fact that he wrote a long typed letter saying that since he was not allowed to bring a lady with him he would not attend the party—he returned his invitation. Happily this tragic piece of news was never broken to the President or his wife.

I remember a headline in bold type—"White House Bars Writers' Family," and underneath that, "Do Not Bring Your Family." It was quite true that fathers, mothers, brothers, sisters, uncles and aunts, and children, were not included. As it was, the crowd was so large, well over a thousand, that it was a good thing these parties were held in the spring, when the grounds could be thrown open.

Mrs. Roosevelt received the guests as they entered. The President usually sat on a sofa in the East Room, listened to the music, and watched the dancing. There were no formal introductions, but people came up and spoke to him, his closer friends among the press sometimes pausing to tell, but more often to hear, a joke. The non-dancing guests would wander at will, or have refreshments at small tables in the foyer.

One thing led to another, and in the campaign of 1936 I found myself, to my own amazement, deep in my only adventure in politics. Eventually it drew a substantial covering press. This adventure took place in and around Grayville, the small town in Illinois where my husband was born and where we spent our summers. After Admiral Helm's death I still went to Grayville. I rode every morning with the old farmer who was then acting as my farm superintendent. He was full of dry humor, and I learned from him more about the townspeople and those in the country around than I could have known otherwise in many months.

Grayville is at the center of three counties, and with President Roosevelt the candidate for re-election I began having regional meetings at my house. I invited people from various farm groups to discuss some of the questions of the time and had speakers in from Springfield and elsewhere.

How much good these meetings did I do not know; but they made it possible for a lot of surplus energy to be spent in that way. I also was asked to go to various spots and speak, which was a distinct disadvantage to the Democratic Party.

But all this gave me experience and it was borne in on me that in the various Presidential campaigns too little attention had been paid to the rural districts of Illinois—and in fact, to any of the smaller farm towns of the Middle West. Most of the Presidential and other candidates seemed to have concentrated on the larger towns.

Before leaving Washington for the summer of 1936, I had asked Mrs. Roosevelt if she and Miss Thompson would not come out and spend a few days with me. Happily, President Roosevelt was going to open the George Rogers Clark memorial in Vincennes, Indiana, so Mrs. Roosevelt arranged to leave the train there and spend three days with me.

I had notified Governor Henry Horner of Illinois, a splendid state executive, that Mrs. Roosevelt would be my guest. He sent his car for me to Grayville, so I could go to get her at Vincennes, and she and Malvina Thompson came home with me. He also insisted that some state troopers should guard the house while she was there.

Malvina and I never dared tell her of this. We knew she would insist that the troopers be sent away. But they came and my good Mary—who has been with me now for thirty-two years—saw that the ice box was always filled so the men on duty at night could find some coffee on the stove and something in the ice box.

Having a President's wife in Grayville was of course a tremendous event for the little town. I had talked over some of my plans with various Grayville friends and I decided to concentrate on the farm people who never would have had a chance to meet a President's wife. So I wrote to the Farm Bureaus of several counties, asking them to have their people come to two afternoon receptions I had planned for Mrs. Roosevelt. The response was excellent.

Catering facilities were non-existent at Grayville and if it had not been for the kindness of my neighbors, who baked vast quantities of cookies to supplement Mary's output, I would never have been able to have any refreshments on those afternoons. As it was, I am afraid the refreshments were disappointing to some of my guests, who were accustomed to the lavish hospitality of country entertainment, which usually included a supper of fried chicken and the trimmings in the afternoon.

On the first afternoon I asked friends in Grayville and Carmi to help me with my guests and see that people had refreshments and also that they went out into the garden, so as not to crowd the house. One of them asked a guest if she would have some refreshments, and she replied: "What have you got?" When she was told there were iced tea and fruit juice and cookies, the guest (a woman) said: "Is that all you've got!" And passed on.

However, most of the people did not seem to mind. There were long lines waiting outside the house to come in. It was an interesting sight to see men and women with children, old men and women, some in working clothes and others in their Sunday best, with adults and children all shined up.

I stood beside Mrs. Roosevelt, to get names and introduce the guests to her. I remember one stooped old man looked up at us—two tall women—and asked, "Which one of you be Mrs. Roosevelt?"

It seemed an endless procession both days, but fortunately cookies and soft drinks held out.

The day of our arrival, Mrs. Roosevelt went to see a Soil Conservation Camp that had been established in Grayville. The second day the town had arranged a picnic for us, to be held in one of the fields near Grayville. We all carried our lunch, and one of the pictures I like best shows Mrs. Roosevelt, Malvina and me sitting on the ground at this picnic. The heat was terrific, but nobody seemed to mind that.

All sorts of entertainment had been arranged—hog calling, husband calling and other amusements of the rural districts. Malvina and I had been on our feet continuously, and when someone came by to say there would be dog races, we hoped Mrs. Roosevelt would not hear; but she did and of course we went to see the dog races in one corner of the field.

During one day, hordes of Roosevelts appeared, and, to our amazement, when F.D.R. was told about them he knew who they were and to which branch of the family they belonged. It was one which had migrated years before from New York, and practically all of them lived in a small county adjacent to Grayville. One old gentleman looked exactly like Theodore Roosevelt.

Some months earlier a congressman from an adjoining district had asked Mrs. Roosevelt to promise she would go down in a coal mine if she ever came to southern Illinois. As soon as he heard she was to be there, he reminded her of her promise.

The only time we could fit this in was on the last morning Mrs. Roosevelt and Malvina were to be with me. We were due back promptly at one, as she was to go to Indiana and the Governor of Indiana had said his car would come for her. That meant we had to get up at four o'clock in the morning. Malvina and I were furious, but Mrs. Roosevelt was gay as a lark and glad to go.

Of course we had a police escort. We dashed through the countryside and whenever we reached a town the escort opened up their sirens and we must have scared many old ladies nearly to death as we raced along deserted streets of little towns and villages with only a stray cat or dog to dispute the right of way with us.

In our party was a local man who was all for promoting stops at every crossroads where fifteen or twenty people had gathered together.

However, we did get to the coal mine but Mrs. Roosevelt did not keep her promise. There is a superstition among the miners that it is bad luck to have a woman go down in the mine when the men are at work, so all Mrs. Roosevelt could do was stand at the mouth of the pit and speak to the crowd of men ready to go down the elevator shaft.

We then visited the largest coal mine in that section, which was not being worked at the time. A Chicago correspondent of the Associated Press, Ruth Cowan, one of the many reporters on this trip, stumbled into a deep hole full of water and got soaked with coal dust. She had to follow Mrs. Roosevelt in that bedraggled condition for the rest of the day.

Mrs. Roosevelt's visit cemented my friendship with the young editor at Grayville, adding greatly to the general interest in life when oil was discovered out our way. He would call me up in the middle of the night, maybe, to say that a new well was about to come in. Up I would get and off we would go in his car, over narrow roads through the underbrush of the Wabash River bottom, for the great thrill of seeing an oil well send up first a shaft of gas and then a shaft of oil, subsiding when "capped."

The time came when I had the really tremendous thrill of seeing an oil well come in on one of my own farms. It was not the Texas type of millionaire-making oil well, but a modest Illinois steady producer of a moderate annual income. Nevertheless, after many early years of living on a financial shoestring among the moneyed, this oil well has gladdened my latter years, and I am very grateful to it.

Chapter 15

THE SOCIAL SECRETARY
IS INVITED OUT

During my years at the White House, I received a great many invitations, not because I could do anything for anyone, but because a White House social secretary, though she has no official rank, does have a certain official standing. She is asked to a great many places—official parties, and, to a certain extent, parties given by residential society.

I really never have been offered anything for White House social favors—never any mink coats; just a few flowers sent me because people appreciated something I did in the natural course of events. But occasionally there were indirect social bribes.

I remember one incident of that kind in the Roosevelt administration. For several years I had been asked to one of the so-called exclusive houses in Washington—not as an intimate but to what the hostess might have called "my receptions, not my small parties." I had always gone with great pleasure and enjoyed looking at her beautiful, highly interesting house, with its many historic associations.

One day I was thunderstruck when my telephone rang and this lady asked if I wouldn't come with an intimate friend of hers the next day to tea. Did I have an engagement? Could I come that day or could I come another day? I said I would be very glad to come that day.

Then suspicion began its dirty work and I wondered why I had suddenly been singled out for this special honor.

The answer was forthcoming.

There was some question of the purchase of the lady's house by the government. Just at the right time, not too soon or too late, I was asked if I would not use my influence with the President to see if the purchase could not come to pass.

I said I would convey the message to the President and I did. The answer was a flat no. At the time, an economy wave was sweeping Congress, and the President said he would not feel justified in asking an appropriation for such a purpose when there was much need for vital projects.

So a little later on my invitations to the lady's house dried up. And that is one of the unhappy things that can happen to a social secretary who is not asked originally to "my small parties."

However, looking back through my scrapbooks I find many other invitations.

An invitation to dinner at the British Embassy in 1935 was worded:

> His Britannic Majesty's Ambassador
> requests the honour of
> Mrs. Helm's
> company at dinner
> on Tuesday, February 19th,
> at 8:30 o'clock
> British Embassy   R.S.V.P.

This particular "Britannic Majesty's Ambassador" was Sir Ronald Lindsay, who with Lady Lindsay gave brilliant dinners. Lady Lindsay was a long-time friend of Mrs. Roosevelt's and I look back with warm remembrance on the friendly kindness which she extended to me as a result of that long intimacy.

That night the Secretary of the Interior and Mrs. Harold Ickes were the guests of honor, and others present were the Minister of South Africa and Mrs. Close—and Representative Edith Nourse

Rogers of Massachusetts. Mrs. Rogers' husband came to Washington during the Wilson Administration as a member of Congress, and after his death she was elected to succeed him and has served in Congress with distinction for many years.

Lady Lindsay had arranged the rooms at the new Embassy on Massachusetts Avenue very well. The reception room, which is really almost like a hall, was attractive with sofas and screens. One thing I remember about the Embassy dining room—the table appeared too narrow for its length.

Every time Lady Lindsay was good enough to ask me to the Embassy, it was always to some agreeable party. When she left Washington, on the retirement of her husband as Ambassador, a group of her friends joined together in giving her a farewell gift and forunately I was allowed to be one of them. In a note thanking me, Lady Lindsay wrote:

"I feel too deeply to be able to put into words what my friends mean to me. You and I have often joked together, have sometimes suffered together, and have always felt together."

Early in 1937, when relations between the United States and Russia were pleasanter than they are nowadays, I received this invitation:

The Ambassador
of the Union of Soviet Socialist Republics
and Mrs. Troyanovsky
request the honor of the company of
Mrs. Helm
at a musicale by Sergei Prokofiev
on Monday, February 8
at the Embassy

The musicale was given at the present Russian Embassy on Sixteenth Street, successor to the building on I Street which I knew so well when Baron Rosen was Ambassador and I was the Baroness' secretary and companion for their daughter, Elisabeth.

An invitation from the successor of Troyanovsky, Maxim Litvinov, to an afternoon reception of the Soviet Embassy, had the Soviet hammer and sickle emblem at the top, in gold. The Troyanovsky invitation was a plain embossed card.

The Litvinovs gave this reception "On the occasion of the twenty-fifth anniversary of the Great October Revolution"—a date which has been celebrated at the Embassy each successive year, with similar events attended by enormous crowds. At that time Russian suspicion of guests prevailed and no one, of course, was allowed to get past the door without an admittance card. Even then, sharp-eyed men peered at one, and each card was checked carefully.

The drawing room of the Soviet Embassy is on the second floor —a great room extending the length of the mansion. In that room, the Ambassador and his wife greeted the guests. I have never seen such masses of food as were on the buffet tables—on one a huge fish in aspic, and of course the choicest caviar.

Poor Litvinov, who was friendly to the West, was recalled to Russia in 1943, and was further "relieved from his duties" with the appearance of the Iron Curtain after World War II. Until his death on January 2, 1952, the Western World had few reports on him. In 1945, a newspaper reporter from this country sought him out, and found him "cut off from all news." He was described as "a bitter, cynical old revolutionary, isolated and alone." In press reports of his funeral in Moscow his British wife was once more mentioned. He had married Ivy Low, a member of the well-known Low family of London, when he was a diplomat there. I have often thought of what must be the special loneliness of her lot as a widow in Russia.

My invitations were not all from the Diplomatic Corps. I note one from the Secretary of Commerce and Mrs. Daniel Roper, to dinner in honor of Ruth Bryan Owen (daughter of William Jennings Bryan), who then was Minister to Denmark. This was the first appointment of a woman to any top diplomatic post, and Mrs. Owen was a very charming and celebrated figure.

I also went to ladies' luncheons galore, to teas large and small, often to help out. I even went to some of the weekly "At Homes" of the Cabinet Ladies. These were like the old New Year's receptions at the White House—open to the public, come one, come all. There are no such "melting pot" affairs now.

The last Cabinet "At Homes" I remember were during the Roosevelt administration, and before they disappeared there were signs that the end of this type of entertaining was in sight. I remember, for example, that Frances Perkins, Secretary of Labor, and some others joined together and had a reception at the Sulgrave Club one winter.

The Cabinet days "At Home" were intended to allow people to meet Cabinet members' wives, and I am afraid that privilege became sadly abused. Such large crowds appeared that they swamped the premises.

There was one poor lady who became quite famous among Cabinet wives—I think she was the widow of some minor government official. She was well known in official circles because she would come to every Cabinet lady's "At Home," carrying a large-size bag which was somewhat greasy as to exterior and surely very greasy within. After eating copiously, she would put sandwiches and cakes in the bag and take them home. She would take a handful and stick it in the bag, then go to another section of the buffet and take another handful.

She had become such a nuisance that a certain Cabinet wife on one of her days "At Home" declared: "If this woman comes here today, I am going to see that at least this once the other Cabinet wives are not afflicted by her."

The old lady turned up in due course and after she had collected sandwiches and cakes, the Cabinet lady said to her: "My car is outside and I know you live some distance away. Won't you let my chauffeur take you home?"

The old lady thanked her and said there was nothing she would like better. The chauffeur reported, when he came home, that she had had him drive her to the entire round of Cabinet "At Homes," and then to her own home outside of town.

Instead of saving her colleagues from this poor old nuisance the Cabinet member's wife had actually provided her with transportation on her rounds.

While I have said I was offered no fur coats while social secretary at the White House, I must admit that my most embarrassing moment while in that post was due to a fur cape which I had purchased myself. That was when I "stole" a blue fox cape and was caught red-handed with the article in my possession.

Sometime before the crime was committed Mrs. Roosevelt and Malvina and I had bought fur capes. The chief merit of these garments was that they were cheap. I have always suspected the animal they came from was a guanaco or a llama, somewhat pleasantly treated so they looked a bit more expensive than would have been possible with fur directly traceable to those useful beasts of burden of the Andes. Anyway, my cape was on my shoulders one afternoon when I went to a tea, where unfortunately there was no checking system. I hung it up with other wraps.

After the tea was over I met Representative Edith Rogers and she suggested that we walk along together. She looked at my cape and said, "What a beautiful cape you have on." I said, "Oh, this old thing," and let it go at that.

The next morning as I was doing the last chores before going to the White House at nine o'clock, a call came from my hostess of the day before, who evidently had a high opinion of my honesty. She said, "I know it is ridiculous and you couldn't possibly have taken a fur cape, but Mrs. So-and-So's daughter has lost a beautiful blue fox."

It took me only one leap to go from the telephone to my closet, and there hanging on a hook was a cape that I recognized as being far superior to the object I had left at the hostess' house.

The awful part of the affair was that the mother of this young girl who had lost the cape was the militant head of a Republican Ladies' Committee—and I was social secretary to the wife of a Democratic President! I called her up and assumed a joking line (I suppose other criminals have done that, too). I said that, as usual, I had left something very poor and taken something very much better. "Yes," she said, "my daughter did not wear your cape home. She was very sad about it. She said, 'Mother, I never expect to see my beautiful blue fox again.'"

As it happened, both capes came from the same shop. Every now and then I have bumped into the mother whose daughter's cape I "stole." With my guilty conscience, on these encounters, I say a few words, stammer, reach for a piece of cake and manage to run from the room.

Chapter 16

KING GEORGE AND QUEEN ELIZABETH COME VISITING

IN THE WINTER OF 1938 it was announced that King George and Queen Elizabeth of England were going to Canada for a visit and would come to the United States.

It was well that we had advance notice of this event, for it was the first time in all our history that a reigning monarch had included this country in a state tour. There was, naturally, no precedent in any records available to us as to what should be done on the occasion of a royal visit. The visit of the King and Queen of Siam in the Hoover administration was unofficial—the King came to this country to consult an eye specialist.

I had kept a diary of entertaining for the President and Mrs. Wilson when they were guests of King George and Queen Mary at Buckingham Palace in 1918. Also, I had in my scrapbooks invitations that went with this entertaining for the Wilsons when I accompanied them (as Mrs. Wilson's social secretary) to Europe after the Armistice in 1918.

The State Department was particularly interested in a folder and dinner list given to the President and Mrs. Wilson at Buckingham

Palace on the night of the state banquet in their honor. This included a chart of the seating, with every guest's name inserted at his or her place around the horseshoe-shaped table. The then State Department Chief of Protocol, Mr. George Summerlin, told me this was very valuable to him and his staff; it was the only thing they had to guide them for similar entertaining in honor of King George and Queen Elizabeth at the White House.

I lent Mr. Summerlin my scrapbook of the Buckingham Palace visit, which was used as a model for the social events scheduled by the State Department. Then at the White House, under my direction, Mr. A. B. Tolley of the Social Office had our own very attractive souvenir program prepared. Copies of this program were placed in the bedroom of the King and Queen, and also in the rooms of members of their staff who accompanied them. Other copies were given to the members of the Cabinet.

Our program, which had an exceptionally handsome engraving of the White House on its cover, gave the King and Queen information about the different events scheduled for their three-day official visit in Washington, June 7th, 8th and 9th. It also gave the plans for their entertainment at the Roosevelt home at Hyde Park that week end, following a visit to the "Century of Progress" World's Fair in New York. By glancing through it they could know what was arranged for them to do during every day of their stay. It gave them the names of the guests who would attend the State Dinner in their honor the first night of their visit. It not only identified official guests, but also listed members of the Roosevelt family, identified as to their relationship to the President or Mrs. Roosevelt. Three of the Roosevelt sons, with their wives, were present at that dinner, and for this important official event the President and Mrs. Roosevelt included from their working household Marguerite Le Hand, personal secretary to the President, Malvina Thompson, and me.

Mrs. Roosevelt had given a great deal of thought to the after-dinner musicale. She planned it to give Their Majesties a picture of the scope of American music, including hillbilly songs, cowboy ballads, and sacred songs. Also American square dancing. And, topping it all off, Marian Anderson singing "Ave Maria" and "My

Soul's Been Anchored in the Lord," and Lawrence Tibbett singing "God Save the King" and "The Star-Spangled Banner."

Mr. Tolley included several pages listing artists, musical numbers and dancers who performed for Their Majesties after the State Dinner. Particularly interesting, we thought, was this foreword about American music:

> American music today is made up of three distinct living idioms—a folk, a popular and an art music. The traditions of all these three derive from Europe; the bulk of our folk music from the British Isles, that of our art music from the great composers of the continent. As in the case of the American language, the folk music has undergone a change in migration across the Atlantic.
>
> In addition, certain other national and racial minorities have created new hybrids, the French in the Southeast, the Spanish in the Southwest, the Germans and Scandinavians in the North. Above all, the Negro has made the most distinctive contribution.
>
> The people sang as they built a country, recalling the old and celebrating the new. The voices of miners, farmers, lumberjacks, workers of all kinds, their wives and children, swelled into a tide of music, rich and strange but vital and undeniably American.
>
> Our popular music, the music of the cities, draws from the sources of both the other and older idioms. Today, like the motion picture, it is an export commodity to all parts of the world.
>
> The selections on this program are drawn from these three musical currents and sung by persons and groups—professional and amateur—who know and sing them best.

It was a worthwhile plan and, I believe, accomplished its objective. It was an interesting and successful musicale. That this was true was in itself a triumph, for if ever best-laid plans seemed likely to succumb to heat and overcrowding, it was on the occasion of the royal visit of June 8, 9, and 10, 1939. June in Washington can be very pleasant and also unbearably hot. Looking back over several decades, those three days, I think, were the hottest I have ever felt in any Washington June.

The sun beat down upon the party as they arrived in their twelve-car blue and silver royal train at Union Station, where they were received by the President and Mrs. Roosevelt in the station's Presidential reception room, newly redecorated for the event.

The royal couple were escorted through a Guard of Honor by the Secretary of State and the British Ambassador, to be received by the President and Mrs. Roosevelt. Next, their Majesties' suite—a very large one, including royal palace officials—was presented to the President and Mrs. Roosevelt; then members of the U.S. reception committee were presented to the King and Queen.

Diplomatic representatives of the British Commonwealth followed with more presentations. The British Ambassador presented Lady Lindsay and members of the Embassy staff. Mr. W. L. Mackenzie King (Canadian Prime Minister who had accompanied the royal party from Canada) presented the Minister of Canada, Sir Herbert Marler and Lady Marler. Sir Herbert presented the staff of the Canadian Legation in Washington.

The Earl of Eldon, lord-in-waiting to the King, presented the Minister of the Union of South Africa and Mrs. Close. Mr. Close presented his staff from the Legation of the Union of South Africa in Washington.

Lord Eldon next presented the Secretary of the Irish Legation and Mrs. Healy, representing North Ireland in Washington.

This ended formalities at the station, but there was much more to follow.

In retrospect it will ever seem sad to me that this visit was not arranged for earlier in the year, as it could have been so very much pleasanter for all concerned. One of the international good will gestures thought up was by the enterprising international wool industry. Mrs. Roosevelt was to wear a dress of sheer British wool, Queen Elizabeth one of sheer American wool. Wool in that weather, be it said, seemed sheer madness. Nevertheless Mrs. Roosevelt wore hers, a notable example of stoicism. The Queen wisely turned to something thinner.

During the procession to the White House, President Roosevelt and King George rode in one open car; Mrs. Roosevelt and the Queen followed in another. The Red Cross had three first-aid stations, with doctors, nurses and stretcher-bearers, along the line of march. Never were precautions better taken. They did such a rushing business that they lost count of the numbers overcome by the heat when they reached well over one hundred. The newspapers said that more than one hundred and fifty in the crowd fainted that day.

The Queen had a very fair skin and by the time she reached the White House, although she had held a ruffled parasol over her head, she was very sunburned. In fact, that night one of her staff told me she was really suffering from a headache and from the effects of the sun.

Awaiting Their Majesties at the White House was a Diplomatic Circle, the title given by the Department of State to the custom of bringing to the White House, right after inauguration of a President and on very important diplomatic occasions, the heads of missions, ambassadors and ministers and their wives. It is a semi-circle really, for the group waiting to be received forms a half circle in the East Room. For the King and Queen there were seventy-eight in the group.

The King and Queen passed slowly around this semi-circle and each diplomatic pair was introduced. As dean of the Diplomatic Corps, Sir Ronald Lindsay, the tall British Ambassador who had just been presented with the Grand Cross of the Order of the Bath, presented the ambassadors and ministers and their wives, in the order of their precedence, while Lady Lindsay presented them to the Queen. The foreign ambassador who at the time has served his country longest in Washington is the dean of the Diplomatic Corps. The rest are ranged in the Diplomatic Blue Book in the order of their arrival and presentation of credentials to the President of the United States. Whenever they appear en masse, officially, they automatically line up in that order.

Mrs. Roosevelt had told Miss Thompson and me to come downstairs and be presented to the King and Queen and their party on their arrival at the White House. This was very formal, of course, and we had little contact with Their Majesties. However, the Queen's lady-in-waiting, Lady Katharine Seymour, stayed in the house and I found her a charming person, very attractive. I saw her very often during her stay there, because often there were questions she wanted to ask me. I have in my scrapbook a charming little note she wrote me after the royal party had departed, which I think is worth quoting. This is the note, written by hand:

THE ROYAL TRAIN
Canada

14 June 1939

DEAR MRS. HELM:

I must send you one line to bring you all my very grateful thanks for your help and advice during our visit to Washington.

You must have been so busy and yet you always had time to help and advise me and I do want you to know how deeply grateful I am.

The visit was so wonderful in every way and everyone was so kind and helpful.

Thanking you so very warmly,

Yours sincerely,
KATHARINE SEYMOUR

The Queen had another lady-in-waiting, Lady Nunburnholme, who stayed at the British Embassy and whom I naturally did not see as often as I saw Lady Katharine Seymour.

I also was able to observe the duties of a lady-in-waiting (a post held by titled English ladies since the early days of the British empire). Lady Katharine was seemingly in constant attendance on the Queen and always relayed messages received or sent by Her Majesty.

An informal White House luncheon crowded hard on the heels of the Diplomatic Circle. I have preserved in my scrapbook a brief typed memorandum concerning a detail of that luncheon. It was in regard to the inclusion of the Prime Minister of Canada, who had been a passenger on the Royal Train when it entered this country at Niagara Falls, as follows:

MRS. HELM,

Confirming telephone conversation, Mr. Summerlin called the Canadian Minister about inviting the Prime Minister of Canada to the luncheon on the day of the arrival of the Royal Party and the Minister of Canada said he thought it would be an excellent idea to invite him here for the luncheon that day.

E.R.

The menu of the King and Queen at their first White House meal, which we gave to the newspapers at the time, was:

        Minted Canteloupe Balls
         Green Turtle Soup
   Broiled Sweetbreads and Mushrooms
Asparagus   Saratoga Chips
Hearts of Lettuce Salad with Roquefort Dressing
     Pineapple Sponge Shortcake
Coffee   Nuts and Candies

After the luncheon, the King and President, the Queen and Mrs. Roosevelt, in the same two open cars, went sightseeing. Malvina and I took ourselves off to be among the envied at the British Embassy Garden Party, which would follow the sightseeing trip.

Now, invitations to British Embassy garden parties long have been more in demand than cards to White House functions. And when their Britannic Majesties were to be present, and it was the only opportunity for resident society to curtsy to British royalty, invitations came to be something very special indeed.

Of course, it was never suggested by anyone that Americans should curtsy to the King and Queen. If an American woman familiar with the Court of St. James in London, or other royal courts, wishes to curtsy, that is all right and occasional curtsiers were watched with interest and perhaps envy by non-curtsiers. The King and Queen always shook hands with Americans.

But the Embassy garden party guest list caused a storm at the Capitol and elsewhere.

As I recollect, Lady Lindsay invited heads of all congressional committees and all members of the Foreign Affairs and Foreign Relations Committees of the Senate and House, as the committees of Congress which deal directly with international problems. But other members of Congress—to whom no precious embossed invitations were delivered—felt they should be on the guest list, too.

Lady Lindsay, who was a New Yorker, American born, had many friends in that city and invited many persons from there, which increased the uproar from senators and congressmen (no doubt with complete concurrence from their wives). Eventually, the guest list was extended to include all members of the Congress and everything was serene or nearly serene.

The crowd was very large, so Malvina and I did not go through the receiving line, feeling this would make two less people for the King and Queen to greet. The day, though hot, was beautiful. From where Malvina and I stood on a small rise in the grounds, we had an excellent view of all that was going on.

The Embassy is a stately residence of traditional British architecture on Massachusetts Avenue in northwest Washington. Its large gardens were laid out by Lady Lindsay, who had studied landscape gardening and loved flowers. The Lindsays were the first to occupy this handsome structure. There are stately trees, a sloping lawn and a lovely rose garden. Everything was at its best that day, with all seasonal trees and flowers in full bloom. Most of the guests were assembled on the lawn.

I had never been to a garden party at Buckingham Palace, so the procedure of this royal function was very interesting.

The King and the British Ambassador, emerging through the French doors opening on a flagged terrace, went in one direction, while the Queen, with Lady Lindsay and Miss Irene Boyle, Lady Lindsay's social secretary, went in another. The crowd was drawn up around an empty space in the center of the lawn below the flagged terrace. As the Queen walked along, Miss Boyle would bring different persons to be presented to Her Majesty. Then the little procession would halt.

The same procedure was followed by one of the Embassy staff members, with the King and the Ambassador.

Her Majesty could not have been lovelier. She was dressed in white—a frock of some diaphanous white material. Her skirt had row upon row of circular, bias-cut flounces. Her wide brimmed hat exactly matched the dress and so did her tiny parasol. She must have been feeling the heat, but she did not look it. She made a beautiful picture.

There were striped marquees on the lawn, farther away from the mansion, with buffet refreshments: strawberries and cream, ice cream, tea and cakes. Tea was served to the King and Queen on the terrace, and more guests were brought to them for brief conversation. I remember Vice-President Garner and J. Pierpont Morgan, New York financier, with the King. There were a few curtsies for Their Majesties—and a traffic jam outside the Embassy on Massachusetts Avenue, through which Malvina and I made our way back to the White House.

The state dinner for Their Majesties that evening after the garden party was as usual at eight o'clock. For this historic occasion, it seems appropriate to reproduce the official guest list:

DINNER

THE WHITE HOUSE

THURSDAY EVENING, JUNE 8, 1939

AT 8 O'CLOCK

The President and Mrs. Roosevelt

Their Britannic Majesties

His Excellency the Right Honorable W. L. Mackenzie King, Prime Minister of Canada
His Excellency the British Ambassador and the Honorable Lady Lindsay
The Lady Nunburnholme, Lady in Waiting
The Lady Katharine Seymour, Lady in Waiting
The Earl of Eldon, Lord in Waiting to the King
The Earl of Airlie, Lord Chamberlain to the Queen
Mr. Alan Lascelles, Acting Private Secretary to the King
Surgeon Captain Henry White, R.N., Medical Officer
Mr. George F. Steward, Chief Press Liaison Officer
Captain Michael Adeane, Assistant Private Secretary to the King
Lieutenant Colonel the Honorable Piers W. Legh, Equerry to the King
Commander E. M. C. Abel-Smith, R.N., Equerry to the King
Mr. A. D. P. Heeney, Principal Secretary to the Prime Minister of Canada

The Vice-President and Mrs. Garner
Mrs. Charles Evans Hughes, Wife of the Chief Justice of the United States

Mrs. Woodrow Wilson, Widow of Woodrow Wilson, President of the United States
The Speaker and Mrs. Bankhead, House of Representatives
The Secretary of State and Mrs. Hull
The Minister of the Union of South Africa and Mrs. Close
The Minister of Canada and Lady Marler
The Secretary of the Treasury and Mrs. Morgenthau
The Secretary of War and Mrs. Woodring
The Attorney General, Honorable Frank Murphy
The Postmaster General and Mrs. Farley
Mrs. Claude A. Swanson, Wife of the Secretary of the Navy
The Secretary of the Interior and Mrs. Ickes
The Secretary of Agriculture and Mrs. Wallace
The Secretary of Commerce, Honorable Harry Hopkins
The Secretary of Labor, Honorable Frances Perkins
Senator and Mrs. Key Pittman, Chairman, Foreign Relations Committee and President pro tempore of the United States Senate
Senator and Mrs. William E. Borah, Ranking minority member of the Foreign Relations Committee, United States Senate
Representative and Mrs. Sol Bloom, Member, Foreign Affairs Committee, House of Representatives
Mrs. Sam D. McReynolds, Wife of Chairman of the Foreign Affairs Committee, House of Representatives
Representative Edith Nourse Rogers, Member, Foreign Affairs Committee, House of Representatives
General and Mrs. Malin Craig, Chief of Staff, United States Army
Admiral and Mrs. William D. Leahy, Chief of Naval Operations
Major General and Mrs. Thomas Holcomb, Commandant, United States Marine Corps
Honorable and Mrs. Stephen T. Early, Secretary to the President
Brigadier General and Mrs. Edwin M. Watson, Secretary and Military Aide to the President
Honorable and Mrs. Sumner Welles, Under Secretary of State
Major General Hugh A. Drum, U. S. A., Military Aide to the King

Rear Admiral James O. Richardson, U. S. N., Naval Aide to the King
Rear Admiral and Mrs. Ross T. McIntire, Surgeon General of the United States Navy and Aide to the President
Captain Daniel J. Callaghan, Naval Aide to the President
Honorable George T. Summerlin, Chief of Protocol
Miss Marguerite Le Hand, Personal Secretary to the President
Honorable Frederic A. Delano, Uncle of the President
Mr. and Mrs. Henry Parish, Cousins of the President
Mr. G. Hall Roosevelt, Brother of Mrs. Roosevelt
Honorable and Mrs. James Roosevelt, Son of the President and Mrs. Roosevelt
Mr. and Mrs. Elliott Roosevelt, Son of the President and Mrs. Roosevelt
Mr. and Mrs. Franklin D. Roosevelt, Jr., Son of the President and Mrs. Roosevelt
Miss Malvina C. Thompson, Secretary to Mrs. Roosevelt
Mrs. James Meredith Helm, Secretary to Mrs. Roosevelt

The state dining room, like the Embassy gardens, looked its best for the occasion. The famous old Monroe mirror-plateau centerpiece never reflected more beauty than that night. Purple-tipped white orchids were massed in the gold bowls. White candles gleamed in the gold candelabra. The gold flat silver was arrayed in rows on the white damask cloth. And for a touch of lacy color there were bouquets of roses, baby's breath and fern.

The Queen, all in white, wore exquisite jewels. And Mrs. Roosevelt, in ecru lace, wore her heirloom diamond necklace. After considerable conversation on table seating, two high-backed chairs matching those of the President and First Lady had been ordered. The President, with the Queen on his right, Mrs. John Nance Garner, wife of the Vice-President, on his left, sat opposite Mrs. Roosevelt; he always occupied the seat nearest the entrance to the State Dining room. He and the Queen led the procession into the room, followed by His Majesty and Mrs. Roosevelt. The King sat on Mrs. Roosevelt's right, and on his right was Mrs. Charles Evans Hughes, wife of the Chief Justice of the United States. On Mrs. Roosevelt's left was Vice-President Garner. There were sixty-two guests.

The menu for this dinner was:

> Clam Cocktail
> Calf's Head Soup
> Terrapin   Corn Bread
> Boned Capon
> Cranberry Sauce
> Peas   Buttered Beets
> Sweet Potato Cones
> Frozen Cheese and Cress Salad
> Maple and Almond Ice Cream
> White Pound Cake
> Coffee

The President proposed the health of the King in a very happy short speech in which he said: "It is because each nation is lacking in fear of the other that we have unfortified borders between us. It is because neither of us fears aggression on the part of the other that we have entered into no race of armaments, the one against the other."

As the King made an equally happy reply, I could not understand why a decision had been made not to have him address a joint session of Congress. The impediment in his speech which was supposed to prevent him from making long addresses was not noticeable that night or at any other time, and I think a very short speech at a Joint Session would have been sufficient.

"The visit which the Queen and I are paying you today is something which has been in our minds for many weeks," was the friendly way the King began. And he closed with, "I pray that our great nations may ever in the future walk together in a path of friendship in a world of peace." In retrospect, the "path of friendship" seems clear enough, but the "world of peace" still far off.

After dinner Mrs. Roosevelt and the Queen went into the Green Drawing Room and I took up different ladies of the party, according to rank, and left them with the Queen for a short interview. After what seemed a sufficient time, I brought up someone else so that the interview could end.

Then came the musicale, an affair that did not go off without incidents although every detail had been carefully thought out and planned beforehand by skilled White House staff members.

Kate Smith had a radio engagement, and her moon had to come over the mountain—it was by special request of the King—at the very start of the program instead of working up a mood for it. Marian Anderson, world-famous Negro singer, became slightly temperamental and wanted to change her number. And a hillbilly folksong singer ran briefly afoul of the White House Secret Service. An erroneous report had come to the Secret Service, ever on the alert, that one of those who took part in the program was supposed to have communistic leanings. The hapless man was thoroughly searched and arrived on the stage rather shaken from his experience. I wondered why his voice did not show up better, and I learned that he was hardly able to croak after his ordeal.

However, the East Room rang right merrily with "Get Along, Little Dogie," and "Buffalo Gal," and the folk-dancing followed in full swing, "Wagon Wheels" and "Ocean Wave." The night was stifling, thermometer in the upper nineties, humidity appalling. Queen Elizabeth had come from cool Canada, and she had had a long day. In the middle of that carefully-planned musicale, Lady Lindsay, wife of the British Ambassador, reported that something must be done; Her Majesty was almost exhausted.

I think they took the Queen out on the South Portico—though the air outside was little better than in the then airconditionless East Room.

On the second day of the royal visit, Lady Katharine Seymour called me and asked if I would come into her room. I went and she showed me an object and said, "I don't know exactly what to do with this or who is to be thanked for it."

I looked at the object. It was one of the most terrible paintings I have ever beheld in my life, supposedly a likeness of the Queen. I said, "Where did that thing come from?" She said, "I don't know. It was in the Queen's room."

After F.B.I. work on the part of the chief usher and me, we found that one of the White House household who thought he had talent as an artist had executed the "object" and induced one of the servants to leave it in the Queen's room. The usher was almost ready to murder the ambitious "artist."

When I told Lady Katharine what had happened, we looked at each other and burst into laughter. I said, "Give it to me and I shall see that it goes back. Don't do anything about it."

That day, Their Majesties received British citizens, resident in Washington, at the British Embassy, then went to the Capitol and were greeted in the rotunda by members of both Houses of Congress.

Immediately after this ceremony, they went down the Potomac to Mt. Vernon on the Presidential yacht *Mayflower,* with luncheon aboard. At Mt. Vernon the King laid a wreath at Washington's tomb—as is always the custom with visiting foreign dignitaries. Malvina and I and the late Mrs. Henry Parish, cousin of Mrs. Roosevelt (who was staying at the White House at the time) went by motor to Mt. Vernon and saw this ceremony.

Their Majesties motored back to Washington, instead of returning on the *Mayflower.* At that time "made work" still was going on as an aftermath of the great depression, and there was a Civilian Conservation Camp on the road from Mt. Vernon, which the King was eager to see. From the camp he drove on to Arlington, to lay another wreath on the Tomb of the Unknown Soldier.

The King had said he would like to meet some members of the President's Cabinet, like the Secretaries of Agriculture, Commerce, and Labor, also others active in various government agencies. These people were invited to tea on the White House lawn the second day of the royal visit.

Some of the officials who talked to the King at that tea were amazed to discover how much he knew about the work of our different government agencies. We had been asked to send him data about these federal agencies and the work they did, and evidently he had studied the data painstakingly. He had a number of questions to ask about details of the work of agencies and departments.

At this tea, members of the Social Staff were presented to Their Majesties by Mrs. Roosevelt. They had much to do with preparing the invitations and all the hard work which led to the visit, and it was only fitting that they should have this opportunity to meet a live King and Queen.

The King and Queen gave a return dinner to the President and Mrs. Roosevelt the evening of June 9th, at the British Embassy. Their Majesties were host and hostess only in name, of course; they were staying at the White House and drove from there to the Embassy, where all arrangements had been made for the party.

Little Diana Hopkins, Harry Hopkins' daughter, was at the White House and was eager for a glimpse of the Queen. Mrs. Roosevelt took the little girl to meet Her Majesty, as she came downstairs dressed for the Embassy dinner.

The Queen, with children of her own and knowing childish thoughts, said Diana probably would like to see her when she really looked like a Queen, in evening dress and royal tiara. I did not get a glimpse of her that night, but I know she was radiantly lovely the previous evening at the state dinner, in a marvelous white dress of some thin lacy material with silver trimming on it, as I recall. I wondered if that was the gown that had to have a trunk all to itself so it would arrive uncreased. It did arrive uncreased and certainly fitted its beautiful owner.

Their Majesties' party was a large one, including two ladies-in-waiting, a lord-in-waiting, a lord chamberlain to the Queen, an acting private secretary to the King, a medical officer, a chief press liaison officer, an assistant private secretary, two equerries to the King, two personal maids for Her Majesty, a first and second valet for His Majesty, a head footman, a Queen's footman, four undesignated footmen, a maid for each of the ladies-in-waiting, a man servant for the lord-in-waiting and the medical officer, a King's page, a clerk, two inspectors from Scotland Yard and several Canadian mounted police who served as orderlies.

The King was given the southwest suite. All members of the royal party who stayed at the White House occupied rooms on the second floor. The British Embassy and three members of the Embassy staff entertained others, while overflow servants slept on the royal train in the railroad yards near Union Station. A car was sent to bring three personal attendants to the White House for their duties on each of the two days of the royal visit.

When the royal party left Washington Saturday morning, June 10th, all details had been planned in advance for their Hyde Park stay.

More than a month earlier, on May 6th, Mrs. Roosevelt had come to a decision which may have disappointed some of her important neighbors living on Hudson River estates near the Roosevelt family mansion. She had decided that no guests were to be invited in after dinner on that Saturday night at Hyde Park.

For the very famous "hot dog" picnic lunch on Sunday, June 11th, a very special group of guests were invited to sit on the porch of the President's cottage, where the King and Queen and the President and Mrs. Roosevelt were served. This small group included the Secretary of the Treasury and Mrs. Morgenthau, the Governor of New York and Mrs. Lehman, the Right Rev. Henry St. George Tucker, Presiding Bishop of the Episcopal Church, and Mrs. Tucker, Mrs. Vincent Astor, Mrs. Price Collier (the President's aunt), Mr. and Mrs. Gerald Morgan (Hyde Park neighbors), Mrs. J. Roosevelt Roosevelt, widow of President Roosevelt's half brother, and Mrs. Myron C. Taylor. And of course, the President's mother, Mrs. James Roosevelt.

The King and Queen went to New York City by train and then to Hyde Park by motor. The day in New York must have been an exhausting one, with all sorts of civic ceremonies arranged for them.

Neighbors of the President and Mrs. Roosevelt had hospitably offered to entertain some of the royal staff and representatives of the State Department at their homes, and to give dinners for these guests on Saturday night, June 10th. The volunteer hostesses included Mrs. Vincent Astor, Mrs. Lydig Hoyt and Mrs. Gerald Morgan.

On the Roosevelt estate itself were four houses, three separated by distances of from two to three or four miles. Mrs. James Roosevelt's house—the President's boyhood home, now owned by the federal government—was always called the "Big House." At the "Big House" were staying the King and Queen and the two ladies-in-waiting, Lady Katharine Seymour and Lady Nunburnholme; Mr. Alan Lascelles, the private secretary to the King; Colonel Piers

Legh, the King's equerry; and Mr. Mackenzie King, Prime Minister of Canada.

The King and Queen dined on Saturday night at the "Big House"—a small party due to limitations of space in Mrs. James Roosevelt's dining room. A few relatives were invited and some members of the royal party, with the President's military and naval aides and the Chief of Protocol.

Malvina and I stayed at Val Kill Cottage, one of the other houses on the Roosevelt estate. Val Kill Cottage also, of course, was filled with guests. This cottage is a small house built by Mrs. Roosevelt as a furniture factory during the depression, when she and two friends joined in financing this factory for handmade furniture to give work to unemployed persons. The beautiful tables, desks and other articles of furniture made there are now collectors' pieces.

After the depression, Val Kill workmen (Val Kill was the trade name used for this furniture enterprise) went to other positions and Mrs. Roosevelt converted the factory into her own residence on the Roosevelt estate. It is a pleasant place and we were very comfortable there.

That Saturday evening—it must have been about six o'clock—disquieting messages began to come to us that Their Majesties had been delayed on the trip from New York and that dinner arrangements for members of their staff and others would have to be delayed. This meant telephoning to each hostess.

It seemed to me that no sooner had I finished one set of phone calls, reporting the royal party would be a half hour late, when another report came in saying another half hour, and so on. What the dinners must have been like when the people finally sat down to them, I cannot imagine. I think the last one must have been served about nine-thirty.

The Hyde Park visit was an epoch-making one for a member of my own household—Mary, who had served me faithfully for many years. For Mary had an unexpected reward when Mrs. Roosevelt proposed that she should go to Hyde Park with us.

I had been several times to Hyde Park before, but this was my first trip on the President's train. We left Washington Friday night, arrived at Poughkeepsie the morning of the 10th, and drove to

Hyde Park. As we got off the train in Poughkeepsie, an amusing incident occurred. During her stay in Washington, the Queen had received quantities of orchids—more than she could wear. One of the White House maids had retrieved the excess supply of corsages and had pinned five on her bosom—and, I will add, she was amply busted. As she walked down the platform, followed by one of the other maids, Bill Hassett, one of the President's press secretaries, said: "Here comes _____ and her lady-in-waiting."

The trip was a "duty" assignment for both Mary and me—I was on duty as Mrs. Roosevelt's social secretary and Mary was to help supplement the staff of servants. My own wardrobe was a comparatively simple affair, but Mary's had to be carefully selected—aprons and morning and afternoon uniforms. Our establishment of two could not be let down!

Mrs. Roosevelt sent Malvina and me over early Saturday morning to see if there were any changes to be made at the "Big House." The rooms, of course, were in perfect order and the house was filled with flowers, arranged by some of the local garden clubs. It was the first time I had ever seen the large flowered clematis used in flower arrangements, and it was exquisite.

Late Saturday evening the royal party finally arrived. On Sunday morning, we were up early to go to the cottage President Roosevelt had built on top of a hill—and no more inaccessible spot can be imagined for a royal picnic than that hilltop cottage. It actually was not finished and the ground around it was quite rough, but the views from the front porch were superb.

Both the President and Mrs. Roosevelt loved picnics. The difficulties of transporting food from the "Big House" to this cottage would have seemed to me insurmountable, but not so to Mrs. Roosevelt.

Some of the White House servants had come up on the train with us and they went with us to the cottage. Then there were the servants from Val Kill Cottage and my own Mary, making a considerable staff.

Two types of "Admit Cards" had been printed for the picnic party. These had been carefully planned and they sounded very well in theory, but did not work out so well in practice.

The idea was that No. 1 cardholders would bring their own lunches. But evidently these cardholders must have liked the looks of the lunch being prepared in the small kitchen at the cottage, better than their own—if they really did bring their own lunches. Of course the picnic food was ample for Their Majesties and the invited guests, but when it came time for Miss Thompson and me to eat, it was as though a horde of locusts had swept over the place. I do not think there was one of the famous hot dogs left. We did not even get any of the wonderful strawberries that the Secretary and Mrs. Morgenthau had sent over from their nearby place at Hopewell Junction.

There were in all some seven tables, seating four each. Here is the menu:

Virginia Ham	Hot Dogs
Cold Turkey	Sausages (hot)
Cranberry Jelly	Rolls
Green Salad	
Strawberry Shortcake	
Coffee	Beer	Soft Drinks

Someone had sent a smoked turkey and Mrs. Roosevelt was especially anxious that the King try it, because he said he had never tasted it. When Mrs. Roosevelt offered a platter of smoked turkey to the King, he took a good-sized slice and pronounced it very good. We had a long serving table in front of the fireplace in the cottage living room. There was regular turkey, too, and we put the platters of smoked turkey on the mantel so as not to confuse the two.

There was a concert at the President's cottage after lunch and two American Indians were on the program. One was a real Indian princess and the other was only part Indian. They had to share the only mirror in the cottage, which was in the bathroom, and the Princess, who was really an artist, was very scornful of the other performer, who was not. Both were in full tribal costume.

Miss Thompson and I had little time to think of food or concert, however, because Mrs. Roosevelt sent for us and said, "Please hurry as fast as you can down to the cottage [Val Kill]. The King wants to go swimming and the party will have to dress at Val Kill. Please put the place in order and make ready for tea."

The swimming pool was at Val Kill, several miles from the President's cottage on the hilltop. So we commandeered a car and rushed down at breakneck speed.

Our rooms at the cottage were on the ground floor, which would be most convenient for the King to use. We ran here and there, putting away articles of apparel, etc., that had been left around by us or the guests.

The Queen did not go in the pool and I discovered later that the King used Malvina's room to dress and the President used the one I was occupying. Malvina was deeply chagrined because she had no shower curtain in her bathroom; she had bought a new one, thrown away the old one and had not had time to hang the new one, never thinking anyone would want to use her room, much less the King of England and Emperor of India.

While the swimming party was in progress, I began to prepare for tea. I tried to find a teakettle, but no one is more inefficient than I when it comes to cooking, and all I could find was an enormous pot. I filled it with water, put it on the stove and started to boil the water. Malvina ran around frantically trying to find some sandwiches and cakes which she knew were somewhere in the kitchen and which she finally unearthed.

Never did I see such scorn on any countenance as on Mary's, when she appeared on the scene, came into the cottage and saw all the disorder I had created. I was relegated to one side and Mary took charge. She said of course she had thought they might want tea and had made it, taken it off the leaves and put it in the refrigerator, waiting to be used.

The crisis was over. When the swimming party came to an end I beheld a procession pushing tea carts. Mrs. Roosevelt's maids were new and rather frightened, so the dauntless Mary led the procession and everything was perfect for a hearty English tea. One of the maids, however, dissolved in tears and was unable to work because she had not been introduced to the King and Queen.

Almost my only recollection of the tea is that Governor and Mrs. Lehman and some of their family came in while Mr. Roosevelt, the

King and some of the royal party were still in the pool. The rest of the affair for me was a blank.

There was one other incident worth mentioning in connection with the royal visit. Before the King and Queen arrived in Washington, Mrs. Roosevelt asked Malvina and me to go through the rooms they were to occupy at the White House and see if it would be necessary to make any changes. Probably she had in mind that books in White House guestrooms apparently were often chosen for their bindings and not for their contents.

"Diseases of Horses and Their Cures" had been discovered in one of the rooms—a bit of lively literature for guests. And Mrs. James Roosevelt had astounded her daughter-in-law by telling her she had found and read a novel in her room which was not at all the kind of novel that should have been found in that lady's bedchamber.

So with this in mind we went into the rooms assigned to Their Majesties, and it was just as well that we did. Next to the King's bed we found a picture that was hastily removed and something more fitting substituted. It was a print of the surrender of Cornwallis at Yorktown.

In the Queen's rooms were some charming prints that had to do with the coronation of Queen Victoria, given to the White House by Mrs. Charles Hamlin, an old friend of the Roosevelts. Those were all right.

Chapter 17

ROYAL REFUGEES; CHURCHILL; AND MADAME CHIANG

WITH THE AWFUL ATTACK on Pearl Harbor, Malvina and I settled into an unreal sort of life. The official social calendar was adjourned, but the days were even busier for us all. The tremendous White House windows had to be equipped with blackout curtains, a bomb shelter was built beneath, machine guns adorned the roof, guarding troops paraded outside.

Royal refugees came and state luncheons and dinners were held for them—Martha and Olaf of Norway, Wilhelmina and Juliana of Holland, George of Greece, Peter of Yugoslavia. And Madame Chiang of China, a law unto herself.

I have a memorandum of state functions for refugee royalty, 1942, after Pearl Harbor:

> H.M. King George of Greece—Dinner Wed. June 10, 1942
>   The President and Mrs. Roosevelt
>   54 at table
> H.M. Peter II, King of Yugoslavia—Dinner Wed. June 24, 1942
>   President Roosevelt (stag)
>   25 at table

H.M. Wilhelmina, Queen of the Netherlands—Dinner Wed. Aug. 5, 1942
The President and Mrs. Roosevelt
41 at table

H.R.H. The Crown Prince and The Crown Princess of Norway—Dinner Jan. 30, 1942
The President and Mrs. Roosevelt
28 at table

The Grand Duchess of Luxembourg was an earlier visitor, a state dinner having been held for her, her consort Prince Felix and son the Grand Duke Jean on Feb. 12, 1941. During the war years Great Britain and the United States and Canada furnished asylum to many royal and ducal personages.

Those days of 1942 after the attack on Pearl Harbor seem almost like a dream or something resurrected from the first World War. Though, of course, the danger was much less in World War I days—that is, danger to the White House and its inhabitants.

After Pearl Harbor, all state receptions were canceled and when the various royal refugees arrived, dinners that were held for them were small in comparison to the state dinner for the King and Queen of England in 1939.

There were joint sessions of Congress at which the President made historic speeches. Mrs. Roosevelt always took Malvina and me with her to the executive gallery in the House of Representatives, from which we had the privilege of listening; but after several of these crowded affairs, I decided it was better to sit at home and get the full import of a speech quietly and without the distractions of watching people on the floor of the House, noting applause and those who did not applaud, also incidents involving people who came along and tried to get into the gallery and had to be ejected as courteously as possible.

Princess (now Queen) Juliana visited the Roosevelts more than once while she was living in Canada as a royal refugee. My first glimpse of her was at Hyde Park when I was staying there sometime during one of the autumns of the Roosevelt administration (not an election night, however). Her Royal Highness was staying with the President and Mrs. Roosevelt at the "Big House"—home of Mrs. James Roosevelt.

Mrs. Roosevelt's house had a large combined living room and library, which was an addition to the older part of the building and a very useful one, because it made a splendid room for large gatherings. It was a very comfortable room.

On the evening to which I refer, only a small group was present. The Princess sat in the corner of a large sofa, before an open fire. The President was busy nearby with some of his stamps. There was not very much conversation. The Princess knitted most of the evening.

I remember that once the President called her "Child" and asked her to transmit some message to the Netherlands Prime Minister.

The next time I saw Princess Juliana was at an informal tea given for her by the wife of the Ambassador of the Netherlands in Washington. Notes of invitation to this affair were handwritten; nevertheless it was a large party and a very pleasant one. The Dutch Legation is a handsome residence and in the spring its display of tulips in front of the house is magnificent.

Mr. (now Sir) Winston Churchill was a frequent White House visitor during World War II, but we of the White House staff seldom saw him. I remember a hush-hush visit during the early stages of the war, when we had been informed he was expected and Mrs. Roosevelt told us (Malvina and me) to be on the second floor so we could be introduced to him when he stepped out of the elevator. That was the only time I recollect that he ever spoke directly to either of us. However, Malvina saw much more of him than I did, because she was at the White House more constantly and she came in contact with his aide, Commander C. R. Thompson.

I remember, though, that Mr. Harry Hopkins had brought his small daughter, Diana, to be introduced to Mr. Churchill with Malvina and me. Mr. Hopkins said, "Come, sweetheart, and meet the Prime Minister," and Mr. Churchill just said, "How do you do."

It is a very amusing but erroneous theory, cherished by many people, that simply because a guest of great prominence is at the White House, he or she drops pearls of wisdom all over the premises before those who stand and wait. I was hardly a "waiter," but I saw Mr. Churchill very seldom and then I can remember only a pleasantly grunted "Good morning" or "Good evening," as the case might be. Certainly no pearls of wisdom.

The great war Premier was no exception to the general rule of White House visitors. If they had anything world-shaking to say they said it only to the President, the President's wife or some other important person. Mr. Churchill, however, has been such an international figure that even the smallest details about him seem to be of interest, and we of the staff did garner a few of those.

We were always informed two days in advance of Mr. Churchill's arrival. He was at the White House oftener and for longer stays than the public realized, I feel sure. Once he and Mrs. Churchill were there for a full month while the Roosevelts were at Hyde Park, and the secret was so well guarded that no word ever leaked out.

His "home" at the White House was the Rose Suite at the east end of the building on the second floor—the suite occupied by Queen Elizabeth of England in 1939 and Queen Juliana of the Netherlands in 1952. During the same period Harry Hopkins lived at the White House for a considerable time, and he was quartered across the hall from Mr. Churchill, in the Lincoln bedroom. Mr. Hopkins was always hurrying back and forth, usually in a dressing gown, as I recall, though I really saw very little of him.

Mr. Churchill, in common with other White House visitors, used the Monroe Room as a personal sitting room. This was convenient, because, like the Rose Suite, the Monroe Room also is at the east end of the building and at the head of the stairs leading to the first floor. Personal callers on such visitors as the British Premier could come to the Monroe Room without using the elevator at the west end of the building, and usually without encountering the White House family or household.

I remember during the Churchill visits that when I emerged from the elevator on the second floor, on the way to my morning conference with Mrs. Roosevelt, I would see bottles of various sizes with appropriate glasses assembled and ready to be carried at the proper time to Mr. Churchill's apartment. After one of his stays President Roosevelt was heard to express the fervent hope that he wouldn't have to drink any cocktails for at least a week.

Mr. Churchill could be very formal in his dress on occasion, but usually at the White House he wore that extraordinary one-piece garment that was called his "siren suit." Why "siren" I do not know, because his figure was not of the slim or sinuous variety which that word suggests.

I remember my delight over being asked to that wartime Christmas dinner at the White House when Mr. Churchill was a guest. It was primarily a family dinner, including only three British dignitaries who were staying at the White House and a few others— among them Lord Beaverbrook, famous British publisher; Admiral of the Fleet Sir Dudley Pound; and Field Marshal Sir John Dill.

Mrs. Roosevelt always seated family dinners. When I went in, expecting to be placed at the foot of the table (where I always put myself when I did the seating) and hoping I might be somewhere near Malvina, I found instead that I was only three places away from the President, between Sir Dudley Pound and Sir John Dill. This was somewhat appalling, for of course it is usually rather hard to find a common meeting ground with absolute strangers.

I can remember little of the conversation that flowed around the wartime Christmas table, because I was trying to summon up courage to ask one question which was trembling on my lips; I wanted to ask about Sir Roger Keyes, who knew my father and whom I had met in London when I was there with President and Mrs. Wilson after World War I. But at the time of this Christmas dinner, he had just been relieved of command of the British Commandos, and as Sir Dudley was Admiral of the Fleet, I hesitated to ask him anything about Sir Roger.

The President spoke a very few moving words about his pleasure in having the British there. He proposed the health of the King and Queen, saying that he knew it was contrary to British custom to drink their health before the dinner was ended. The Prime

Minister replied, also in a few words, and those seemed to be the highlights of the dinner.

Memory also takes me back to a wartime visit of the Duke and Duchess of Windsor when they stayed with Lord and Lady Halifax at the British Embassy. Lord Halifax then was British Ambassador to Washington.

Mrs. Roosevelt was doing some work with Civilian Defense and had an office outside the White House, in a building on Dupont Circle. The Duchess had said she wished to see the work that Mrs. Roosevelt was doing. Malvina Thompson and I had enormous curiosity, like the rest of the people of our country, to see the famous Duchess. So *we* were appointed a committee of two to go to the British Embassy and conduct her to the Dupont Circle building.

Arriving at the Embassy in a White House car, we were shown to a small sitting room where Lady Halifax met us; and then, in order, arrived Lord Halifax, the Duke of Windsor and last the Duchess with a small dog. We went down the stairs in a solid procession, entered the car with a British Secret Service man on the box, and drove down to Mrs. Roosevelt's office. The Duchess was very agreeable on that short trip.

Arrived at the building, hordes of photographers were waiting to take pictures. The Scotland Yard man protested that they should not be allowed to photograph "Her Grace"; but Malvina, with commendable energy, seized the initiative. She said Mrs. Roosevelt always allowed photographs to be made of her, most willingly, and Malvina could not see why they should not be made on this occasion of the Duchess of Windsor. After a somewhat spirited exchange, the photographs were taken.

There was tremendous interest shown throughout the country as soon as it was announced, early in 1943, that Madame Chiang Kai-shek was coming here to enter the Columbia Presbyterian Medical Center in New York.

The brave struggle of Nationalist China against the Japanese had roused admiration and keenest interest throughout the United

States—and, indeed, the world. The lovely, flowerlike wife of the Generalissimo, who was educated in the United States and speaks English better than most of us, had become a heroine for all of America. No visiting royalty ever attracted more attention.

I fear some of our illusions about this extremely interesting woman—one of the most able in the world today—were dispelled a little even before she came to Washington, when it was published in the papers that she had taken a whole floor in the Harkness Pavilion of the Medical Center. This has never been contradicted and I imagine it was the case. That such enormous expense should have been incurred, when the Chinese were starving, was the subject of some criticism in the newspapers.

Unlike many of the royal or other State visitors to this country, Madame Chiang came on the personal invitation of Mrs. Roosevelt. Partly for this reason, her visit caused us many difficulties. We could not communicate with her through the Chinese Embassy and therefore we worked under a serious handicap.

I do not know the inside story of the many complications Madame Chiang's visit caused the Chinese Ambassador then in Washington, but from what I gather, the Chinese Embassy even had to ask the State Department to try to find out when the Generalissimo's wife was coming and the hour of her arrival. Had she come with her husband and had the visit been arranged officially through the State Department, no such difficulties would have been encountered prior to her arrival.

I have heard that Madame Chiang told a friend she had the greatest difficulty with her entourage on this visit, because racially they considered themselves superior to all members of the white race. With this there need be no quarrel, but certainly with an older civilization should come corresponding civility.

The attitude of superiority was unmistakably reflected in two members of Madame Chiang's entourage who stayed at the White House and who made no secret of their feelings that we were inferior. It may have accounted for some very curious orders which were given and of which Madame Chiang may have known nothing. For instance, before her visit we were told that Mrs. Roosevelt could speak to her on the telephone only on one day—the Saturday before her arrival at the White House, at six-thirty; not before, not after, but promptly at six-thirty. This, even though at the time Madame Chiang had left the hospital.

My troubles began on the morning after her communication with Mrs. Roosevelt. I understood that in their conversation she had said very definitely she would make only one speech at Congress and that would be before a Joint Session of both Houses.

At this point I must explain that the two Houses of Congress meet in Joint Session only on rare occasions and that to address one of these sessions is a very great honor. At such times members of the Senate go to the House, which, with 435 members to the Senate's 96, is much more spacious than the Senate Chamber. Usually members of the U.S. Supreme Court, top-ranking diplomats, and Cabinet members also attend these rare events.

Looking back, I recall Joint Sessions addressed by Presidents Wilson, Roosevelt and Truman; by British Prime Minister Winston Churchill; by Queen Wilhelmina of Holland, and later by her daughter, Queen Juliana; and by General Douglas MacArthur. King George VI of Great Britain did not appear at the Capitol in this way, but not because the Congress would have been unwilling to hear him in Joint Session. His Majesty, as was well known, had a slight impediment in his speech and apparently it was thought better for him not to attempt a speech before such an audience.

So it can be seen that when Madame Chiang announced she would make only one speech before Congress, and that before a Joint Session, she was asking to be accorded an honor which would have been unusual since she was not a guest of the United States government, and was here as a private citizen of China.

The situation was further complicated because on that Saturday when she made this statement to Mrs. Roosevelt, Mr. Sol Bloom, the Chairman of the Committee on Foreign Affairs of the House, had talked to Mrs. Roosevelt about Madame Chiang's visit, and said he was speaking for a Joint Committee of the Congress. But of course these details could be settled only by the two joint committees of the Senate and House, and apparently the Senate had objected strenuously to having matters settled for them by a member of the House.

I was plunged into these difficulties and had to talk to a very irate Chairman of the Foreign Relations Committee of the Senate, Senator Tom Connally of Texas. In substance, Senator Connally said Madame Chiang was not a ruler like Queen Wilhelmina of Holland, who had addressed a Joint Session of Congress when she was in Washington not long before Madame Chiang's visit, nor was she the wife of a ruler. Therefore, the Senate would be very glad to have her appear before that body and speak, if she so desired, and then proceed to the House, but there would not be a Joint Session in her honor. In other words, she could take it or leave it.

From what I have known of Madame Chiang, I think she was trying to force the Congress to accord her at least the same honor as Queen Wilhelmina.

On Monday morning an emissary from the Chinese Embassy, Mr. J. Z. Huang (identified in the Diplomatic List as Attaché) came to the White House. I had already asked Mr. Stanley Woodward, State Department Chief of Protocol, to come over and help me, because I had no authority to make arrangements for Madame Chiang. Mrs. Roosevelt was in either Hyde Park or New York. All I could do was to speak as Mrs. Roosevelt's social secretary, and I felt I needed all possible advice from a member of the Protocol Division of the State Department. Evidently the Embassy had been unable to reach Madame Chiang, but this young man, Mr. Huang, told us he would get in touch with her that night and find out her wishes. Through Mr. Huang, she found she could not force her way. She accepted the thinly veiled ultimatum of the Senate but said she would make a speech only in one place.

What actually happened was that when she got to the Senate she made a very excellent extemporaneous speech which, I think, like all her other "extemporaneous" speeches, was prepared in advance. Then in the House of Representatives she read from a prepared manuscript. And I might say in passing that I have never heard a better delivered speech, nor one more beautifully phrased or spoken in a lovelier voice.

I shall never forget Madame Chiang's appearance in that Chamber. She was slight and very small, which made the men who preceded and followed her seem more than usually tall. She was a dauntless figure, very composed, with head erect and an excellent carriage.

When Mr. Bloom called Mrs. Roosevelt on that Saturday before Madame Chiang's visit to the White House, he also said that Representative Edith Nourse Rogers, a member of the House Foreign Affairs Committee, had announced that she would invite Madame Chiang to lunch at the House after her speech.

Mr. Bloom felt this would be overriding him as Chairman of the Foreign Affairs Committee, and he felt the luncheon should be a joint one, including all members of the Foreign Relations Committee of the Senate and the Foreign Affairs Committee of the House. This was the arrangement which was followed.

When I talked to Mr. Huang of the Chinese Embassy, Mr. Stanley Woodward, State Department Chief of Protocol, was present merely as an interested observer, because the State Department could take no part in the discussion with Senator Connally and Representative Bloom about her appearance at the Capitol, since her visit was not an official one.

However, Mr. Bloom was most co-operative and the arrangement about Madame Chiang's Capitol appearance was confirmed in telephoned calls which I recorded in these memos:

February 15, 1943
5 P.M.

Senator Connally, Chairman of the Foreign Relations Committee of the Senate, telephoned me at five P.M. today and said that he spoke for a Joint Committee of the Congress with respect to plans for Madame Chiang's visit to the Capitol.

He said that the Senate wished to extend a cordial invitation to Madame Chiang to appear before that body on Thursday, February 18, and that the House extended a similar invitation to her to appear on Friday, February 19th. The hour would be 12:15 P.M. in each House.

Senator Connally added that Madame Chiang's appearance would be very greatly appreciated and that she might make her principal speech in either Chamber, or if she preferred she could make her main speech before one body and put in a short appearance with a few words of greeting before the other body.

And a half-hour later:

Monday, February 15
5:30 P.M.

Representative Bloom, Chairman of the Foreign Affairs Committee of the House, telephoned me at five-thirty P.M. today and said that since Senator Connally's call earlier, other arrangements had been made by the Joint Committee of the Congress with respect to the plans for Madame Chiang's visit to the Capitol.

Congressman Bloom said that Madame Chiang would be received by the Senate at 12:15 P.M. on Thursday, February 18th, and that immediately *after* her appearance in the Senate she would be received by the House of Representatives in that Chamber. Mr. Bloom added that arrangements had been made for a broadcast of her speech from the House.

Immediately following the session in the House, a Joint Luncheon would be offered by Senator Connally and Congressman Bloom. In addition to Madame Chiang and Mrs. Roosevelt, the Chinese Ambassador and two or three members of Madame Chiang's party would be invited; also the Vice-President, the Speaker, and other Majority and Minority Leaders of the House and Senate.

The lady arrived at the White House late Wednesday afternoon, February 17th. Mrs. Roosevelt asked Miss Thompson and me to take care of the tea table—Madame Chiang was to be given tea, according to the usual White House custom when important visitors arrived at or just before teatime. It was then that Malvina and I had our first and only intimate view of Madame Chiang.

The President of course also appeared for the welcoming tea. The tea table was set in the upstairs West Hall which Mrs. Roosevelt often used to receive friends and formal visitors. Madame Chiang made herself most agreeable to everyone.

The wife of the Chinese Ambassador had sent Mrs. Roosevelt some very special tea—I have forgotten whether it was one hundred or two hundred years old—carefully preserved in an airtight tea caddy, which was used that afternoon. When Mrs. Roosevelt told Madame Chiang about it, her sole comment was that tea kept so long was used only for medicinal purposes in her country. After tasting the ancient brew, I did not question her statement.

The Chinese party was assigned to a suite on the second floor of the White House, overlooking the Treasury Department and Pennsylvania Avenue, a suite ordinarily used only for Very Important People.

Madame Chiang's bedchamber was the Rose Room. This, with accompanying rooms across the long corridor which runs east and west in the White House, affords considerable privacy. White House family bedrooms, sitting rooms and elevator are at the opposite or west end of the corridor, and the place is so large that these rooms seem quite remote from each other.

There were three Chinese who came with Madame Chiang— two of them definitely men and one of these identified as Madame Chiang's nephew, Mr. L. K. Kung.

One of the President's Secretariat, under whose direction came arrangements for news photographs of Madame Chiang, said Mr. Kung was most insolent to him and he was sure there would have been many difficulties in the session with news photographers at the White House if Mrs. Roosevelt had not been there as a steadying influence.

At intervals from her White House suite appeared another curious little person, whom I first took to be a child of about sixteen and who we finally learned was Madame Chiang's niece, Miss Kung. It really was difficult for a person not familiar with Chinese costumes to tell whether she was a boy or a young woman, because she had on a sort of skirt and boy's shoes. For that reason, word came down to the usher's office that there was a mistake, that the name on the door of Miss Kung's room said "Miss Kung," but it should have been "Mr." Further, instead of a maid, one of the men in the House who served as a valet was busy unpacking her belongings.

Well, that error was straightened out in due course of time and a maid was assigned to care for her, but it cropped up again at luncheon, when the President looked benignly across the table and said, "Well, my boy, I understand you have been sightseeing today." Then some one of his family must have nudged him, because he instantly said, "You know, I call everybody 'My boy,' whether they are boys or girls."

Madame Chiang's room was closely guarded, but I remember that when I came down from my third-story office to talk to Malvina one morning, she told me I must do something to keep "one of these people" from going unannounced into Mrs. Roosevelt's room. I met the young lady to whom Malvina referred as she was going into Mrs. Roosevelt's study, and suggested that she tell me what she wanted and I would relay the message to Mrs. Roosevelt—that was the customary procedure. This had the desired effect.

There were difficulties, too, with Mr. Kung—for example, we never knew whether he would be in or out for lunch. The table had to be set and could not be left with a vacant place for him. So I called promptly at nine o'clock every morning to ascertain his plans for the day so that the ushers could be told and the table set for the correct number of people. Could I have taken a sadistic pleasure in making this early morning call? Anyway, undisturbed he slept until noon.

It had become usual procedure during those years for distinguished guests to remain at the White House three days. The ambassadors of the countries concerned arranged with the State Department the necessary procedure and the State Department's Division of Protocol had handled the arrangements. I imagine, though, that the invitation had been extended by Mrs. Roosevelt for as long as Madame Chiang wished to stay.

At any rate, we had been very curious to find out how long Madame Chiang's party was going to stay, and driving home from the Capitol after her speech, I showed Blair House to Miss Kung. Blair House is across from the White House on Pennsylvania Avenue. I remarked, "That is where you will go after your visit to the White House." And she replied breezily: "No, we expect to stay all the time at the White House."

It was extremely difficult to find out in advance the plans of Madame Chiang and her party, and whether they would or would not accept invitations extended to them. For example, Lady Halifax, wife of the British Ambassador, telephoned me to ask Mrs. Roosevelt if she and Madame Chiang would come to the British Embassy to lunch.

I telephoned to Miss Boyle, Lady Halifax's secretary, to explain that Mrs. Roosevelt could not accept and that the invitation had been duly transmitted to Madame Chiang. They heard nothing from her for several days and finally, I understand, Lady Halifax wrote a note which was answered in the negative.

The Chinese Ambassador gave a reception for Madame Chiang at the Shoreham Hotel on Friday afternoon, February 26th, which was a sumptuous affair. I did not go but the papers carried details of the lavish display—food, champagne and every other kind of drink.

Like many Americans who had tangible assets, I was receiving daily appeals for aid for China in one form or another. Also many letters passed through my hands, before Madame Chiang's arrival, addressed in Mrs. Roosevelt's care, containing small sums of money for Madame Chiang to distribute to the needy in her country. All these were acknowledged by me before being sent to the Embassy to be held for her. These were not from the well-to-do, but from people who had obviously made a tremendous sacrifice to send the few dollars they enclosed.

And here I would say further that during the war period the most rigorous self-denial was followed at the White House. Food was plentiful but simple, not elaborate, and the small teas which were held for groups were of the simplest variety, with a few hot biscuits and some cookies plus tea, nothing else.

Another uproar in the newspapers had to do with the silk sheets Madame Chiang used on her bed, but there was really a very simple explanation for those. She came to this country to get treatment for a chronic skin trouble and she could not stand cotton or linen sheets. Silk in China was cheap and her sheets probably were little more expensive than cotton ones here—perhaps even cheaper. She slept between something that looked like two down comfortables sewed together. These were lined every day with the silk sheets, which made them a sort of sleeping bag, and I can look back now and see the White House maids on the third floor near my office, down on the floor basting in the silk sheets every day.

One of the best photographs I have of Mrs. Roosevelt was taken with Madame Chiang. She had promised photographers to pose on the lawn south of the White House, and she did. It was when this picture was taken that my friend in the Secretariat had such a difficult time getting Mme. Chiang to pose as the photographers desired, until Mrs. Roosevelt poured oil on the troubled waters.

There was another incident which kept me in uncertainty for several days after Madame Chiang's arrival.

It is customary for White House visitors from foreign countries to pay their respects to certain of our country's national shrines. Almost always, they visit the tomb of George and Martha Washington at Mt. Vernon, and the tomb of the Unknown Soldier in Arlington National Cemetery, and lay wreaths at each place. The wreaths, of course, are provided for them. The visits always are widely publicized and photographed.

On February 18th, I sent Madame Chiang a memorandum through Mr. Kung, telling her Mrs. Roosevelt would like to know if she would care to visit Mt. Vernon on Washington's Birthday, and also go to the tomb of the Unknown Soldier.

Visits to Mt. Vernon had become such a routine with foreign dignitaries that they required little planning. With Madame Chiang, however, it involved a lengthy exchange of memos back and forth for two days among Madame Chiang, Mrs. Roosevelt, Grace Tully, secretary to President Roosevelt, and me. In the meantime, Mr. Kung had reported that Madame Chiang was not so well and stipulated that the Mt. Vernon engagement must be tentative and have no publicity.

However, on February 18th, Madame Chiang appeared with Mrs. Roosevelt at a press conference for ladies of the press, who quite evidently shared the admiration of most Americans for the Generalissimo's beautiful wife. The press conference was not unprecedented—Queen Wilhelmina of Holland also had held one under Mrs. Roosevelt's wing—but it created great interest and Madame Chiang answered questions freely and ably.

Malvina was present to take down what was said and she kindly allowed me to use her transcript. In view of events since then, I think some portions of this mass interview are of definite historic interest.

For example, Madame Chiang was asked about the food situation in China. She replied:

"As you know, the Japanese armies have occupied our port cities and most of the strategic railway points. Therefore, transportation is a very great difficulty in China. China produces enough food for her people, but the point is, how to bring certain foods from one point to another point. That is our great difficulty."

And when a companion question followed: "Have you any idea how many Chinese the United States should help feed after the war?"—she said: "I do not think we expect the United States to feed any of our people."

At one point Mrs. Roosevelt made a suggestion. She remarked to Madame Chiang: "You once told me something that I think you ought to tell these people here. That the Chinese people had hope and were alive, all working together, and a new spirit was abroad in the whole land; that they are not fighting for themselves alone but for a better world for everyone and that they worked with a determination which was missing where people lacked hope and vision."

The Chinese visitor smiled and said: "You have told it better than I can."

What irony, to recall those words and think of Communist China, and of the Generalissimo and his army on Formosa!

Madame Chiang also told of her orphanages—in which were sheltered 30,000 war waifs—and of millions of broken families.

The ladies were allowed to ask her direct questions, but not to make direct quotes except in one instance. Replying to a question as to what particular quality of the Chinese had made them endure the Japanese invasion, she said: "I think we are a very old nation and we realize that spiritual values are eternal." Here she gave permission to quote: "Spiritual values are eternal."

But she gave the gist of the reason for her visit to this country in a question and answer interchange on which Malvina Thompson took shorthand notes. From the original transcript, I quote:

Question: Of all that China needs now from the United States, what is the most important?

Madame Chiang: Ammunition and ammunition, and when I say ammunition, I wish you all to understand that we take our partnership in the United Nations very seriously. We feel we are contributing and we have contributed our part and we intend to keep on contributing and what we haven't is ammunition, and in accepting ammunition we are, so to speak, getting the results of the common pooling of resources, because, if you remember, your President spoke of America as the "Arsenal of Democracy" and we are all fighting for common cause and we are providing manpower, flesh and blood to get rid of our common enemy in that part of the world and therefore in accepting ammunition we are accepting part of common resources which we have pooled.

Question: Do you mean ammunition or munitions?

Madame Chiang: I am afraid the question to me was ammunition. No, I mean the materials of war—munitions.

Question· If what is needed is guns, airplanes, etc., to what extent are these needs being met?

Madame Chiang: We need more and more planes and everything that goes with planes, gasoline and spare parts because they wear out terribly quickly. We need heavy arms; we can manufacture light arms.

In recalling Madame Chiang's White House visit, I do not want to do her injustice. This unusual woman has her place in history. Nationalist China as we have known it in recent years was certainly as much her creation as it was her husband's. She had a tremendous influence in rousing sympathy for her country in its fight against Japan; she was noted for relief work; she played an important role in securing the release of her husband when he was kidnapped in the Sian mutiny which rent his party in 1936.

In retrospect I would say that we are an emotional and sentimental people and that the build-up for Madame Chiang was extraordinary throughout the country. Since then her importance and prestige have diminished. China today is a greater world problem than it was when Madame Chiang paid her visit to the White House in 1943.

Chapter 18

IN COMES THE MAIL,
OUT GO THE SOUVENIRS,
ON WITH THE WAR

WHILE LIFE IN THE WHITE HOUSE was different in time of war from that in time of peace, there was a certain routine of sameness which no doubt added to sanity. The letters continued to roll in, literally by the bushel. Groups intent on worthy causes continued to be asked in at teatime. There was a regular routine for showing wounded servicemen from the nearby hospitals through the White House. And family friends were invited in, though not so often as in previous years. Mrs. Roosevelt's press conferences went on.

The daily luncheon table, presided over by Mrs. Roosevelt, continued to be the place where people with new ideas were allowed to outline their projects. When I first came to the White House, Mrs. Roosevelt had invited me to lunch there regularly, but I preferred to break my day by going out to my own apartment. However,,when anyone really interesting was to be there, Malvina told me, and I stayed. The President always lunched in his Executive Office, and hot trays were wheeled across to him and to as many as might be lunching with him. In all the years Mrs. Roosevelt was in the White House, I doubt if she ever sat down to any meal alone or with only Malvina Thompson. Although persons obsessed by various causes sometimes ran away with the conversation, usually Mrs. Roosevelt kept the talk in balance and on the whole the luncheons were very interesting. Luncheons were always comfortably small. The family dining room accommodates only twenty.

Naturally, these luncheons were bright spots for Malvina and me as interruptions in our unceasing labors on the ever-piled-high mail. There is no question that I am asked more often than about that mail. Down the years, I have more or less analyzed it, and am able to give samplings.

Requests come for discarded clothing. Usually the President's wife has persons or institutions to whom she has given these articles for years, and a polite little note has to go back to the writer of the request, regretting that she cannot add to this list.

Letters come from mothers of servicemen, wishing to get them out of the service. Only one I remember ever came asking that a man be kept in; I think his wife considered him a "black-hearted villain" and did not want him running loose. Anyway, her request would not have had much weight with the military authorities, for he would have been kept in as long as he behaved himself.

Many of the letters are pitiful. There are questions of illnesses in the family and pressing reasons why men should be allowed home on furlough.

All these letters having to do with the military discipline and the relaxing thereof had to go to the military authorities. Occasionally a request for a report on some of the cases is sent along with the letters, and almost invariably it is found that the decision of the man's commanding officer is a wise one. Or, as he is human like the rest of us, if he has made a mistake, some relief is granted.

Then there are requests from school children and ladies who are writing papers to deliver to an admiring circle of friends. Some of these have come to me and have seemed to indicate a feeling that I should write the paper.

Here is a sample:

> I am a Senior at ___ High School and I want to enter a Declamation Contest. I would highly appreciate it if you could

write me one entitled "What Women Can Do in This Great Emergency."

My superintendent and I thought that would be a grand subject since conditions are as they are, and we have not been able to gather enough material for it. Since you are very famous everywhere, as well as with me, we thought you could probably help me. I will deliver it the best I know how. Hoping you can help me and thanking you in advance for your kindness, I remain,

Cordially yours,

Collectors of every kind of item write for articles from the President's family, and since it would not be possible to send something to all, a note explaining this goes to each writer. People are particularly interested, it seems, in collecting buttons, salt and pepper shakers, neckties, demitasse cups and saucers, spoons, and stamps.

Each mail brings requests for autographs and photographs of the President's family.

Churches and other organizations ask for personal articles to be sold at their bazaars, as an article from the President's family always adds interest. No personal items ever were donated during the time of my service at the White House, but the President's wife did send a small engraved card with a picture of the White House. This engraving has proved very popular, and many people reported that at church auctions it helped to raise a goodly sum.

Women, particularly food editors, are interested in recipes which have been used in the family of the President.

Once in a while someone desires to make a visit to Washington and thinks the White House would be an ideal stopping place. This is an actual quote: "Please let me come and stay a week with you. I haven't any close (sic) or money, so you will have to pay my way to Washington—I am sorry if I get tears on the letters, but I can't help it, I want to come."

One young girl apparently thought the White House an ideal setting for her wedding. She wrote Mrs. Roosevelt:

> In 1934, when I was graduated from a Grammar School in Louisiana, I sent your husband an invitation to my graduation. He did not come, of course, but sent me a very sweet and short

note—wishing me many happy returns and stating his regrets for not being able to come to my commencement exercises.

This year, *1944,* I am in Washington and working as a Stenographer in the Navy Department; and this is my purpose of writing today: My boyfriend, a sailor (stationed in Maryland), and I have our licenses to be married this week-end. And we ask for the honor and privilege to be married in the White House either the 11th or 12th of this month. We plan to leave soon after we are married for his home in West Virginia. (We both have a 10-day leave.)

I pray that you take our wishes into consideration, and let me hear from you early Friday morning on GEorgia-5——.

Love,

An enterprising young man wrote Margaret Truman on behalf of his mother, but couldn't resist giving away that his real purpose was to meet Miss Truman:

Enclosed is a snapshot of myself and my mother, who arrived here two days ago. After a tour of sea duty, I came to Washington in March of this year for new duty (writing training course books) in the Bureau of Naval Personnel. Unfortunately, I haven't had much time to show my mother the town and introduce her to various people, since I work at the Bureau during the day and attend classes at Columbus University Law School 5 nights a week.

Because of the cost involved, my mother travels very little. Thus, I would like to make her stay an enjoyable one, and one which she will always remember. As a furtherance of this end, it would be nice if I could acquaint my mother with some of the well known social events that transpire in Washington and have her introduced to worthwhile people. Thus, I wonder if you could help me in this matter.

From what I have heard about you, I would like very much to meet you.

Anything that you would do for my mother would be sincerely appreciated.

Sincerely,
(signed) _____Lt. (jg)USNR

P.S. That frown of my mother's isn't always there!

People send gifts too. During my time at the White House there was a rule that no gifts of value could be accepted, so many of these had to be returned. It is particularly sad when some aged person with no close relative or friends wishes to place a valuable collection of books, music, furniture, etc., in the hands of someone who would care to have them. When possible, these persons are directed to libraries or museums where their property might be accepted.

Some people send small gifts for no reason at all. Others follow the gifts with a request for a favor. There was a woman who sent in a ragged pair of shoes to show how hard she had worked in a campaign—and asked for a personal reward.

Another woman, without giving her name or address, sent a complete outfit of clothing, including costume jewelry, for the President's wife to wear at a special official event. The dress was completely unsuitable.

Some people are very businesslike in making requests. For example: "Dear Madam: I would like to have some money for my personal needs. Kindly inform me whether or not you can comply. Yours very truly."

Personal suggestions are made—a picture of a First Lady showing one hair style or one style of hat brings many suggestions as to a better style. Letters of criticism are all too frequent, but occasionally someone writes commending the President or his wife. Mrs. Wilson received this letter of high praise:

DEAR MADAM:
We, the teachers and pupils of —— High School, want to express our appreciation of your democratic spirit which was shown by the fact that you did not courtesy to Mrs. George V. Windsor. We congratulate you for being a true American.
                              Yours respectfully,
                 (signed)_____Supt.
                      "   Prin.
                      "   Assistant
                            Seniors   Juniors

Many people in foreign countries write to the wife of the President in an effort to obtain relief from their sufferings or in an effort to speed up immigration proceedings. Many ask the President's wife or family to act as sponsors, as they have no one in this country to vouch for them.

Particularly sad requests come from sufferers of tuberculosis and other maladies who cannot find a way to buy the new wonder drugs of which they have read and which offer hope to them.

The temperance people are ready to criticize any publicity concerning the serving of liquors, and equally ready to praise when it becomes known that a member of the family is abstemious.

One woman wrote that she was fifty-two years old and deep down in her heart there had always been a yearning for a big beautiful doll. This she would like the President's wife to send her.

A great many people do not understand the working of the Federal Government, nor whom to approach when they need help. For instance, this appeal: "Dear madam: Will you please send me a good man from Washington, D.C. to see about some business Uncle Sam left undone."

Malvina Thompson drew down wrath upon Mrs. Roosevelt's head when she answered a letter in her own name, writing for the President's wife.

The letter she answered was intended to be a kindly one. The writer had invoked a blessing upon the President's wife. Malvina replied:

MY DEAR ——
    Mrs. Roosevelt asks me to thank you very much for your letter. She deeply appreciates your greetings and good wishes and thinks it was very kind of you to write.
                      Very sincerely yours,
                        Malvina C. Thompson
                        Secretary to
                        Mrs. Roosevelt

This was the wrathful response:

    If the President and Mrs. Roosevelt do not deem the blessing of sufficient import to require acknowledgement by their own hands, I am asking God to let the blessing return to me.
    If you *have* and *do* presume to dispose of it as common mat-

ter, without calling their attention to it, I am asking the *curse* of *God* upon you. This is not the work of a crank but the *servant* of *God.*

Very truly,

I must admit that the letter which follows was received with gales of laughter, and I feel that so many years have now passed that it may be shared more widely without betrayal of a confidence.

SECRETARY TO THE PRESIDENT
Washington, D.C.

MY DEAR MR. SECRETARY:

An object both patriotic and news-producing is back of a campaign that the _____ News will launch.

The patriotic object is to contribute as many dollars as possible to the Red Cross. It is to be done by selling at a big public auction here, kitchen aprons made from the shirt tails of famous men, and others.

Making aprons from shirt tails is a trick well known in households where economy is enforced. They are aprons any woman is glad to wear, when made cleverly.

Will you not secure a cast-off shirt of the President's and send one of your own, as contributions to the cause? We should like to have the two shirts identified, and if possible, a little history of the President's garment, relating what important functions it has attended, social or business. They should be mailed to the Auction Editor _____ News.

Whatever your decision, please do not make this letter public.

Sincerely,

Auction Editor

Along came wartime restrictions, and cut off the surplusage in men's shirts, women's skirts, and even the cuffs of the trousers.

When a new laugh broke the humdrum of the day, Malvina and I would chuckle in reminiscence over past laughs of more peaceful days.

There was one incident that figured in the newspapers. Apparently a member of one of the congressional committee said Mrs. Roosevelt had snubbed him—that he and his wife never had been invited to the White House. We produced the records showing when this committee member and his wife had been invited, and received no denial of the truth of our evidence. But this letter came to the White House:

DEAR MADAM:
It matters not a hurrah to me whether Rep. _____, his wife and all his children were ever invited to the White House. But from the record and "for the record," it seems to me some one should be advised that there is a difference between invitations to the White House.
I always receive an invitation from The General Motors to their Fall Exhibition but Mr. Sloan has never taken me by the arm and invited me to his house for lunch.
Yours truly,

A gentleman, replying to his "Mr. and Mrs." invitation, wrote:

Mrs. _____ would greatly appreciate Mrs. Roosevelt's invitation were it not for the fact that she is as yet nonexistent.
Mr. _____ nonetheless appreciates Mrs. Roosevelt's kind expression of anticipation for him of a more abundant life.

Responses to White House invitations ordinarily were in accordance with accepted etiquette but occasionally there were deviations. For example, one from a lady who, I fear, did not love her husband's secretary. The lady wrote:

DEAR MRS. ROOSEVELT,
As I have not rec a invation to the White House Garden party for the twenty forth of May kindly write me why my Husband Sec rec one instead of me, my husband is Congressman in the _____ dst kindly let me know at once.
Resptfully
_____(Republ)

Sometimes an irate letter to Mrs. Roosevelt expressed the opinion that her social secretary, being only a government employee, could be fired. But I think that probably the most scathing letter I ever received was addressed to me formally. I do not remember just how I had offended, but it must have been one of those unfortunate occasions when a lady of importance was invited to one White House function and yearned to go to another. For here is the reply to a note I had written:

United States Senate
Washington, D.C.

Mrs. J. M. Helm,
Secretary to Mrs. Roosevelt,
The White House
Washington, D.C.

My dear Mrs. Helm:

As one Secretary to another, I am writing to ask what the point is in your letter of April 25th, 1936, addressed to Senator ————.

Did you write to criticize yourself for inviting Mrs. ————, who is a daughter of Senator ————, to the White House in the evening instead of in the afternoon? Or to criticize Mrs. ———— for going, on the theory that she might have gone in the afternoon instead, thus making room for someone else with no better claim to importance or name, and with nothing to approach her personal distinction or charm? Did you fail to connect Miss ———— of yesterday with Mrs. ———— of today? If I were in charge of lists, Mrs. Helm, I would remember your name as such, and if in addition you happened to be the daughter of Senator Blank I should not let your surname cause me to become confused.

Your letter indicates that you have not even a passing acquaintance with Senator ———— and his family, and their instinctive familiarity with the proprieties in important places at home and abroad.

I suppose you have gate crashers of all kinds, and I suppose that you are driven to writing some of the oddest letters conceivable, but I would hardly expect you to find any contributions to social irregularity from Capitol Hill, or at least from families of the United States Senate, or to comment upon them if you did.

Sincerely yours,
Secretary to Senator ————

But I can add an incident which, I think, tops all these. The most peculiar request which ever came to me as the result of being social secretary was by telephone. I was dead tired that night, and when an insistent ringing aroused me at ten P.M. I really thought it was past midnight. On the phone was a woman I had known in a friendly but most casual fashion. She said she was having dinner guests, among them a relative of the White House family, and a pipe had burst in her sink.

"My kitchen is afloat," she said. "Will you please send the White House plumber over right away?"

I had to confess that the White House plumber was not at my beck and call, even were he on duty at that hour, which he wasn't.

As Malvina and I worked in war days, a couple of gas masks, on which we had received instructions as to donning, always hung in a nearby closet. We had been told our stations in case of air attack, and we had one or two evacuation drills to impress upon our minds the routine of getting to them if necessary. We all trooped silently down the stairs to the stations to which we had been sent.

Somehow, somewhere, Malvina and I heard that microphones were being installed in the White House. Later we discovered there was no truth in the rumor, but for a time we feared some of our conversations had been overheard.

We searched all over Malvina's office and could find absolutely nothing that looked suspicious. However, when I went back upstairs to my office, which had been a third-floor bedroom, converted for my use, I looked in the closet where I hung my hat and coat, happened to glance up at the ceiling and saw a queer-looking metallic object inserted in the plaster.

I called Malvina and said, "I have found it! It's here in my room!"

Together we went down to the usher's office and demanded indignantly to know if that was a microphone in my office. The usher looked bewildered. He said, "We have put nothing of the kind in your office, Mrs. Helm." So then he came upstairs with us and identified the queer-looking object I had discovered. It had something to do with de-mothing the closet.

Teatime as well as lunchtime was often very interesting in the Roosevelt White House. I recall one noted visitor particularly—

Gertrude Stein, author, who came with her faithful shadow, Alice B. Toklas.

Mrs. Roosevelt had screened off the end of the west hall on the second floor, looking toward the old State, War and Navy Department Building. She used this as a somewhat more formal sitting room than the room which adjoined her bedroom, both overlooking the South Grounds. In the west hall she had Miss Stein and Miss Toklas to tea.

When the two ladies came in, accompanied by their Washington hostess, there could be no doubt about which was Gertrude Stein. Happily she did not talk in those extraordinary sentences which distinguish her books, and which have to be dissected in order to catch their meaning—at least, by anyone born in the 1800's. Probably twentieth-century children can understand her.

She was quite deaf, but was an insatiable conversationalist. I remember that Mrs. Roosevelt tried to inject a few words, but Miss Stein, like a glacier, maintained her conversational advance. Mrs. Roosevelt was as interested as the rest of us in meeting the famed author and listening to the famed Stein conversation. It was Miss Stein's hostess who tactfully stemmed the tide of words and brought the tea party to an end.

This informal White House sitting room was a pleasant place at teatime. The tray was placed on a small table beside Mrs. Roosevelt, who poured for the small groups who came to tea. Even the wartime emergency failed to interfere with this tradition of the Roosevelt family.

The war emergency also did not seem to take the edge off the appetite of the souvenir hunters—and the larger the group that came calling the more likelihood that someone had tucked away a silver teaspoon marked "The President's House." Apparently, visitors did not think it dishonest to pick up a spoon or a napkin marked with the insignia of the executive mansion.

At some time in more recent administrations some bright soul at the White House devised a scheme to prevent this. Instead of using embroidered napkins and engraved spoons, which carry their own identification as having come from the White House, plain napkins and plated spoons were substituted. Even plain teacups and saucers were used for White House teas—very nice china, of course, but not the expensive Lenox, of which a complete set may have to be bought for a new administration on account of breakage. For a large crowd cups have to be washed quickly and there is likely to be breakage in the pantry.

There was one terrible scene I remember very vividly. After a certain group which shall be nameless had been received, *every* spoon had disappeared—and they were heavy solid silver spoons. Some newspaper got hold of it. To the embarrassment of officials, the story was printed. And it was perfectly true.

The White House had its own little match folders—red, white, and blue and bearing the President's seal—which were used at White House dinners and other functions. I remember after some of the teas not a match folder was left in the place! But they are inexpensive trifles.

On a certain afternoon, as I was starting out from the second-floor study after having been with Mrs. Roosevelt, I met the President, who was going down to his office after lunch. He said, "We have just been naming some ships this morning." I looked at him, not knowing just why he was telling me that, and he said one of the ships had been named the *Helm*.

I was overjoyed. I knew it would have been the one thing my late husband, Rear Admiral James Helm, would have wanted above all others—to have a destroyer named for him. Every time I think of it my heart grows warm to the President for selecting my husband for this honor.

When the *Helm* was launched a year or more later, I was the sponsor for her. She and another destroyer were built in the drydock at the Norfolk Navy Yard, and instead of sliding down the ways, the customary manner for launching a ship, water was let slowly into the drydock and as it reached a certain point on the keel, the sponsor was supposed to break the bottle.

That was an unhappy circumstance for me. I had christened two other ships, the first when I was a girl of fifteen at the Navy Yard in California when I sponsored, with another young girl, the first *San Francisco*, a cruiser. I broke the champagne bottle there in fine shape. Then, in 1913, a destroyer named for my father, Rear Admiral A. E. K. Benham, was launched at the Cramp shipyard in Philadelphia. That ceremony went off all right, too; I broke the bottle as the ship started down the ways.

This time, however, with the *Helm*, a young aide had been assigned to me by the admiral in command of the naval station and he told me not to break the bottle as I had done previously, with a heavy blow across the bow, but to beat it against the side of the destroyer. I could make absolutely no impression that way, and I think if I had not shifted to the old style—a good crack on the sharp pointed bow—that bottle never would have been broken. Ships start off very quickly and the *Helm* would probably have been well down the James River before I caught up with her and achieved the necessary breaking.

Those of us who had worked as volunteers in the First World War were anxious to do something in the new conflict. Mrs. Mason Gulick and I offered our services to the War Hospitality Committee, which was organized to include representatives of agencies and groups wishing to promote the welfare of members of the armed forces passing through Washington.

My first service was well after Pearl Harbor, when I served for one winter at the information desk established in a room at Union Station which ordinarily was reserved for the use of the President in receiving distinguished guests whom he met there. The room was inadequate and still is for the vast numbers of service men who have passed through its doors.

I worked Sunday afternoons—the only time I had free—and I could serve only during the winter, as I went to Illinois for the summer. My place was filled the following year by others who could give time summer and winter.

The Travelers' Aid Society—an agency of the Community Chest—was the one under which we operated. We served no food, as we had done in the canteen where I worked during the First World War. There was no space for food service in the reception room, but later a sort of canteen was established outside where service men could buy food at reduced prices.

My job was to sit at a desk and answer questions. When a service man came and asked where he could leave his bags, I directed him to a little checking room we had set up in a corridor behind the reception room. Questions were always asked about sightseeing trips and lodging, and we had a long list of places where the men could stay—some in basement dormitories churches had established, others in various houses which had been taken over by certain groups for this purpose, and of course the Soldiers, Sailors and Marines Club, which always was filled to overflowing.

This Union Station service was one of the most rewarding things of my life. When it was first suggested that I go down there I said the men would probably prefer to see something young, but I was assured that those who were going overseas and were blue would rather see someone old than one of the engaging young creatures I was suggesting for my position.

Questions came to us about everything—there is even one story that we were asked to arrange for a wedding. Then there were shopping services—anything that could be done to help a man in uniform.

Perhaps some of my activities were not entirely those that a refined elderly woman should have engaged in. When a man came in a little the worse for liquor but not obstreperous or noisy, we tried to keep him from being picked up by the M.P.'s. I remember very well going out one day with Mrs. Gulick, who had been my "commanding officer" in the old canteen days of the First World War, with a garrulous Marine whom we were trying to shield from the M.P.'s, and getting him pointed to a cab and homeward bound. Remember that Mrs. Gulick's husband had been a General in the Marine Corps and mine had been a Rear Admiral in the Navy!

We also had a wake-up service and we used to pin tags on the men who were to be called for trains. They were young and could sleep anywhere, in chairs and, occasionally when it was very crowded, even on the floor.

Another of our duties was sending mothers with babies over to the United Nations Hotel nearby. One day Mrs. Roosevelt came down to visit us. She was interested in all these activities, and had worked in the First World War canteen. She went through the

United Nations Hotel to see what arrangements were made for the men there. She was particularly interested in the nursery for babies whose mothers could leave them there while they went out shopping or spent the day with their husbands.

Mrs. William Galvin, who was the secretary of our organization and still is, was a dynamo of energy and efficiency. While I have not been active as a worker for some years, I understand there still is hospitality service for young men of the armed forces under Mrs. Galvin's direction—though of course not on such a large scale as during the Second World War.

Mrs. Roosevelt had asked me one night to go with her to visit some of the typical activities for service men and women conducted by the Catholic and Protestant Churches and various organizations throughout the city—I think we went to ten or twelve. Mrs. Roosevelt scorned elevators and I can see myself dashing up and down stairs, following in her wake.

She also could see more at a glance than most people can see in a half hour. This visit of hers was not announced in advance. She wanted to see just what was being done and not to have a show put on for her benefit.

One of the best-kept places was a small house which was run by colored people for colored service men. Mrs. Roosevelt went from cellar to garret, with me in her wake; I have never seen a cleaner place. They had very little money to work with but every cent was carefully spent and the women certainly did their share.

However, I think women did this everywhere—with the U.S.O. and in all other activities for service men and women.

There also was the Stage Door Canteen, which I think was a favorite spot. Usually when I mentioned that to any of the service men who asked where they should go for recreation, they seemed to feel it was the spot for them. This Canteen, in the old Belasco Theater, was close to the White House. It put on an excellent floor show and furnished light refreshments for men who came there in the evening.

Indicating the interest shown by all in doing something for our men in uniform was a telegram which came to Mrs. Roosevelt from someone in Pennsylvania recommending a "memory pianist eighty-eight years old," who evidently was not considered by the sender or anyone else as too old to entertain the soldiers. This lady said she could go from camp to camp. No mention was made of any attendant to help her from camp to camp or pick up her remains if by any accident her life were cut off prematurely.

Mrs. Roosevelt, of course, referred this offer to the proper volunteer organization which provided soldier entertainment. I do not know the outcome.

Chapter 19

THE END OF THE ROOSEVELT ROAD

FRANKLIN ROOSEVELT had four inaugurations, and I helped engineer the social events of three of them. The fourth, on January 20, 1945, the unprecedented one which was held on the South Portico of the White House, placed the heaviest responsibilities on me. This was the one and only all-White House inauguration. It was held with as little fanfare as possible, and with no parade or other demonstration. However, I can report that even this most simple of inaugurations was not as simple as it seemed.

I have preserved in my scrapbook a typed copy of the statement of the Joint Congressional Inaugural Committee headed by Senator Harry F. Byrd of Virginia, which announced the South Portico ceremony. This is how it read:

> The President of the United States, with the privilege of choosing where the Inaugural Ceremonies may be held, has informed the Joint Congressional Inaugural Committee that he desires to be inducted into office on the South Portico of the White House. This ceremony will, of course, include the inauguration of the Vice-President at the same time. This message from the President has been conveyed to the Committee

through two of the Capitol officials, Edwin A. Halsey, Secretary of the Senate and Secretary to the Committee, and David Lynn, Architect of the Capitol, whom the Committee had designated to call upon the President to ascertain his wishes in this matter.

The choice of the South Portico of the White House eliminates the customary expenditure for Inaugural Stands at the Capitol. This choice has been made by the President in view of the war conditions which necessitate the abandonment of normal ceremonial activities, the restriction of travel, scarcity of hotel accommodations, shortage of critical materials, the economics involved, the comfort of the guests, and the convenience of the main participants. It is understood that the President desires that the Congress, the Cabinet, the Court (Supreme), the Diplomatic Corps, the other distinguished guests, and the wives of those included be invited to witness the ceremony.

Before this official announcement, there came my old friend, General Edwin Watson, whom I had known first as a young aide under President Wilson, and who was President Roosevelt's principal military aide and close friend. General Watson was the President's representative in conferences on arrangements for the simple ceremony.

The South Portico could hold only a few persons and General Watson had been told by the President that just one hundred forty could be invited. Any person who has seen an inaugural crowd at the Capitol will be able to picture the problems with which we were faced.

There was a room in the West Executive Office wing of the White House, known as the Fish Room because its furnishings included an aquarium and stuffed fish. It also had inherited the old Cabinet table, used by many Presidents but superseded recently by one given by Mr. Jesse Jones to President Roosevelt. We began our conferences around that old Cabinet table.

In the group were representatives from Washington's police department and the press, Mr. Tolley and I from the Social Office and some others. Discussions became quite heated at times and every now and then the General would burst out with a "Damn!" or worse. Then he would look at me—the only woman there—like a guilty little boy.

We did our best, but when Inauguration Day came, with all the pushing and shoving of people to be admitted to the South Portico, not all went according to plan.

Before President Roosevelt's second and third inaugurations, he had attended services at St. John's Church, across Lafayette Square from the White House. This was a short and simple service and a very beautiful one. Not only did members of his official family join with him, but certain friends also were invited.

Instead of going to St. John's before his fourth inauguration, the President invited a smaller group to a service in the East Room. It was a bad day. Many of the people at the service had not been invited to go on the South Portico, but they remained and some of them began to surge toward the Portico in a wave that could not be stopped. The crowd on the Portico became terrific.

Then there were various disgruntled persons, notably members of Congress, who had to stand on the ground below the South Portico exposed to all the vicissitudes of January weather. A large canvas borrowed from some government agency was spread on the ground, but I do not think it provided sufficient standing room for all the people who witnessed the ceremony from that exposed spot.

Only one member of the Diplomatic Corps—the dean or ranking member in length of Washington service, who at that time was the Ambassador of Belgium—was on the South Portico. But Chiefs of Mission (heads of the various embassies and legations in Washington) were invited to watch the ceremony from the South Grounds and were invited to stay for luncheon. The Right Reverend Angus Dun, Episcopal Bishop of Washington, gave the invocation, and the benediction was pronounced by the Right Reverend Monsignor John A. Ryan, of the Catholic Welfare Conference.

A rope was drawn across the end of the canvas, below the Portico, to separate the sheep from the general-public goats who were allowed at the extreme end of the South Lawn.

For this last inauguration of President Roosevelt, there was a tremendous buffet lunch with 1805 guests. All his sons, his daughter, all his grandchildren were there. Long tables were set up in the East Room, the State Dining Room and the basement corridor. To this luncheon were invited diplomatic heads, governors of states, members of Congress, Democratic National Committee officials, a group accompanied by Jo Davidson, famous sculptor, Supreme Court and Cabinet, and Democratic state committeemen and women, also state Democratic chairmen and vice-chairmen.

There also was an inaugural tea with 875 guests. A group of 197 Democratic members of the Electoral College were received by the President at 4:45 P.M., and other guests (678) by Mrs. Roosevelt and Mrs. Harry Truman, wife of the new Vice-President, at five.

In the latter group were heads of independent government agencies; the "Little Cabinet" (Under Secretaries and Assistant Secretaries of government departments); family friends and some miscellaneous guests; "important members" of the Democratic National Committee and its Women's Division who could not be invited to lunch; and finally, a list of guests compiled by Mr. David Niles, one of the President's secretaries.

After this inauguration on January 20, 1945, I had this note from Mrs. Roosevelt and an official one from the President, which took in my staff. The following are copies:

The White House
Washington

January 22, 1945

EDITH DEAR:

I am dictating this to Tommy because I'm afraid you would not be able to read my handwriting very easily.

I am sure I do not have to tell you how much I appreciate all you do for me at all times, and how especially grateful I am for the magnificent job you did on the Inauguration.

Everything went smoothly to all outward appearances and while I know you had many exasperating periods, the result was excellent.

Please take things easy for a while and get some rest. We won't have another Inauguration (I hope) but there will always be something to make you overwork.

You certainly have earned the title of super-expert Inauguration manager!

With love and affection
E.R.

January 22, 1945

Dear Edith:
I want you and all your staff to know how deeply I appreciate the very fine and efficient job you did in connection with the Inaugural ceremonies. I know how hard you have all worked during these past weeks, and I congratulate you all on the fine results of your efforts. Will you please thank everyone on my behalf?
With every best wish to you and the staff,
Very sincerely yours,
FDR

The warmth of these two letters stayed with me through the following weeks which were filled with battle victories, indicating the successful wind-up of the war in the not-too-distant future.

One of the most interesting gatherings at the White House in my entire recollection had been on November 9, 1943, when a meeting was called there to sign the United Nations Relief and Rehabilitation agreement. That ceremony was held in the East Room, and was the first portent that an organization of nations somewhat similar to the one that President Woodrow Wilson had envisaged, could come to pass.

A long table was set up to accommodate representatives of the forty-four countries signing this agreement. The President, as host, sat at the middle of this long table and at his right was left a vacant space so that each representative, as he came up to sign, could sit down beside the President and affix his signature to this historic document. Behind the table, seats were arranged for the distinguished guests in a semicircle.

The roll was called alphabetically, with Australia leading.

The Supreme Court adjourned and came to the White House in a body for this important occasion. There were many other distinguished guests, including of course members of the Cabinet, representatives from the Senate and House, heads of the military services and also representatives of the State Department.

Mr. George Summerlin, the Chief of Protocol, would call the name of a country and its representatives would rise, walk over and take his seat in the chair left for his use at the President's right.

After the Fourth Inaugural, the talk at the White House hinged much about the proposed United Nations Organization. As March merged into April, it was decided that President Roosevelt would go to San Francisco for its launching, and that Mrs. Roosevelt would accompany him. Mrs. Roosevelt so announced at her morning press conference on April 12, 1945. It was a journey never to be taken. That very day the Roosevelt administration ended with the death of the President at Warm Springs, Georgia, where he had begun his remarkable recuperation from infantile paralysis, and where he had started a foundation for other victims of that disease. He had gone to his cottage there for a rest.

The afternoon President Roosevelt died I was at the hairdresser's and Malvina telephoned me there that "the person in whom we have been interested has just died." I thought she meant little Johnny Boettiger, son of Anna Roosevelt and her second husband, John Boettiger, who was ill in a hospital at that time. Then it occurred to me that there was no reason why Malvina should telephone me about Johnny, much as we would have been shocked and grieved if anything had happened to him.

A few minutes later one of the women at the hairdresser's told me information had come over the radio that President Roosevelt had just died at Warm Springs. I went to the White House at once.

Mrs. Roosevelt was sitting in the office, very calm and collected. She said it was much better that the President should die this way than to live and suffer. That was the gist of what she said—her exact words I have forgotten. She had been at a charity benefit and had hurried home from there. A few minutes after I reached the White House she left by plane for Warm Springs.

Mr. and Mrs. John Boettiger were living at the White House at the time and Mrs. Roosevelt had asked Mrs. Boettiger (Anna Roosevelt) to make the necessary arrangements. That evening about eight o'clock Anna Roosevelt had Malvina and me, Mr. Jonathan Daniels, one of the President's press secretaries, and Major Harry Hooker, an old friend who was staying in the White House at the time, meet with her to talk about plans for the funeral.

Mr. George Summerlin, Chief of Protocol, came over from the State Department and brought a card from the Department's files which had been used for the funeral of President Harding. Mr. Tolley, of the social office, kindly made a tracing from the original, and this duplicate of the President Harding card was used to admit those who attended President Roosevelt's funeral.

I quote below the wording of the card used in connection with the death of President Harding, which, with necessary changes, was duplicated for President Roosevelt:

Funeral Services
of
WARREN GAMALIEL HARDING
Late President of the United States
August Eighth Nineteen Hundred and Twenty-Three
at eleven o'clock A.M.
Admit to the Rotunda of the United States Capitol

Mr. Tolley had searched the Social Office files and had found no precedent for the religious and other ceremonies in connection with the death of a President.

A state funeral was held at the Capitol for President Harding, but Mrs. Roosevelt had decided to have the funeral services for President Roosevelt in the East Room at the White House.

Of our meeting that evening after the President's death, I remember very little except that we were trying to formulate the plan for persons who should attend the services—such as diplomats, high government officials, etc.—and to restrict the list as much as possible because of limited seating space in the East Room.

I do remember, though, that during the discussion about funeral arrangements, the telephone rang and the operator asked for Jonathan Daniels. He carried on a lengthy conversation in a low voice, while the rest of us continued our discussion. When he hung up the telephone Malvina asked to whom he had been talking and he said: "That was the President of the United States." Meaning, of course, President Truman, who already had been sworn into office.

Malvina hesitated a moment, then told Mr. Daniels that remark hurt her more than anything before in her life.

I shall never forget the scene at Union Station when the train bearing the President's body backed up to the station platform. His was the last car and the guard of honor which had come with the body from Warm Springs was standing at attention outside. Mrs. Roosevelt spoke to us and to the various officials who had been admitted to the platform. We waited until the casket was removed from the train and then we took our places in the cars assigned to us for the procession to the White House. The trip from Union Station was a slow one and we had an opportunity to observe the crowds that filled the sidewalks all the way from the plaza in front of the station to the White House.

Comment has frequently been made about the stunned silence of the crowd. I was deeply impressed by that at the time. We rode silently through what was almost a vacuum of silence.

Occasionally along the line of march I would see people kneeling at the edge of the pavement in prayer. There were no sounds at all except that occasionally a mother would tell a child to come back after straying past the line of soldiers stationed all along the route to hold back the crowd.

I had been in the funeral procession of President Wilson. He was an ex-President and an invalid at the time of his death and was not as much loved by the people as was Franklin Roosevelt. I think universally, here and throughout Europe, President Roosevelt was looked upon as the people's President and that would account for the deep sadness of the "little people," who thought they had lost their best friend.

Funeral services in the East Room were conducted jointly by Bishop Angus Dun of the Episcopal Diocese of Washington; Dr. Howard Wilkinson, rector of St. Thomas' Church in Washington, of which the President had been one of the vestrymen for many years; and the Reverend John Magee of St. John's Church (the parish church of the White House).

Two hymns, favorites of the President, had been selected by Mrs. Roosevelt—"Eternal Father, Strong to Save," and "America." I telephoned these to Bishop Dun, who felt that the choice of "America" was not a happy one. Dr. Wilkinson suggested two additional hymns which also were favorites of the President and were more suitable for a funeral. Of these two, "Faith of Our Fathers" was chosen.

Mrs. Roosevelt also requested me to ask Bishop Dun to incorporate in some part of the funeral service these words from the President's first inaugural address: "So, first of all, let me assert my firm belief that the only thing we have to fear is fear itself—nameless, unreasoning, unjustified terror, which paralyzes efforts to convert retreat into advance."

After the President's burial at Hyde Park, Mrs. Roosevelt hurried to leave the White House and all its sad associations. I marveled at the speed with which she worked—I think it took her only five days to make the change. As I passed through the halls I saw packing cases, furniture being carted out, and all the paraphernalia of moving day on a large scale—all the personal belongings of the President and Mrs. Roosevelt.

Malvina went to New York with Mrs. Roosevelt and I stayed on to see that there was an easy transition for Mrs. Truman. In an interview I had with Mrs. Truman, I think at the time Mrs. Roosevelt showed her around on the second and third floors of the White House, I told her I expected to leave and, as usual, various names of possible social secretaries had been suggested to her.

A few days later Mrs. Truman was good enough to ask me if I would reconsider my decision to retire. I said I had thought things over and decided I would like very much to be with her and to keep on with all the pleasant associates I had at the White House. This was a wise decision and I am thankful to have made it.

Mrs. Roosevelt allowed me to keep her files for a year before sending them to Hyde Park. They were very valuable in making it possible for me to check on various references to things which were done in the Roosevelt administration. Of course this was simply courtesy from her to me. She knew I would take the best of care of these files and that they would be open only to Mr. Tolley and me.

It is very difficult to write about Mrs. Roosevelt, whom I love and admire and with whom I had a long and happy association as friend and secretary. As the years go by, my admiration for her has increased. While she was in the White House, she was a strong and forceful woman, and she has developed into a really great personality.

The work she has done in the United Nations is outstanding. She was a popular figure in the country—and a controversial one—both admired and disliked, but always a strong character. Now she has become internationally known and respected, and the people who have served with her in the United Nations, as I have heard frequently, have only the greatest praise for her and the work she did on the Human Rights Commission. This admiration is not confined to her own political party.

If anyone were to ask me what I consider Eleanor Roosevelt's most characteristic gesture, I could answer instantly. I have never stepped into her study with even a casual mention of a pathetic case or a worthy cause but that she automatically reached for her checkbook. I had to learn to think carefully before making any comments which might inspire such sweeping generosity.

Chapter 20

WHITE HOUSE LIGHTS
GO ON AGAIN

I HAD KNOWN MRS. TRUMAN, of course, when she was the wife of the Vice-President, but my first real impression of her, of her kindness and sympathy, was on the day of Franklin Roosevelt's funeral.

I think Malvina and I must have been two extremely woebegone objects, sitting together in the East Room. My head must have been down, because the first I knew a sympathetic hand was put in mine and I looked up, and there was Mrs. Truman, just going out with the new President after the funeral service. Yet she had time to think of an unhappy friend of F.D.R., saddened by his death.

That kindness and understanding lasted through the seven years I worked as Mrs. Truman's social secretary. She has been more than kind to me in her estimate of the little I was able to do for her.

I have said of President Truman that if I ever should be in serious trouble I was sure he would help me if he could—and if he couldn't, at least he would see that I had a comfortable cell. And I know too that I shall always be able to count on Mrs. Truman's friendship.

I admire President Truman greatly, and I feel that his place as one of the great Presidents of our country is assured. And I like him for himself, for his human qualities. I hardly need to mention that Mr. Truman had many enemies and detractors, some of whom were in the habit of saying what a wonderful job Mrs. Truman did and how much she added to the dignity of the White House, etc. This was perfectly true but the remark always irritated me, coming from these sources. Usually I felt this was said with a mental reservation that the people who said it did not think so highly of President Truman. Supersensitive on my part, perhaps, but still a fact. I realize that often people were trying to be polite and say something pleasant about an administration they disliked.

The same was true to some extent in the Roosevelt administration. I remember one person who disliked both Mrs. Roosevelt and the President, who came up with the astoundingly perceptive remark that "certainly Mrs. Roosevelt is a very energetic woman."

In considering the vagaries of public and friends, I think what I have always called "bearing testimony" was one of the most persistent obligations which afflicted me as a White House social secretary in my unofficial contacts with the rest of the world. I refer to the political angle of my affiliation with the administrations under which I served.

For example, at a dinner party in a strong Republican household, the host and hostess evidently would resolve to abstain from any partisan remarks that would hurt the feelings of a Democrat—to wit, myself. Sometimes this resolve would last through the soup and on to the roast. Then about the time the roast appeared, the strain would become too great. Someone would start an attack on the Democratic Party, particularly during the administrations of Roosevelt and Truman, and that always led to the veiled or unveiled query—how could I reconcile with my conscience my service for such people, etc., etc.

Sometimes I met this head on when I saw the danger signals start to fly, by saying that I hoped everybody would enjoy himself and say just what he felt. I could be sure, if we did weather the roast, that the dam would burst by the time dessert and finger bowls were reached. Well, it gave vent to a lot of pent-up emotion and also gave me an opportunity to follow the Biblical injunction to "bear testimony."

Administrations changed, but there always were administration critics to carry on. It would be hard for me to say whether I was called upon to "bear testimony" for one more than another of the three Presidents with whom I was associated.

Mr. Truman is still in the spotlight, and, as I have said, my personal opinion is that he will rank as one of our great Presidents. But I know no President can be fairly assessed until many years after his death, and I am willing to accept history's verdict on this man who talked in plain words to plain people, had the courage of his convictions, made momentous decisions and carried them out.

I can also say that I believe Mr. Truman was one of the few musical Presidents we have had. Among them all, probably only Thomas Jefferson understood music as well as he does. Mr. Truman really loves music and both he and Mrs. Truman did all they could to further music in Washington.

I remember watching him after a small tea at the White House, shortly after his accession to the Presidency.

After the guests had gone, he went into the entrance foyer and talked to the leader of the Marine Band Orchestra which had played for the party, also to some of the men, asking them technical questions about the instruments. He showed not just a polite, casual interest, but a genuine understanding of the part each man had in the ensemble and the particular instrument each played. And then, in his usual friendly fashion, he invited them to come into the dining room and have some refreshments.

The President and Mrs. Truman came to the White House shortly before the end of the war in Europe and Japan. But the White House did not return to its former social schedules immediately after the close of hostilities.

After the official mourning for President Roosevelt was over, in the spring of 1945, Mrs. Truman received the wives of ambassadors and ministers, and the Woman's National Democratic Club seems to have gone to the White House that year. Mrs. Truman had been a member of the club for a long time.

A request also came that spring from the various veterans' hospitals in Washington for sightseeing tours through the White House to be arranged for convalescent veterans. I know all the staff were glad to collaborate in showing these groups around and explaining different points of interest to them.

An official guest of that early postwar period was General de Gaulle, who came to tea. He came unsmilingly into the Red Room and never seemed to relax from his stiff position all during the afternoon. He has been often pictured, but I think no picture can give the idea of how ramrod-straight he is and how long his neck is. Another colorful visitor was the Regent of Iraq, His Royal Highness Abdul Ilah, who came to the White House the last of May, 1945, and had tea in the Red Room the day of his arrival. The President and Mrs. Truman and Margaret were there.

Mrs. Truman's Spanish class also received considerable mention after she came to the White House. Mrs. Truman had attended this class for about two years, and during her first year as wife of the President, she and her personal secretary, Miss Reathel Odum, were faithful attendants. But later she became so busy it was not possible for her to continue with it, and then the class moved to other quarters.

I had an invitation to belong but decided I was too old to take part in any such cultural activities. However, I did share in the benefits of a luncheon of Latin-American dishes, at the end of Pan-American Week in 1946. The women who were studying in the class came to the White House early in the morning and helped prepare the Latin-American luncheon under the direction of the Spanish professor in charge.

The Truman administration brought me another delightful working partner in Miss Odum. She is a very pretty and extremely efficient young woman who worked in the Truman office on Capitol Hill while Harry Truman was Senator from Missouri and Vice-President of the United States. She brought to her work at the White House her wealth of detailed knowledge from that experience.

I first saw Reathel on one of the days when Mrs. Roosevelt was hurrying to move out of the White House. Malvina and I received word that Mrs. Truman's personal secretary, Miss Odum, would come over to the White House, so we both took her in hand and introduced her to the members of the Social Office.

We had heard that Reathel Odum was young and very pretty, but that description was really not adequate. She is a lovely-looking creature and as good and sweet as she is good to look at. In addition to serving as personal secretary to Mrs. Truman, she took care of Margaret Truman's engagements and Margaret's increasingly huge correspondence. And when celebrities from overseas came to pay their respects to the President and Mrs. Truman, it was Reathel Odum and I who "poured" at opposite ends of the tea table. Usually, I poured tea, Reathel poured coffee.

Reathel and I charted our working days much as Malvina Thompson and I had done, managing to have time at some point to share a few laughs. I continued to work in my little third-floor office at the White House; Reathel took over the little office beside the elevator which had been Malvina's.

One chortle, I recall, was over a new title bestowed upon the White House social secretary. In my time, I had been addressed by many titles, but this one, on a letter from France, was unique. It addressed me as *Madame Helm, Secrétaire Générale de Monsieur le President Truman à Maison Blanche, Washington, U.S.A.*

Another came later when I received this definitely "out of the ordinary" response to a White House invitation:

> The _____ Ambassador is deeply grateful to the President and Mrs. Truman for their invitation to dinner on Monday, April 4, at 8 o'clock.

And that was all the acceptance we had from that particular Ambassador, to that particular dinner!

Another element had entered the White House mail which at intervals added lightness to our days. We now had a President and First Lady with a charming young daughter of university age—Miss Margaret Truman, who was attending George Washington University not far from the White House. Letters came from utter strangers expressing interest in her college career, solicitude for her future happiness, and even one or two thinly disguised suggestions of matrimony. There was, I recall, one letter from a "pure, intelligent bachelor."

Miss Truman greeted this with the same good-natured laughter with which she met all the varied rumors of her engagement that confronted her during the more than seven years her father was President of the United States. Her interest was concentrated on a musical career. My newspaper friends sometimes tried to tease me by saying that Margaret was wrecking any chance I might have had, as social secretary at the White House, of helping stage a wedding there for a President's daughter. Before I became social secretary at the Wilson White House, my predecessor, Belle Hagner, had helped arrange the weddings there of two of President Wilson's daughters. The ladies of the press suggested that I try to use my influence on Miss Truman.

The Trumans were a close-knit family, and Margaret had a large circle of young friends who added much to White House gaiety.

Mrs. Truman's mother, Mrs. David Wallace, a mentally alert, aristocratic lady in her eighties, always was part of the family circle. The Trumans lived in her home in Independence, Missouri, just as the Roosevelts had lived in the home of the President's mother, Mrs. James Roosevelt at Hyde Park, New York, a rather remarkable coincidence. But Mrs. Wallace always lived at the Truman home in Washington, while the elder Mrs. Roosevelt had merely been one of the most frequent White House visitors.

In October, 1945, when it was time to give out dates for the White House social season, Miss Odum and I announced for Mrs. Truman that there would be no formal state receptions and dinners that winter, as there still were food shortages and so many families had men serving abroad that it was decided not to have these parties, which always had been a feature of peace-time Washington. The last previous reception—for the Army and Navy—had been held in February, 1941.

However, it was announced that there would be informal afternoon teas and some luncheons after the first of December.

In that first winter in the White House, Mrs. Truman also continued the "get together" luncheons Mrs. Roosevelt had originated at my suggestion. Both Miss Odum and I went to these ladies' luncheons, because Mrs. Truman felt it was helpful to have someone see that the guests were introduced and that no one was left alone through lack of meeting people. Margaret, of course, was a great help when she was there, but that was not often, as after she finished at the university she started her singing career.

In the autumn of 1945 a luncheon planned by the wives of Senators for servicemen was given at the White House. Mrs. Truman had served at one of the U.S.O.'s during the war, when her husband was a Senator; she also, of course, as a Senator's wife, had taken part in all activities of the "Senate Ladies," as they were called, and as wife of the Vice-President had been President of their very exclusive club which meets regularly at the Capitol to sew for the Red Cross.

One hundred servicemen from hospitals in Washington were invited to this White House luncheon. The Senate Ladies brought food, and of course it was heated and served by the White House staff. As wife of the President, Mrs. Truman was honorary chairman of the Home Hospitality Committee in Washington, and also of the War Services Committee. Both were organized to provide entertainment for the armed forces.

When Mrs. Truman asked me to continue at the White House as her social secretary, I had no premonition that I would have the responsibility of meeting the press as her representative. That blow fell the autumn following President Roosevelt's death.

After President Truman assumed office, Mrs. Truman decided that she would not hold press conferences as Mrs. Roosevelt had done. This was reverting to the custom of former President's wives.

The women's section of the press complained about the lack of the news which was formerly released to them. Mr. Charles Ross, who was then White House press secretary, felt it was advisable for someone to give out lists of Mrs. Truman's engagements. After some consultation, Mrs. Truman agreed that Reathel Odum and I should see the press women at regular intervals—the time to be decided by the press women.

Now, holding press conferences for the wife of a President is no light responsibility, though it must be made plain, of course, that our meetings with the press were minor events compared with the give and take of Mrs. Roosevelt's press conferences which were held weekly, except for the vacation season, for more than twelve years. Mrs. Roosevelt faced the press frankly, answered their questions freely, and sometimes drew violent public criticism upon her head.

Miss Odum and I had the apparently simple responsibility of giving out Mrs. Truman's engagements, which of course were legion—appearances for this charity and that, teas and receptions at the White House.

But I had been present at literally hundreds of Mrs. Roosevelt's press conferences. I knew the public interest which attaches to the wife of a President. Everything she does or says—even the hat she wears to church on Easter Sunday, and her haircut—is news. I am sure most American women will remember reading about Mrs. Truman's "poodle" bob!

Whatever is made public about a President's wife is matter for vital concern to her husband and his administration. Errors of judgment can be disastrous. And I knew that when I was brought face to face with press women who had asked Mrs. Roosevelt searching questions, I might easily make one of those disastrous errors of judgment.

So the first time we met the press, in the little dining room at the White House, Miss Odum and I felt and looked like condemned criminals. Frankly, we were terrified. One of the newspaper women, Doris Fleeson, summed up the way we looked, as I recall, with these words: "While they showed no trace of personal resentment against anybody, their attitude toward this part of their duties clearly was that there must be an easier way to make a living."

It is all very well to laugh about this now, in the light of all the press meetings that Miss Odum and I have held since then, but there was no humor in it for us at that time. However, the meetings continued and it was good at first to have the backing of that small, pretty person, Miss Odum. This was withdrawn later, when she went with Margaret to New York, and I had to conduct these meetings on my own.

When the assignment was given Miss Odum and me to hold

meetings for Mrs. Truman with the women of the press, I had to see the Press Secretary to the President more often. If it had not been for the aid given me by "Charlie" Ross, the task would have been very difficult. I always looked forward to my visits to the office of that gentle, considerate man, never too busy to be helpful.

There were several other Presidential Secretaries during my years in the White House, and with some of them I had closer contacts than with others.

First should come William (Bill) D. Hassett, to whom I turned often for advice and who never failed to deliver learning salted with humor.

Another, Lowell Mellett, was one of the correspondents who covered President Wilson's trip to Europe. I had known him pleasantly for many years.

A third, Jonathan Daniels, is the son of the late Secretary of the Navy and Mrs. Josephus Daniels, the latter one of the most lovable women I have known in official life. I am glad my friendship with the Secretary and Mrs. Daniels has continued with their son.

One of the events which gave us a feeling that our press group had become a "going concern" was the visit of Mrs. Truman's bridge club.

In the spring of 1946, Mrs. Truman invited as visitors to the White House the whole group of women who had played cards with her at Independence, meeting from time to time at one another's houses. I recall this group of women as among the nicest I met during my entire service at the White House.

Some people, when they came to the White House, rather assumed the attitude that it was just one more incident in their lives. But Mrs. Truman's friends were genuinely thrilled and delighted at the idea of being there and seeing Washington from the inside of this center of national life.

Some landed at the airport and were asked if they would have their photographs taken, which they did willingly; and everything else they did was on the same pleasant basis.

I knew all about bridge clubs, particularly in small towns. We had them in Grayville, where I have spent so many summers. The same pattern is repeated all over the country. A wave of spontaneous interest in these visitors was evident in newspapers all over the country.

Some of the ladies in this group from Independence had been in Washington before, some had not. They made endless trips around the city. The indefatigable ones saw everything of interest in the Capital of these United States of America. Of course, the highlight of their visit was a large luncheon which Mrs. Truman gave for them.

I shall always think of the springtime visit of the Independence ladies as symbolizing that song this country so hopefully sang, "When the Lights Go On Again All Over the World." For a short while our lights did go on again. In the fall of 1946, the Truman Administration launched a full-fledged official social program, pressed down and running over, with two Diplomatic Dinners where only one had been before.

Looking back over old records, I noted that in 1916 there were only thirty-five chiefs of mission to be invited by President and Mrs. Wilson; in 1934 there were fifty-four chiefs of mission, who with their wives plus the Secretary of State and his wife made a total of ninety-three attending that year's Diplomatic Dinner.

In the long interim between the two World Wars, during which this country had become the world capital, official guest lists had doubled. Official receptions which once could be limited to around a thousand now had two thousand definitely eligible. The State Dining Room, seating one hundred four somewhat less than comfortably, no longer was large enough to seat even the sixty-two heads of the Diplomatic missions and their wives, let alone the additional guests that are always a part of every state dinner.

The Diplomatic Dinner, therefore, was of necessity divided into a pair of dinners. Thirty-one Chiefs of Mission with their wives were invited to the first dinner; these and other guests made a total of ninety-two. The remaining thirty-one Chiefs of Mission with their wives attended the second dinner of ninety-four.

The Diplomatic Corps concurred heartily in this division. The dean, of course, was invited to the first dinner. Then No. 2 in precedence (according to length of service in Washington) came to the second dinner; No. 3 to the first, and so on alternating down the line, with No. 4 following No. 2 at the second dinner.

Diplomats are very tenacious of their rank and if one man at one of these dinners is improperly seated a little ahead of another, there is a hard time for the Chief of Protocol. I remember hearing that a tape measure was brought out before one of the Diplomatic Dinners to make sure that the representative of one country which hated another was precisely placed in point of inches from the President so that the representative of neither country could have the slightest advantage in sitting closer to the President.

That social season of 1946-47, full-swing with voluminous "New Look" ballgowns after the long and weary scrimping of the war, with long-unused tail coats coming out of the mothballs, will ever stand out in my mind as among the most spectacular of my long life. Every Tuesday night the White House blazed with reassuring light from many windows.

This was to be the only full-fledged official social program which the Fates vouchsafed the Trumans during more than seven years in office. Here is their complete schedule for that gala first post-war season.

> November 26, Tuesday, Diplomatic Dinner, 8 P.M.
> December 3, Tuesday, Diplomatic Dinner, 8 P.M.
> December 10, Tuesday, Judicial Reception, 9 P.M.
> December 17, Tuesday, Cabinet Dinner, 8 P.M.
> January 7, Tuesday, Diplomatic Reception, 9 P.M.
> January 14, Tuesday, Dinner to the Chief Justice and the Supreme Court, 8 P.M.
> January 21, Tuesday, Reception to the Officials of the Treasury, Post Office, Interior, Agriculture, Commerce and Labor Departments and Federal Agencies, 9 P.M.
> January 28, Tuesday, Dinner to the President Pro Tempore of the Senate, 8 P.M.
> February 4, Tuesday, Army and Navy Reception, 9 P.M.
> February 11, Tuesday, Speaker's Dinner, 8 P.M.
> February 18, Tuesday, Congressional Reception, 9 P.M.

There was, of course, no Vice-President at the time, as Mr. Truman had been elevated to the Presidency from that office. But for whatever precedent it may establish in any similar situation in the future, the dinner honoring that office was not omitted; it went to the President Pro Tempore of the Senate who assumed the presiding chair when Mr. Truman became President.

The receptions, especially, of the Truman period marked the very peak of official entertaining in the old White House—and spectacular events they were. To make it possible to receive the tremendous numbers who came, lines marched four abreast through the East Room. They were opened with elaborate formality.

As Cabinet members and their wives arrived, they were shown to the President's study on the family floor. The President and Mrs. Truman joined them there.

At 8:45 P.M., fifteen minutes before the hour set for the reception, four young service men—a soldier, sailor, air force man and marine—reported to a designated military aide in the main corridor near the foot of the stairway. Marching two abreast, they followed the aide upstairs and into the President's oval study where the President sat at his desk flanked by two flags, the flag of the United States and the President's own flag. The aide approached the President, saluted, and asked permission to remove the colors.

The four young service men, who had halted three paces from the flags, saluted and stood at attention. Two of them removed the colors from the standards, marched down the stairs, and took stations to the right and left of the door leading from the corridor to the Blue Room. The aide and the two other color bearers followed the colors down the stairs, saluted, and retired.

Precisely on the stroke of nine o'clock began the ceremony of the "Little Procession," when down the stairway came the President and his wife, followed by the Cabinet Members and their wives in order of precedence. The entire group went through the guarded door, the President and Mrs. Truman to take their handshaking stand under the chandelier in the Blue Room, the Cabinet to less formal positions in the Red Room. The first two service men stood guard for twenty minutes.

Each twenty minutes during the evening, the two young service men on duty were relieved by the two who had retired twenty minutes earlier. At the conclusion of the reception, the colors were carried back up the stairs but the "Little Procession" was not repeated. The President and Mrs. Truman always went directly to the elevator and upstairs—the Cabinet did not follow them. President Roosevelt also rode up on the elevator, usually alone. Mrs. Roosevelt left him there and remained to mingle with their guests for a time.

It was only when the "Little Procession," which was dropped during the Roosevelt Administration because of the President's lameness, was resumed, that one realized how much dignity and drama it added to this Flag ceremony which is one of the most moving of all White House rituals.

Thousands and thousands of people who have attended White House receptions down the years must remember a pair of uniformed young service men standing at the right and left of the entrance to the Blue Room, eyes front, stiffly erect, each holding a magnificent silk flag—one the flag of the United States, the other the flag of the President. But very few indeed have ever been told that these are the flags that stand behind the President when he is at work at his desk in his private study in the White House.

The next social season, that of the winter of 1947-1948, the official social program again was cut down, this time because of hunger abroad. The White House put into effect an austerity program, eliminating all the state dinners, since this nation was sending abroad shipload after shipload of wheat and other food to aid war-devastated nations. The official receptions, which required no great outlay of food, were continued.

It was at the Army and Navy reception in 1948 that General and Mrs. Dwight D. Eisenhower made their last public appearance before their departure for Europe where the General was to take charge of the North Atlantic Treaty Organization. I remember walking along the White House corridor and seeing a group collected around two people, who turned out to be the Eisenhowers. I recall watching them as they talked gaily and happily to their friends, and thinking what a pity it was that two such lighthearted people were leaving Washington.

I thought back to another meeting with them when they were

living at Fort Myer, just across the Potomac River from Washington, at the end of the Second World War when General Eisenhower was Chief of Staff of the Army. I must have been looking very tired at the time, for Mrs. Eisenhower had said to me. "Don't you want to come over sometime and just rest outdoors on our porch? It would be a change away from the city and away from the White House." Those were two pleasant memories of a man who later would become President, and his wife.

At the Departmental Reception of 1948, the last one for that season, and one of the largest, President Truman noted that the East Room chandelier above his head was tinkling in a strange fashion. This was the signal which spelled shut-down for us all, though we did not know it at the time.

While the President and Mrs. Truman and Margaret were off campaigning in the Whistlestop tour that resulted in his re-election, a very detailed study was made of the White House as a fire and structural hazard. Immediately after the President's return, it was condemned for occupancy and had to be completely reconstructed within its old walls.

I was among the evicted. I had to depart from my little third-floor office where I had worked for so long. An office was found for me on the second floor of the East Wing, which had been converted from a ceremonial entrance into an office building by Franklin Roosevelt during the Second World War. It was much more convenient and better suited to my purposes than the one I had occupied. I settled like a satisfied pussycat into its day-by-day pleasantness, close to the Social Office, just above a conference room where each fortnight I had my morning meetings with the women of the press.

Chapter 21

BIG DOINGS IN
LITTLE BLAIR HOUSE

THE PRESIDENT AND MRS. TRUMAN briefly had occupied Blair House, diagonally across Pennsylvania Avenue from the White House, at the time when Mrs. Roosevelt was packing up for the move back to Hyde Park and while the White House was being renovated for the Trumans to occupy. They loved this historic old home, famed as the residence of Francis Blair of Andrew Jackson's "Kitchen Cabinet" and his son, Montgomery Blair, Postmaster General in Abraham Lincoln's administration. Blair House was filled with the furniture, silver, china, art, books and even the cartoons of many generations of Blairs. So when the White House was condemned for occupancy, the Trumans moved back to Blair House, and the bulk of the White House furniture and silver was sent into art gallery storage space.

Enough of the choicer pieces, however, were moved across the street to give a miniature White House atmosphere to Blair House, or rather to Blair-Lee House, for the two government-owned guest houses were joined by cutting out an inner connecting door between two front rooms. Three drawing rooms in Lee House became miniature Green, Blue, and Red Rooms.

Blair House dated back to earliest Washington. Lee House had been built adjoining it shortly before the Civil War by old Francis Blair for his daughter who married Captain Phillips Lee, a first cousin of Robert E. Lee. Blair House and Lee House have individual front entrances. They also have individual dining rooms. Some of the most famous pieces of White House silver became temporary decorations of the Lee House dining room, which was most used in the official entertaining. The dining room of Blair House, while used for some official dinners, had more of the atmosphere of a private dining room for the Truman family.

In these greatly reduced quarters, the President and Mrs. Truman continued to offer a proportionately reduced scale of official hospitality. Dinners were of a family size, never more than twenty. For teas, one hundred fifty was the maximum, even when the weather was warm enough to use the garden. And when a high official from another nation was entertained, a State Dinner was held at the Carlton Hotel nearby. There the White House ushers took over and carried forth the White House traditions of table chart, place cards and floral decorations.

The Trumans lived at Blair-Lee House from the autumn of 1948 until the spring of 1952. It is no exaggeration to say that during all that time official entertaining was conducted under great difficulties. However, many a guest enjoyed the greater intimacy that a visit with the President and his wife gave in such circumstances.

A little office was found for Reathel Odum on the top floor of Blair House. There I visited her as I made my daily reports to Mrs. Truman, and when we met the press together, she came over to my offices in the divided White House establishment.

It was my custom during my years at the White House to go to my apartment on Connecticut Avenue each noon for lunch. Mrs. Truman, out of the goodness of her heart, had assigned a car and chauffeur for the necessary transportation—a very great help for an elderly social secretary in the season. My office was now almost two blocks away from Blair House, and when I was heavily laden with papers for Mrs. Truman's attention or signature, I usually was driven around to Blair House from my office. Otherwise, I preferred to walk. I talked over with Mrs. Truman the requests that came for her to make personal appearances, and every engagement she had. She would mark the ones she wanted me to give out to the press women. Some of her personal engagements and a few of her parties she did not mention.

Mrs. Truman was habitually friendly, good-humored, and forthright. She made her decisions promptly but thoughtfully, and stuck to them. She merited the high acclaim that she received as the wife of the President of the United States.

All over Washington I heard from people—many of them no friends of the Truman administration or its ways—nothing but praise of Mrs. Truman, her dignity and her unfailing cordiality when hostess at the White House. Many also commented on her really extraordinary memory of names and faces, even with persons she had not seen for a long time. Certainly, I can say in all truth that no adverse criticism of her has ever come to me.

When President Truman was inaugurated in January of 1949, it involved a change of inaugural locale. The closed White House was useless except as a symbolic background for the reviewing stands of the Inaugural Parade. Of course there could be no large entertaining in Blair House, which is modest in size compared with many private residences. This led to the biggest Presidential reception in history.

The Trustees of the National Gallery of Art had offered the Gallery for the inaugural reception and no more beautiful place could be imagined. They did their part in making it even more attractive, with shrubs and flowers and plants placed in just the right positions. No human being could have been more considerate and helpful than Colonel Harry McBride, Administrator of the Gallery, who was our liaison man for the affair.

Originally the number of invitations sent out was to have been held down to four thousand. Since the usual attendance at White House functions averages sixty percent of the number invited, this would have meant around two thousand four hundred.

Finally, however, with additions from the Democratic National Committee and with requests from the committees of Congress which had to do with the Inauguration, also from senators and representatives, plus just people who asked for invitations (friends and the like) the list swelled to the enormous total of ten thousand.

The usual approximately sixty percent of attendance held good at this affair. With ten thousand invitations sent out, 5628 persons attended. Mr. Tolley and his staff, and all the extra persons who had to be pressed into service to issue invitations and admittance cards, managed to survive—how I do not know. We were a battered-looking lot after the thing was over.

There are three entrances to the National Gallery, which faces on Constitution Avenue at Sixth Street just off Pennsylvania Avenue. The West Entrance was reserved for the President, the Vice-President, their families and house guests (a total of fifty persons) and a small buffet was set up with some refreshments for them.

My place was at the South Entrance. Through this entrance came the Electors, the Supreme Court, the Cabinet, the Joint Congressional Committee on the Inaugural, heads of independent agencies, the Little Cabinet, and representatives of the religions—Archbishop Patrick O'Boyle of the Roman Catholic Church, the Right Reverend Angus Dun, Episcopal Bishop of Washington, and a leading rabbi of Washington, Dr. Norman Gerstenfeld. Then there were some family friends, the ranking officers of the Army, Navy, Air Force and Marine Corps, and a few others.

If any unauthorized persons tried to use this entrance, I was supposed to shoo them gently away to another part of the building. By unauthorized persons I do not mean those without invitations, but persons whose invitations directed them to some other entrance.

There were military and naval aides all over the place to help me with this, plus some of the Secret Service. So things went very smoothly, with only one incident that I can recall.

A lady, one of the Electors, came with a friend. She had a South Entrance card and the friend had a North Entrance card. She protested vigorously when she was separated from her friend, but later went very happily with the other Electors into a room reserved for them. There was so much space at the Gallery that it was possible to put all the distinguished people into rooms allotted to them.

It was obviously impossible for the President and Mrs. Truman and Vice-President Barkley and his daughter, Mrs. Max Truitt, who acted as his hostess at the time, to shake hands with all the 5081 persons who entered by way of Constitution Avenue. A stand was built in one of the courts, from which the President made a brief speech and gave a symbolic handshake to all the people within sight. His welcome was carried over loudspeakers throughout the building.

The President and Mrs. Truman and the Vice-President and Mrs. Truitt did shake hands with the smaller and more official group which entered through the South Entrance, numbering 547.

Another incident, which might have had disastrous results for this reception, was told to me by Mr. Tolley.

The social staff had worked night and day getting out invitations and proper admit cards, and it was agreed with the officials of the Gallery that all necessary records and lists would be in the office of the Gallery at four o'clock on Inauguration Day, so that the doors could be opened and the guests assembled for five o'clock, the hour of the reception.

A Lincoln car with uniformed chauffeur was provided to transport Mr. Tolley, his staff and all the records from the White House to the Gallery. Police blocked off the Gallery and all surrounding streets, to make room for the long lines of private cars and taxis which soon would bring thousands of guests to this largest of all inaugural receptions. Without Mr. Tolley and his lists for checking cards of admission, and without his staff to serve as doorkeepers, everything would have been chaos. It would have been impossible to go on with the reception.

But the Lincoln car displayed a windshield card which was guaranteed to pass the party through police lines. With all records safely in the car, they left the White House for the short ride to their destination.

A couple of blocks from the Gallery they were suddenly stopped by a police officer, who held up both arms and with all the majesty of the law, announced in a loud voice: "No cars pass this point!"

The agonizing thought flashed through their minds that there would be no reception that afternoon if they didn't reach the Gallery with their records. They could have carried the records, but it would have been harder for them to get through police lines on foot and without identification, than in the White House car with approved windshield card. In fact, it would have been impossible. The chauffeur turned to Mr. Tolley, wondering what the next move would be. In desperation, Mr. Tolley lowered the window and in as stern a voice as he could muster in the circumstances, said to the officer: "This is an official White House car."

The policeman looked straight at Mr. Tolley, whose manner evidently carried conviction. Finally the policeman said: "Well, go ahead then!"—and with a sweep of his arm waved them on their way.

The social staff reached the Gallery promptly at four o'clock and the day was saved for everybody.

Inauguration that year was on a Thursday, making a long week end crammed with parties. Blair-Lee House was filled to overflowing with house guests, mostly members of the Truman and Wallace families in from Missouri. On Inauguration night, the President, Mrs. Truman, Miss Truman and the house guests attended the Inauguration Ball held in the National Guard Armory.

Surprises can come to a social secretary and one of the surprises of my life was in the winter of 1949, when Mrs. Truman told me she wanted to have a luncheon party in my honor. This was the first time I had ever had a White House luncheon given for me, and naturally I was excited.

Mrs. Truman asked me to suggest some of the guests, so I did suggest some mutual friends—including Mrs. Perle Mesta, who later became Minister to Luxembourg; Mrs. Angus Dun, wife of the Episcopal Bishop of Washington; Mrs. James L. Houghteling, daughter of Mr. Frederic A. Delano, President Roosevelt's uncle; Mrs. D. Buchanan Merryman, whose niece is the Duchess of Windsor; Mrs. Charles Warren, one of my old friends from the Wilson administration; Mrs. Albert P. Niblack, widow of Vice-Admiral Niblack, who for years was American representative at Monte Carlo in connection with deep-sea surveys sponsored by the Prince of Monaco. (The Vice Admiral had the impressive designation "Director and President of the International Hydrographic

Bureau of the Principality of Monaco, stationed at Monte Carlo," which demonstrated that something besides roulette went on at Monte Carlo.)

Others on that list were Mrs. James Thomson, a neighbor of mine in Virginia and daughter of Champ Clark, who was one of our most famous Speakers of the House; Mrs. Edward B. Meigs, a very active member of the Woman's National Democratic Club; Mrs. Orme Wilson, whose husband had been a minister to Belgium and Ambassador to Haiti; Miss Isabella Wells, an old Washington resident originally from St. Louis; and Mrs. Harry Vaughan, the wife of the President's Military Aide.

There is a beautiful set of Lowestoft china that belongs to Blair House. Mrs. Victoria Geaney, Blair House housekeeper, remembered my admiration for this china and she had it taken out of its cabinet and used it to set the luncheon table. Mr. Robert Redmond, the White House florist, made an exquisite centerpiece of blue and gold to go with the blue and gold of the lovely Lowestoft ware.

It was not just because it was my party that the table seemed the loveliest I have ever seen. It was. Just to admire that priceless china that goes with the dining room in Blair House would have been enough for me—to have sat down without food and felt what an honor it was to have a party given for me there. But the menu I know was delicious, even though I was too excited and happy to pay much attention to such material things as food.

This luncheon was one of my prized triumphs over my good friends, the ladies of the press. They never knew it was given and there never was any notice of it in any of the papers. They know so much and find out so many things that I have always been astonished that these clever women did not find out about this one little, but very important to me, episode in my life.

Mrs. Truman had continued the buffet luncheons originated by Mrs. Roosevelt and ladies of the Roosevelt Cabinet for the Senate Ladies' Luncheon Club, and these were continued even in the limited confines of Blair House. They began as picnic affairs, with some of the cold dishes contributed by Cabinet ladies, but after the first one there was a food census because many of the ladies had hit on the same cold dish and this did not make for variety in the menu. Later the expense was divided on a pro rata basis, with each Cabinet lady contributing her share, not only for food but also for incidentals.

Menus were submitted to Mrs. Truman and then in turn submitted to the Cabinet ladies for their approval. They were very simple and of the picnic variety. A sample menu was: jellied madrilene; cold sliced tongue, chicken and ham; fish salad, mixed vegetable salad; potato chips; celery, carrot fingers and olives; corn sticks; ice cream; cake; coffee.

When Mrs. Roosevelt had first started these informal luncheons, no invitations were issued; the Vice-President's wife just stood at the door and identified the ladies as they came in. But invitations became necessary when White House security regulations were tightened during the Second World War.

Later on, when the White House was closed and picnic luncheons were held at Blair House, these were very crowded affairs because of the limited space. Fortunately, most of them fell on good days, when the little patio garden hidden to the rear of Blair House could be utilized for tables.

The demands on the time of the wife of the President are always heavy. A random sampling of a two-week span in the spring of 1949 shows thirteen engagements for Mrs. Truman. They included lunch with the Senate Ladies on Capitol Hill; a Congressional Club breakfast; a reception at Blair House to a branch of the American Association of University Women; a reception given by the White House aides at Anderson House; a musical luncheon given by the Democratic Women's National Council; a benefit tea for the Goodwill Guild; the opening of the Spanish Class to which she had belonged; a handshaking with a group of Home Demonstration agents from Vermont; a Women's Luncheon of the United States Chamber of Commerce; a luncheon with the 74th Club, an organization of the wives of men who entered the House of Representatives in the 74th Congress. Mrs. Truman opened the Annual Flower Mart on the Pilgrim Steps of Washington Cathedral. She attended the Thrift Shop White Elephant sale. And she received the Society of Sponsors of the United States Navy. So went the busy days.

Junior White House aides added to pleasant informal entertaining by giving a cocktail party with the President and Mrs. Truman and Margaret Truman as their honor guests. This started out as a rather small affair; the first one, I recollect, was held in a Georgetown house rented by several of the aides, and the house next door was turned over also for the overflow of guests. These yearly parties, all in honor of the Trumans, grew in size and were moved to Anderson House, the beautiful home on Massachusetts Avenue which was built by Mr. and Mrs. Larz Anderson, now owned by the Society of the Cincinnati, a national patriotic organization.

One of the pleasantest customs established by Mrs. Truman at the Blair-Lee House were afternoon parties for hospitalized service men. She did this shortly after the Korean war opened in June, 1950. Only one hundred men could be invited at one time, because of the comparatively small rooms at Blair-Lee House. There also could be no stretcher cases such as those that came to the Veterans' Garden Parties on the White House lawn, because the steps are steep and a small elevator held only two or three persons. I always wondered at the courage of some of the badly crippled young men who climbed those steps outside Blair House.

Mrs. Truman asked young friends of Margaret's to come each afternoon that these groups were received. There also was another party touch, a Marine Band orchestra of four or five musicians which played in the hall of Lee House.

Mrs. Truman received the men in the drawing room of Blair House, which faces on Pennsylvania Avenue and from which a wide doorway opens into the rooms where the guests assembled. After greetings from Mrs. Truman, the men went into the larger drawing room of Lee House and refreshments were served in the dining room there.

The men seemed to enjoy these parties greatly. They came in buses furnished by the Red Cross or the various hospitals. The volunteer bus drivers, men and women, also were received by Mrs. Truman and stayed for the party.

President Truman always attended all of these teas, though his name was not on the invitation which was sent to the heads of the two service hospitals—Walter Reed and the Naval Hospital. No invitations were issued in advance to the men who attended, because at the last moment a man might not be able to come and a substitute would be put in his place. Word was passed around in the hospitals that a party was to be held, and the men put down their names.

There were always more names than space, but I think the commanding officers of these hospitals did a wonderful job of selection. The White House had nothing to do with the selection, nor did we know on what basis the men were chosen; but it always seemed to me they were excellent representatives of the hospitalized group. After these parties an engraved invitation was sent to each person who had attended, bearing his name—as a souvenir of the affair.

When the teas were planned, President Truman inquired about refreshments and when told that only soft drinks and coffee were to be served, he said a very light beer should be added. That proved to be a very popular move on his part. There was not enough alcohol in the beer to hurt anyone, and yet it made the men feel they were being treated as real service men.

Of course Margaret was the great attraction when she was able to be present. Time after time, however, as I served coffee, men would come up to me and say they could hardly believe they had met the President of the United States, talked to him, and had been asked questions about themselves. President Truman knew all the ways of service men. He had served in the first World War and had firsthand knowledge of G.I.'s and their problems and the usual gripes that all of them have. But none seemed to have any gripes on those afternoons. They just had a good time.

I remember one boy who played the piano very well; he sat down at the piano in Lee House and played until it was time for him to go back to the hospital with his companions.

I remember also one of the disabled men who picked up a spoon and said, "I think I'll take that along with me." I said, "You know it's government property and you're liable to prosecution if you take government property." He put it down immediately.

Some of the service women came to these parties, too—some who drove the Red Cross Motor Corps vehicles, some from the hospitals and some who were ill, either sent back from Korea or who had seen service in other places, and of course some of the regular Army nurses. The commanding officers of the hospitals turned up, too, and so did some of their subordinates. Altogether, these were happy parties and never marred by an unpleasantness. Many hundreds of disabled veterans were entertained in this way.

In the autumn of 1950, some charming friends of Mrs. Truman's came from Independence to visit her. She and the President took them down the river on the President's yacht *Williamsburg*, and I was fortunate enough to be in the party.

It was one of those heavenly October days. We went down as far as Mt. Vernon, lunching on board, and then sat in the sun. On my place card this was written by the President:

As usual, a pleasant day
with
Mrs. Helm

10/29/50   Harry S. Truman

Only a few days later, on November 1, 1950, an assassination attempt was made on the life of Mr. Truman at Blair House where he had just gone for lunch. If the President and Mrs. Truman had been living in the White House, which is much more easily guarded, the President might have been spared this ordeal and two lives would have been spared. A policeman was killed protecting the President, and one of his assailants was killed by the police.

I had gone to my apartment for lunch as usual. On the way back to the White House, the chauffeur, for no reason that I can recall, drove down Seventeenth Street instead of taking our usual route down Sixteenth. And because of that slight change, I had a partial glimpse of the shooting scene.

As we crossed Pennsylvania Avenue, the chauffeur, Sergeant Collins, called my attention to police cars, quantities of police, and an ambulance, all in front of Blair House. I supposed there had been an accident on the street, although there seemed to be too many police for that. I never thought of the President at all. We drove around the South Grounds of the White House to the East Wing, still knowing nothing about what had happened. I was met at the door by a guard, who broke the news to me. In addition to the shock of knowing that the President's life had been in danger, it was horrible to think of the White House policeman who had been killed. We knew them all, of course, pleasant, agreeable and efficient men, who went about their work as we went about ours and who co-operated with us in every way.

I do not remember when I first saw the President after this terrible thing happened, or that he ever spoke of it in my presence. The papers, of course, told of his courage—how he ran to a window when he heard the shooting, how he went on schedule at two P.M. to an Arlington Cemetery ceremony, and was out for his walk at seven o'clock next morning, as usual.

The whole thing was so horrible that it left me almost in a daze. I do not remember exactly, but I must have seen Mrs. Truman right afterward—I do not even remember what I said to her. Mrs. Truman is a very self-contained person, but I do know the assassination attempt was a great shock to her and she probably was more affected by it than she would acknowledge.

I also know she was very much concerned to keep it from her mother, Mrs. Wallace, who was old and frail. I think she was successful at the time. If Mrs. Wallace ever knew about it, it was very much later.

After that day, the Secret Service greatly strengthened the security regulations. White House policemen had always been on duty in sidewalk sentry boxes in front of Blair House while the President lived there. But until the assassination attempt, pedestrians had passed and repassed at will. From that time on they were shunted to the other side of the street. The sidewalk was blocked off. Even the streetcar loading platform was removed from the Avenue directly in front of Blair House. And the President was required to make his trips back and forth from the Blair House to the White House and vice versa in a guarded automobile.

When Vice-President Alben W. Barkley married Mrs. Hadley, a very beautiful woman, the President and Mrs. Truman entertained in their honor at dinner at Blair House. In December, 1950, there came to me an invitation to dinner with the Vice-President and Mrs. Barkley, who were, in turn, entertaining in honor of the

President and Mrs. Truman. It was hard for me to decline this invitation, but some time before I had firmly decided that Washington was overloaded with widows—and that in my own case an elderly example of the clan was better by her own fireside. So I felt I should regret even the Barkley invitation—a real test of my retirement from the social dining-out scene, for Mrs. Barkley is a charming person and of course everybody who knew Vice-President Barkley loved him. I shall not deny, however, that it was music to my ears to hear people sometimes say that they regretted the fact that I no longer accepted dinner invitations.

Many distinguished foreign visitors to this country, chief among them the President of France and Madame Auriol, and Princess Elizabeth of Great Britain with the Duke of Edinburgh, enjoyed a hospitality here that was more than a little restricted by the small size of Blair House. And it was nip and tuck as to whether or not the White House would be completed in time to entertain Queen Juliana and Prince Bernhard of the Netherlands.

When it was announced in 1951 that Princess Elizabeth and the Duke of Edinburgh would be in Washington for the usual three days of official visiting, excitement mounted. Since the Princess then was not a reigning sovereign, it was decided by the State Department that there would be only a small dinner at Blair House, followed by an equally small reception for about one hundred fifty people. It was too bad that these affairs had to be given in Blair House and that more people could not be invited. And all the time Princess Elizabeth and the Duke were in Washington, they were on such a tight schedule that we only saw them whisking in and out of cars.

The afternoon Princess Elizabeth arrived I was watching at one of the windows in Blair House, and that first glimpse surprised me because the Princess was smaller and slimmer than I had thought. My impression of this royal party was the youth of all its members, headed by very young royalty. Princess Elizabeth's lady in waiting, the Honorable Mrs. Elphinstone, looked just about the age of the Princess, who was twenty-five at the time. Mrs. Elphinstone, wife of a clergyman, also was very pretty. Her husband, the Rev. Andrew Charles Victor Elphinstone, was the Princess Elizabeth's first cousin on her mother's side.

The Princess seemed quieter than her gay and charming husband. She had brought a very beautiful antique over-mantel (a gold framed mirror with a painting above, to be hung over a mantel) which she presented in behalf of the King and Queen of England to President Truman.

The presentation ceremony was held in the rose garden adjoining President Truman's office. It was a miserable day in November, with rain threatening, but fortunately none fell; however, I noticed that the lovely mirror was hurriedly packed up and taken inside, so that no rain should mar it.

After the ceremony, we went with the President on a tour of the White House, which meant that Her Royal Highness and the Duke (as well as the rest of us) jumped over pipes and all sorts of debris left there by workmen who had moved out for a few hours to allow the British party to be shown some of the rooms and the spot over the Blue Room fireplace where the President hoped the over-mantel would be hung. (The White House Renovation Commission later decided that was not the place for it.)

It still seems to me too bad that the President of the United States had no place in which to hold a small ceremony of acceptance of a rare gift from the King of England except a rose garden in which he was subject to the vagaries of wind and weather.

Of course, this was a special emergency, with the White House torn apart from roof to basement; ordinarily, the ceremony would have been held in the East Room. And the rose garden is a secluded spot, which the President can call his own. The little patio terrace at Blair House would have been even more unsatisfactory as a background for the presentation. And it certainly could not have been held in any of the small rooms of that substitute Presidential residence.

One real advantage of the White House over Blair House is that it affords the President and his family some ranging room. I am sure President Truman, whose informal morning walks are famous, must have chafed under Secret Service orders when he was forced to ride in a White House automobile back and forth from Blair House across Pennsylvania Avenue to his offices in the west office wing of the White House, after the assassination attempt of November, 1950.

Chapter 22

AN OLD-NEW WHITE HOUSE

Two TOPICS WERE WORN rather threadbare in public prints and private conversation in the early months of 1952. The major one was: would President Truman run for re-election? The other, of great importance to the White House social staff: would the reconstruction of the White House be completed in time to entertain there Queen Juliana and the Prince of the Netherlands? The answer to the first one was: no. The answer to the second: barely.

Almost at the close of the long period of suspense, Mrs. Truman gave the newspaper women who attended my fortnightly conferences a personally conducted tour of the new White House. She knew the answer as to her husband's running again, but kept the secret well, sidestepping all questions. The President made his dramatic announcement at the Jefferson-Jackson Day Dinner before the Trumans moved back across the street from Blair House. So we all knew that when we started the White House entertainment ball rolling again for royal visitors we would be engaged in a closing-out operation for the Truman administration.

In these circumstances, the Trumans extended a maximum of

official hospitality. Literally thousands were invited to tour the White House, the press and Congress seeing it professionally in advance of its opening and all of officialdom seeing it socially immediately afterward.

While I believe that the Franklin Roosevelts made the all-time record for sustained brilliant official entertaining, the Trumans topped all previous crowd statistics for a single season, that spring of 1952 when the beautiful old mansion emerged in fresh magnificence after its two-year blackout. During those spring months Mrs. Truman shook hands with more thousands than ever were greeted by her closest competitor, Mrs. Roosevelt, in the same length of time. Everyone wanted to come to the White House. It seemed to me everybody did.

Many people are under the impression that the President and Mrs. Truman made all the decisions on the rebuilding of the White House, which was markedly changed in appearance, even in the State Rooms. That is not the case. Congress set up a Commission on the Renovation of the Executive Mansion, with Senator Kenneth D. McKellar, then Chairman of the Senate Committee on Appropriations, at its head. On the Commission were two senators; two representatives, Douglas W. Orr, then President of the American Institute of Architects; and Richard E. Dougherty, then President of the American Society of Civil Engineers. The last two named were considered by Congress as representing the public.

Executive Director of the work was Major General Glen E. Edgerton, and Lorenzo S. Winslow, Architect of the White House, served as its secretary. The Commission met often in the same conference room where I met the ladies of the press. They called in consultants on design and decoration, and made all final decisions.

It was a Sunday late in March, 1952, when a record-making gathering of press women assembled in the first-floor lobby of the East Office wing. Mrs. Truman was to meet them on the remodeled second floor and show them through the family living quarters. Every accredited member of my press conference was on hand, and some press representatives from out of town who had come on for the occasion.

Mrs. Truman appeared from Blair House, wearing a plain green two-piece suit. The tour was informal; newspaper women clustered around Mrs. Truman or went on their own through second- and third-floor rooms.

She answered questions about details of the redecoration—Margaret's suite in palest rose and green, the President's bedroom with severe "man-type" furnishings; her own room in deep mauve; the President's study with its hangings and furniture done in brocaded designs symbolic of the President's office; the redecorated Monroe Room; the Rose Room first used by Queen Juliana as a guest room; the Lincoln bedroom across the hall, assigned to Prince Bernhard and furnished not only with the authentic Lincoln bed, dresser and other items of the period, but also with Victorian carpet and embroidered window curtains.

The family floor where Mrs. Truman acted as guide had been made much more comfortable for family living and the entertainment of heads of state. While no main architectural features had been changed, some well-placed partitions had made of it a home and not just a public building.

Always its long upstairs hall, running the length of the building from east to west, had presented a difficult decorating problem. Mrs. Roosevelt had solved this as well as was humanly possible by screening off the west end for a small sitting room, which she made gay and cheerful with bright chintz slipcovers on chairs and sofas. This had always seemed to me really the most cheery and comfortable spot in the White House. But I realized that even this sitting room beside the great fan window had been a little shabby. After all, the White House all during the war years had been allowed to go unpainted and with no new hangings or furniture covers. President Roosevelt had decreed this as a symbol of wartime austerity. For several years it had sadly needed the decorator's hand.

Now this West Hall had become a real room with solid partitions blocking off the rest of the long hallway. The window which so dominated it was covered in sheer and elaborately fluted white silk, framed in an old Colonial print on toile, red figures on a beige background depicting Franklin and Washington in various well-known scenes in their lives. This fabric was also used to cover a love seat and two large chairs, and for the pillows on the red satin sofas. The chenille carpet was beige-color.

Blocked off with high screens, the central section of the upstairs hall had been in the Roosevelt days a dreary spot at best. Against its walls were bookcases on which framed photographs stood; and above the bookcases were a number of portraits and some of the overflow of the President's tremendous collection of ship prints. There was a sofa or two, some easy chairs, and tables to hold the current magazines.

With modern indirect lighting it was possible to make this inner area an appropriate anteroom for the President's study and bedroom, which was essentially its purpose. Its most satisfying feature was the cabinetwork—bookcases and wall-niches for art objects. The upholstery and carpets in this room were of the same materials as was used in the West Hall.

A different and more formal decorative scheme was used in the East Hall, the small sitting room between the bedrooms used by visiting heads of State. There the fanlight was draped in emerald-green satin, more elaborately arranged than the toile in the West Hall.

For all of the rooms on this floor, except the Lincoln Room, some "museum print" of the Georgian period had been found and used as inspiration for the rest of the decoration. The one which had been used in Mrs. Truman's sitting room off the West Hall was a floral print of amethyst-colored flowers and green leaves on an ivory background. The carpet there was amethyst-colored chenille. In Margaret Truman's room a Louis XVI print in shades of green and rose on white was used.

Perhaps the change which I welcomed most was really modern bathrooms. All the White House second-floor bathrooms had been monstrous in size and almost early-Roman in design, with huge bathtubs and much marble.

The women of the Washington press needed no guide through the familiar State Parlors, now different in detail but holding to traditional color schemes, and to much of the original decorative detail. Nevertheless, a representative from General Edgerton's office called their attention to some of new features in which the Renovation Commission took special pride.

Chief of these was the more open Grand Staircase, coming down into the Foyer instead of into the Long Corridor as in the past. The Foyer itself had been lightened and made much more impressive by a rich marble wainscoat and marble pilasters and columns.

The East Room had been newly woodpaneled to the ceiling. The old plaster decorative designs, blurred from many repaintings, were now sharply etched in hardwood, painted white. The cranberry-red silk draperies which had hung in this room had been replaced by a white and lemon-gold silk damask of authentic eighteenth-century design.

The Green Room had been completely redecorated, the monotony of its color scheme relieved by a love seat and two occasional chairs upholstered in a much lighter shade of green than the walls, rug and armchairs. The lovely parquetry floor of the Blue Room was left bare as in the old days. Its walls were newly covered in a blue silk-satin with a large gold decorative motif. Hangings, too, were blue and gold; the furniture white, blue and gold. It was much livelier than the old Blue Room—indeed I heard one press woman complain, "It hits you in the eye." The Red Room, on the other hand, was toned down a bit, three of the chairs having been upholstered in off-white where all had once been red.

No one could have missed the improvement in the White House chandeliers. The enormous East Room trio, installed during the Theodore Roosevelt renovation, had been cut down in size—they had been large enough for the Palace of Versailles in Paris. When musicales had been given in the old East Room, singers' voices had seemed to hit the crystal and bounce in various directions, with unhappy and unmusical results.

It was Mrs. Herbert Hoover who had originated the movement to have the Victorian chandeliers in the White House replaced with early American crystal. During the reconstruction, several beautiful chandeliers from anonymous donors had been added to the White House collection of authentic antiques. The most beautiful went to the Family Dining Room, which had never had a chandelier. When the White House was reopened after the reconstruction, there were fourteen fine specimens.

Of all these famous rooms, the State Dining Room, hung with gold draperies, looked least like its old self. English oak wall paneling from floor to ceiling, which dates back to the Theodore Roosevelt remodeling, was covered with paint of a soft green shade.

To me anything was better than the horror of past years, when that famous wall paneling was first installed and was adorned with heads of hartebeests, antelopes, et al., shot by Theodore Roosevelt. A glorious change indeed! However, the old wall paneling had its ardent admirers and one hears in Washington sad laments about the "desecration of painting over that beautiful woodwork."

The press women climbed to the third floor and saw suite after suite with modernistic bedroom, small sitting room and bath; solarium overlooking the South Grounds; and a new playroom for White House children and child visitors.

At that time Mrs. David Wallace, Mrs. Truman's mother, was very ill and it was known she could not live long. Mrs. Truman, a devoted daughter, shrank from publicity about members of her immediate family. As I recall, the only information she did not give the press women on that tour was about her mother—she did not say which room Mrs. Wallace was to occupy during what was her last illness.

As I went with the press women through the State Dining Room, I noted that the Healy portrait of Lincoln had been returned to its place over the mantel; and that the over-mantel presented by Princess Elizabeth had been hung on the north wall of that room, over a console table.

This Healy portrait of Lincoln closely resembles the same artist's portrayal of the Civil War President at the conference with his generals on the *River Queen* just before the close of the Civil War. The portrait dominates the State Dining Room in a remarkable way. It always reminded me of Robert Lincoln, the President's son, and of his wife and their daughter, Jessie, who cherished it for many years before it came to the White House.

I knew the Robert Lincolns years ago in Manchester, Vermont, and later here in Washington. Both Jessie and I belonged to the

Society of Sponsors, U.S. Navy. She bore a strong family resemblance to her grandfather.

The Lincolns, when they came to Washington, took an old house on N Street in Georgetown and Mrs. Isham, another daughter, came down from Manchester to live with her mother. The house was large enough for Mrs. Isham to live in one section and have her own housekeeping arrangements, while Mrs. Lincoln occupied the main section. This was very satisfactory, because Mrs. Lincoln was a very old lady and kept, I imagine, early hours. When Mrs. Isham died, the portrait, which Robert Lincoln had considered the best likeness of his father, came to the White House. I think one of the conditions of the gift was that the portrait should be hung in a place worthy of it—and it was.

I thought also that the over-mantel was excellently placed, but that the lighting in that part of the room was not good. This beautiful antique work of art does not show up as it should, when viewed from some distance away, in its present location against the north wall; but perhaps some form of indirect lighting will be added, so it will not be necessary to get quite close to the mirror to appreciate the beauty of the eighteenth-century painting which adorns it.

Some people objected to the incongruity of hanging a portrait of Abraham Lincoln in the same room with the eighteenth-century over-mantel. But since President Lincoln is looking away from the over-mantel, he can scarcely be disturbed by what he does not see.

As we made this trip through the White House, more than a hundred years old as to its outer walls, but spic-span new in every other way, I realized how fond I had become of the women of the press who once had filled me with fear and trembling. Never in my wildest dreams had I ever aspired to be "a White House spokesman." Yet giving out social news of the Executive Mansion had long since become routine to me.

In my first few meetings with the press women, I had taken with me memoranda of engagements to be read off to them, a slow process involving spelling of names. I soon decided it would be better to have mimeographed copies of the entire engagement list distributed to the newspaper women. In these lists I included, as a source of further details, the name of the person who had asked

Mrs. Truman to receive a group, or to appear at some event. I believe Mrs. Truman was the first wife of a President ever to have such a mimeographed record made of her comings and goings. I kept a file of these "press releases" which were handed to the newspaper women each fortnight. Looking them over now, I think the one I gave out at the time of the visit of Her Majesty the Queen and His Royal Highness the Prince of the Netherlands was the most interesting!

Mrs. Truman's Engagements to be given to the press
Tuesday, April 1, 1952

April

Tue. 1st —Mrs. Truman will attend a tea to be given for the benefit of the Thrift Shop at the Sulgrave Club at four o'clock. (Mrs. D. Lawrence Groner, 2101 Connecticut Avenue.)

Wed. 2nd —The President and Mrs. Truman will give a dinner at the Carlton Hotel in honor of Her Majesty the Queen and His Royal Highness the Prince of the Netherlands
8:00 P.M.

(There will be no formal tea when Her Majesty the Queen of the Netherlands arrives at the White House. They will be served tea in their rooms, in order to allow them some time to rest prior to the dinner that night.)

Thu. 3rd —Mrs. Truman will go to the Capitol when Her Majesty the Queen of the Netherlands addresses a Joint Meeting of Congress.

Thu. 3rd —The President and Mrs. Truman will give a Luncheon at the White House for Her Majesty the Queen and His Royal Highness the Prince of the Netherlands and the members of their party.
1:15 P.M.

Fri. 4th —Mrs. Truman will accompany the President when he addresses a meeting commemorating the Third Anniversary of the signing of the North Atlantic Treaty at Constitution Hall.
11:45 A.M.

Fri. 4th — Mrs. Truman will accompany the President to the
3:30 P.M.   ceremony at Meridian Hill Park when Her Majesty the Queen of the Netherlands will present to the President a Carillon as a gift from the people of the Netherlands to the people of the United States.

Fri. 4th — The President and Mrs. Truman will attend the
8:15 P.M.   dinner to be given in their honor by Her Majesty the Queen and His Royal Highness the Prince of the Netherlands.

Sat. 5th — Mrs. Truman will receive the members of the Na-
5:00 P.M.   tional League of American Pen Women. Mrs. Barkley will assist her. Approximately 800. (Miss Maurine Emrick, 1300 17th Street.)

Sat. 12th — Mrs. Truman will attend the House and Embassy Tour Tea for the benefit of the Home for Incurables at the Admiral's House, Naval Observatory grounds. (Mrs. Wm. F. Newton, 2800 P Street.)

Mon. 14th — Mrs. Truman hopes to go to the Missouri tea to be given in the Williamsburg Room of the Mayflower Hotel from 3:30 to 5:00 P.M.

Tue. 15th — Mrs. Truman will attend the opening of the Fash-
2:30 P.M.   ion Tea sponsored by Archbishop O'Boyle at the Statler Hotel for the benefit of the Christ Child Farm for Convalescent Children. (Mrs. James Murray, The Westchester.)

Wednesday evening, April 2nd, dinner at the Carlton: Mrs. Truman will wear a smoke-gray mousseline de soie trimmed with sprays of embroidered lace down one side of very full skirt.

Friday evening, April 4th, dinner at the Netherlands Embassy: Mrs. Truman will wear white lace trimmed with navy velvet over navy taffeta.

Suits at other events.

On file with this example of my press release is another memorandum—a note I handed to Mrs. Truman before this press conference in order to get details I felt would interest the press.

Mrs. Truman:

At the press meeting next Tuesday, I will probably be asked what you will wear:

1: When you meet Queen Juliana at the airport;
2: At the dinner that night;
3: At the presentation of the Carillon;
4: At the dinner which Queen Juliana gives for you and the President.

May I have this Monday, please?

Edith Helm

Mrs. Truman's answers, written in her own hand on this memo, were characteristically terse. After Question 2, she had written "Call Agasta." I called up her dressmaker, Madame Agasta, and received considerable detail as to Mrs. Truman's dress for the Carlton dinner. To Question 4, she replied "White lace." Her dressmaker told me the rest of it. There was no answer to the other two questions, and so I could not provide the press with details of Mrs. Truman's attire at the daytime affairs.

It was not always easy to satisfy the newspaper women with my mimeographed lists of engagements. They wanted to know more than the bare bones of news items, and it was my responsibility to give them what I could. There were times when I phoned Mr. Tolley more than once during a press conference, asking him for details I was unable to supply myself.

Queen Juliana and Prince Bernhard, who were the first guests at the White House after it was reopened in the spring of 1952, were attended by a larger retinue than that which accompanied Princess Elizabeth and the Duke of Edinburgh, but smaller than that brought by their Britannic Majesties in 1939.

Miss Marie Ann Tellegen, Director of the Cabinet of Her Majesty Queen Juliana, stayed at the White House. The Queen's lady-in-waiting, Baroness van Boetzelaer van Osterhout, whom I had met before in Washington, also stayed there. Reathel Odum and I were presented to the royal party shortly after their arrival.

As portions of the rebuilt White House were completely new, I was quite unfamiliar with some of the innovations. I had heard there was a second staircase from the third story which led directly down into the apartments assigned to the Queen and Prince Bernhard, at the east end of the second floor. Miss Tellegen was assigned one of the third-floor suites, and I located this staircase for her all right, but she and I reached the bottom only to find the door locked. We had to creep up the many steps back to the third floor and go down on the elevator, the location of which was unchanged. I found later that the door we could not open was some sort of trick affair which opened out and not in.

There was some public comment because the Trumans entertained for Queen Juliana and Prince Bernhard at the Carlton Hotel instead of the White House. The Presidential family, however, had moved back into the White House barely in time to welcome their royal visitors. While the place was equipped with the most modern and complete kitchens and was amply supplied with servants and every convenience, there had not been time enough for stocking up the place and trying it out. It was therefore decided to postpone the initiation of the new kitchens until the luncheon party the next day.

The Carlton did a splendid job on the dinner. They had a large horseshoe table, seating fifty-seven, in a very large room. The guests were received in a smaller room which was really not adequate for such a large number of people, but in all other particulars the affair was beautifully arranged.

After dinner, as usual, the Cabinet and other ranking officials and their wives were taken to the Queen and presented to her, some by Mr. John Farr Simmons, the State Department Chief of Protocol, and some by me. I think that everyone had a chance for a word with her.

The Queen was handsomer than when I saw her as a Princess at Hyde Park. The years had greatly improved her. In a strapless full-skirted gown, a lovely greenish-gray color, and a diamond necklace, she looked quite beautiful.

In accordance with diplomatic usage, the American Ambassador to the Netherlands had come home to accompany the royal party and attended this dinner. In addition to the official guests (who are "musts" for such a party) there was an American naval officer, Rear Admiral Emmet Forrestel, who had been assigned as aide to the Queen. (During the visit of the King and Queen of England, both a military and naval aide had been assigned to them.)

Also present were representatives of the American and Netherlands press. Mr. Merriman Smith, who covers the White House for U.P. (United Press Association), and Mr. Paul Saunders, correspondent for Dutch papers, were there with their wives. These gentlemen were invited to give official recognition to the importance of the public information phases of a royal visit, and also to report to their colleagues the details of the dinner.

The next day there was a small luncheon numbering twenty-two at the White House—an historic occasion, because it was the first formal luncheon after the White House reopening. Everything passed off very well and the new kitchen evidently gave no trouble.

The new Truman Lenox china was used for the first time at this luncheon for Queen Juliana and Prince Bernhard. It is beautiful china, banded in soft green with gold, bearing the Presidential seal in the center of each piece.

The following day there was a very large reception at the Army and Navy Country Club given by the Queen. The club was an excellent place for such a reception, because its large rooms could accommodate all the guests invited. My invitation read:

> Upon Instructions of Her Majesty the Queen
> and His Royal Highness the Prince of the Netherlands
> The Netherlands Ambassador
> requests the pleasure of the company of
> Mrs. J. Meredith Helm
> at a reception
> on Thursday, April 3rd, 1952, from 4:15 to 6 o'clock
> The Army and Navy Country Club, Arlington, Virginia
>
> Please reply to the   Day Dress
> Protocol Section of the Embassy   Uniform

The royal party was to leave the White House at 8:30 A.M. on April 4th. I had not expected to go down to the White House that morning, which was a Saturday, but about eight o'clock, just as I had started to dress, I was called from the White House and Miss Tellegen told me they hoped they would see me when they left. I said of course, and how I got into my clothes and how the car got up from the White House and had me there well before 8:30, I do not know. It was all done without running through any red lights, too.

When I arrived, Miss Tellegen told me the Queen had a gift for me, which turned out to be a silver compact decorated with the initials J and B—a memento of a very gracious lady.

There was one instance of breaking with tradition in the Truman administration which probably never will occur again.

Some time before the White House was reopened, President and Mrs. Truman decided that they would hold their state receptions in the afternoon instead of the evening.

In essence they were the same as the evening receptions; the same groups were invited to them. But the hour was five o'clock in the afternoon, instead of nine at night. They were held in April and May, 1952.

These first receptions in the rebuilt White House were informal in that they were given in the afternoon, though I do not think that any reception at the White House, particularly where diplomats are involved, can ever be really informal.

Of course there were some mutterings because they were not held at night, but the consensus was that it gave the guests an opportunity in spring afternoons really to see the "new" White House.

Mrs. Truman did little personal entertaining that last year in the White House, largely because of the illness of her mother. However, on November 19th, after the election, she gave a luncheon for the wives of heads of the various divisions in the White House and also for the women who held such positions on their own.

She included two members of my staff, Miss Ida Andrews and Miss Edithe Rowley, and Miss Irene Orndorff of Miss Odum's office. These three capable women had been there so long and transacted so much business for Mrs. Truman that she wished especially to invite them, even though they were not division heads.

Garden parties had never been so lovely as they were that spring, for the entire Executive Mansion had been repainted, and the grounds handsomely re-landscaped and brought into better proportions.

The last luncheon party which Mrs. Truman held for the Senate

Ladies also took place on the grounds. The weather was perfect and one of the rare flowering trees in the White House grounds was covered with blossoms. After the luncheon was over, a number of the ladies—including Mrs. Robert Taft, who came that day—made a tour of the White House to see the ground floor and first-floor rooms. Mrs. Taft's husband was of course at that time a strong contender for the Republican nomination.

Members of the Congress and their wives had made a similar tour immediately after the remodeling was completed, but not all the furniture was in place at that time and many of the Senate ladies either had not come or wanted to see the place again.

The Trumans had only about nine months in the beautifully remodeled White House before their departure on January 20, 1953, with the beginning of the Eisenhower administration. Although Mr. Truman was President for nearly eight years, he was out of the White House from November, 1948, until April, 1952, a period of more than three years.

Mr. Truman had followed the remodeling with keenest interest. The very first tour of the "new" White House was conducted by the President in person, when he showed it to White House correspondents while workmen still were far from finished with this multi-million-dollar reconstruction job. He made a vigorous protest about a lanternlike fixture he didn't like in the entrance foyer. A beautiful antique chandelier was installed in its place.

And when the mansion finally was reopened he put on a television program for the nation, giving an informal lecture on White House history, while he showed his far-flung audience the state rooms, basement broadcasting room, library and other points of interest.

Although the "new" White House is comfortably air-conditioned, Mrs. Truman left it in the summer of 1952 and went to the family home in Independence, Missouri, as usual. The Trumans' last months in the White House were saddened by the lingering final illness and death of Mrs. Truman's mother, Mrs. Wallace. But I am sure both the President and Mrs. Truman, and Margaret, in her not too frequent home visits, appreciated and enjoyed the beauty and comfort of the remodeled mansion.

Chapter 23

AN OLD-NEW HOME
AND A FAREWELL

My interest in the white house reconstruction was keen, but my grief at parting from the place was less great because I, too, had an old-new home of my own.

My only close relative, my nephew, Harry Benham, had moved as a small boy to Boyce in Clarke County, seven miles out of Winchester, Virginia, when his mother remarried after the death of my brother, Lieutenant Henry K. Benham, in 1903. He is now a lawyer in Winchester, where he and his family live.

Some time ago Harry acquired The Briars, a farm which was formerly a part of Pagebrook, the lovely old place where he had lived with his mother and stepfather. On one of my visits to Winchester, I drove with him out to The Briars and saw the dreary, half-ruined old house. Originally the home of one of the famous and numerous Pages of Virginia, it had been occupied by descendants of the Pages until the 1880's, when they left and various farmers took the place over. They cut down the oak trees near the house, tore out the mantelpieces and stripped away all woodwork except the staircase, which was badly in need of repairs. The house had no electricity, no central heating, no indoor plumbing. Hams had been hung in what is now my living room. I am sure the plaster was ham-scented.

But the old house was built like a fortress, with native-stone walls two feet thick. Standing on high ground, it had a beautiful view of the mountains on three sides—Massanutten, the ridge which cuts off the Valley of Virginia to the South; the Blue Ridge to the East; the Alleghenies to the West. A small oak grove at the entrance to the place had survived the axes of the succession of farmer owners. And on one side of the house was a natural rock garden.

An idea took shape—to sell my house in Grayville, where I had spent so many summers, and to restore The Briars for a summer home. I would, however, keep my husband's Illinois farms which stretch along the Wabash River bottom lands.

As one of my friends said, I "certainly had my courage with me" when I started to do over the old Virginia house. Furniture, garden tools, even lily bulbs from Grayville were piled into a van and trekked east to The Briars, where they rested while repairs were made over a period of nearly two years.

My nephew and I agreed on the amount of land I would need to make a proper setting for the old house, and he gave me this generous tract. Then I had a stone wall built around it, with a wide-open entrance to the north and a wrought-iron gate—chiefly for ornament—to the south.

In 1946 I moved into The Briars, and every year finds me happier there. No one ever had more delightful neighbors than mine in Clarke County and Winchester. My heart grows warm when I think of the friendship and affection that greet me when I return every spring; then also I am near my nephew and his wife and small son.

My nephew's cattle graze on fields bordering my stone wall. I always look on these Herefords, with their white faces, as part of the scenery. They add to the charm of my rural landscape, I am sure. Often they stand gazing longingly through the north gateway at my flowers bordering the wall within, and my vegetable garden in a small enclosure of its own. My flowers and vegetables are protected by cattle traps—strips of metal laid flat on the ground, with spaces between. These cattle traps have always interested me greatly. Instinct tells the animals their hoofs might be caught in the spaces, and they stay on their side of the open gateway.

My house itself is unpretentious. The main section is not unusual in design—three stories high, including a roof with dormer windows, two rooms to each floor; a central hall and graceful stairway. In the ell, which I rebuilt completely, are my dining room, kitchen, and Mary's bedroom. I also added a third dormer window for architectural balance. Screened porches at both ends of the main building not only enable me to get maximum enjoyment of those mountain views but also greatly improve the appearance of the house.

In the main building, the two first-floor rooms now are living room and old-fashioned parlor. The parlor is filled with Japanese and Chinese things, from the U. S. Grant voyage of my childhood. In the living room I have an interesting little gallery—autographed photographs of the Captains and the Kings of two generations, and also of the Queens and Presidents and their wives. These are ranged on the chair rail all around this room and on shelves. In front of the sofa there is a souvenir which I perhaps prize most of all. It is a coffee table, with a glass top over a curious cardboard plaque, at the center of which is inscribed, in Mr. Tolley's best penmanship:

Testimonial Luncheon
June 7, 1952
to
Mrs. James M. Helm
(née Miss Edith Benham)
White House Social Secretary
under
Woodrow Wilson, Oct. 22, 1915 to Apr. 20, 1920
Franklin D. Roosevelt, March 4, 1933 to Apr. 12, 1945
Harry S. Truman, April 12, 1945 to —
25 years of unique service to this country, particularly through World Wars I and II.

The press women who met with me regularly gave me this plaque at a luncheon at the Mayflower Hotel after I announced that I would retire from the White House at the end of the Truman administration. It was a perfect luncheon in every way.

Mrs. Truman had gone west for the summer, but Margaret Truman came, and Reathel Odum. Emotionally, I was so disorganized by this honor that I wanted to get up and speak and thank my friends of the press every few minutes.

Bess Furman of the New York *Times* and Ruth Cowan of the Associated Press were the prime movers in this affair. Bess was the first speaker, and after she had spoken I tried to get on my feet; but no, Bess pulled me down. Ruth Cowan came next and after she was through I tried again, and again I was pulled down. Frustrated, I had to listen to all sorts of wonderful things said about myself, by Bess, Ruth and Mrs. Alice Frein Johnson of the Seattle *Times,* from which barrage of compliments I emerged with a dazed feeling that they could not possibly be about me.

Some bright soul who had seen a White House table plat complete with stickers inserted in tiny slits for shuffling names of guests in seating arrangements, produced an exact duplicate for the party table, with a sticker for each guest. Everybody signed her own sticker and inserted it in the plat where she sat at table. There were slits at the corners of the plat for the names of a few members of the press conference who could not be present.

Mr. Tolley later confessed that he had made the table plat and stickers on his own time at home, so they would be a complete surprise to me. The press women used the plat as an inset in the coffee table which they gave me as a parting gift, and which is a permanent memorial of happy hours and happy friendships.

As a grand climax to the luncheon, Bess read aloud a note from Mrs. Truman.

The White House
Washington

June 4, 1952

Dear Bess Furman:

I am extremely sorry to miss your luncheon on Saturday, especially so, as it is in honor of Mrs. Helm.

My husband may think (according to the press) that there is no indispensable *man*, but so far as I am concerned, there is one indispensable *woman* and that one of course is Mrs. Helm.

I know your party will be a gay one and I shall be wishing I could have been there.

Sincerely,
Bess W. Truman

The party *was* a gay one, even though it was the beginning of the end of a long and pleasant association. It was a farewell party, though my farewell to the White House was still six months in the future. Some of the newspaper women I had known well through attending Mrs. Roosevelt's press conferences; they now were my closest friends in the group—among these Isabel Griffin, Esther Tufty, Martha Strayer, Ruth Cowan, Ruth Montgomery, Bess Furman, Doris Fleeson and May Craig. But all of the press women were my friends, and all of them I shall always remember affectionately.

To May Craig, who writes for Maine papers, I owe my valued friendship with Senator Margaret Chase Smith, of Maine. Though of the opposing political party to my own, I admire Mrs. Smith as a remarkable woman who never compromises with her conscience.

As the time approached for leaving the White House, press questions centered on details of the Trumans' move to Independence.

As I answered these questions, I thought back over past inaugurations when there had been a change in Presidents. It seemed extraordinary to me that the barbaric custom of ignoring completely the outgoing President should have been allowed to continue over the years. Some Presidents who have been frank have been heard to comment on this utter lack of courtesy. The biographers of others have made mention of it.

I can only give my own personal feeling as the departure of President Truman came closer. He was, of course, to be provided with police escort through the Inauguration Day crowds to the Georgetown home of his friend and Secretary of State, Dean Acheson. That was only proper and right. But no thought was given to making his farewell a natural and pleasant one. Many of the White

House staff would have liked to go down to the station that evening to wave him farewell. But it was literally impossible for those without their own cars to do so, and those with cars would have to park them many blocks from the station. The crowds on Inauguration Day are simply beyond belief. Taxis are impossible to obtain. The Inauguration Parade, which continues far into the evening, cuts off streetcar and bus transportation. I knew that I should have to tell the Trumans good-by at the White House.

My "farewell" press women's party was held in June, 1952. Mrs. Truman already had gone to Independence for the summer, and I was about ready to go to The Briars. This was as it had been ever since I had moved into my old-new summer home; but in the summer of 1952 it was different.

I was coming back to the White House in the autumn, but for the last time. I soon would say farewell to all my associates, to the White House itself, to the President and Mrs. Truman, whose kindness to me had been great.

I could look back upon the years and feel that the memory of many sorrows which had come to me, as they come inevitably to everyone in a long life, should be offset by other memories. Most particularly, memories of the three "officers and gentlemen" with whom my life was so intimately bound up—my father, my brother and my husband. And I could think with gratitude and affection of my nephew, who carries on the heritage left by those three who have gone.

I could think, too, of my mother and of how, during the years of her widowhood when I was helping earn a living for us both, she made our small income cover our necessities. As it had been when my father was living, we never knew the burden of debt.

All these things I could remember gratefully. And I could be grateful for my years at the White House, and for the associations there—although it was those associations which made the break difficult. Thus the weeks and months passed—Election Day, Thanksgiving, Christmas, New Year—finally my last week at the White House, when I faced reluctantly the necessity of saying good-by to my office staff, just as I now have put off writing these last words in my recollections.

No words can ever tell what I feel in gratitude for the kindness and help of these people who have worked with me. There has been no task too hard for them to do for me, no situation they did not try to soften for me. To express my feeling for them, I can only think back to some of the lovely words in *The Bridge of San Luis Rey*—that the important thing in life is love; certainly I was surrounded all my years at the White House by the affection and love of my friends in the Social Office and elsewhere. God bless them all.

I did not leave the White House with a heartache for the job that someone else can do just as well as I have done, or perhaps better. I have done my best and I am sure my successor will do hers.

But I could not leave the White House itself without a heartache.

One day during that last week, I walked through all the State Rooms. I walked through those rooms because I never expected to be in them again. They are very quiet rooms when the day's crowd of tourists has come and gone. I walked through them silently and alone, thinking of the many people who had been there. They were filled with memories.

The State Dining Room, where Malvina Thompson and I had poured at so many large teas; the truly glamorous dinners there, the throngs at state receptions. The Red Room, with more intimate memories of small groups and important personages, all vivid and alive again. The Blue Room, where I had time and again witnessed three Presidents in their own years of power shaking hands with thousands filing by from the Green Room. The East Room, peopled and re-peopled with evening parties, daylight gatherings, tourist crowds.

And dominating all these, the somber memory of a flag-covered casket guarded by four service men; of a man whose earthly career had ended—my friend, Franklin Roosevelt.

I had come to say good-by to the memories and to the White House itself. I cannot explain this feeling, but after a certain length of time in the White House, its atmosphere envelops one.

It has seen many tragedies.

Perhaps the spirit of Abraham Lincoln most pervades the place, because he suffered so much personally, and so much more for his divided country. It has seemed to me Bess Furman expressed this in her book *White House Profile,* when she called Lincoln's administration "the saddest of them all."

But there was tragedy in my time, as well.

I saw a great man stricken before his life work was finished. Not like Franklin Roosevelt, of whom one can write, "Well done," Woodrow Wilson was cut off before his purpose was achieved, before he could earn his "Well done" with an ideal brought to fruition.

So my memories went with me through the State Rooms—the Dining Room, the Red, Blue and Green Rooms, the East Room—as I walked through them all and said good-by.

Index

Abbott, Grace, 171
Abdul Ilah, Regent of Iraq, 253
Abel-Smith, Commander E.M.C., 194
Acheson, Dean, 129, 297
Adeane, Captain Michael, 194
Agasta, Madame, 288
Airlie, Countess of, 86
Airlie, Earl of, 194
Akron, dirigible balloon, 18
Alexander, Grand Duke of Russia, 31
Alexandra, Queen, 75-76, 90
Allen, Corporal, 93
American Commonwealth, Bryce, 45
Anderson, Mr. and Mrs. Larz, 272
Anderson, Marian, 187, 198
Anderson, Mary, 171
Andrews, Ida, 144, 291
Armistice Day, 55
Army and Navy Reception, 148
Around the World with General Grant, Young, 11
Asquith, Mrs., 73-74
Astor, Mrs. Vincent, 201
Atlanta, U.S.S., 26
Audubon, John James, 7
Auriol, President and Madame, 276

Balfour, Arthur James, 96
Baltimore, U.S.S., 26
Bancroft, U.S.S., 26
Barkley, Alben W., 268, 275-76
Baruch, Bernard, 102, 110, 115, 131, 132
Beaverbrook, Lord, 211
Belmont, Mrs. O.H.P., 30
Benham, Admiral Andrew Ellicott Kennedy, 6, 9, 15, 18, 19, 21-24, 25-26, 29, 33-34, 40

Benham, Harry, 293
Benham, Henry K. (Harry), 6, 12, 15, 18, 21, 25-26, 31, 39, 40, 293
Benham, Commander Timothy Green, 6, 8, 15
Bennington, U.S.S., 22, 26, 33
Benson, Admiral, 96
Bernhard, Prince, 276, 279, 281, 286-91
Best, Mrs. Livingston, 36
Biddle, General John, 73, 75
Biffal, General, 103, 104
Big Four Conference, 102, 105, 112
Birds of America, Audubon, 7
Blair, Francis, 264
Blair House, 264-78
Blair, Montgomery, 264
Blake, Dr., 90
Bloom, Sol, 195, 214, 216-17
Bodisco, Russian Minister, 17
Boehinger, John, 245
Boettinger, Johnny, 245
Boetzelaer van Osterhout, Baroness van, 288
Bones, Helen, 46, 47, 49
Booth, Susie, 79
Borah, William E., 195
Boyle, Irene, 193, 220
Brandeis, Louis, 127-29
Breeze, Mrs., 30
Brest, France, 65-66, 99-100, 122
Brooklyn, New York, 21
Browning, Elizabeth and Robert, 56
Brownson, Captain Willard, 33
Bruschi, Countess, 80, 84
Brussels, Belgium, 113-18
Bryce, James, 45
Buckingham Palace, 74-79, 113, 186

301

Butterfield, Katherine, 15
Byrd, Senator Harry F., 240

Caffery, Jefferson, 124
Calais, France, 72
Callaghan, Captain Daniel J., 196
Caraman-Chimay, Countess de, 123
Carnot, President of France, 32
Castellane, Count Boni de, 33
Catt, Carrie Chapman, 138-39
Chesapeake & Ohio Canal, 39-40
Chiang Kai-shek, Madame, 170, 207, 212-23
Churchill, Winston, 77-78, 209-11
Clark, Champ, 270
Clauneh, Charles, 141
Clemenceau, Georges E. B., 69, 87, 104, 106, 107, 112, 121
Clemens, Samuel, 32
Cleveland, Grover, 26, 27-28, 35, 39
Clifton, Staten Island, 18
Close, Mr., 93, 101, 116, 118
Close, Minister of South Africa, 181, 189, 195
Coke, Lady Katharine, 76, 79, 86
Collier, Mrs. Price, 201
Collins, Sergeant, 274
Colonna, Prince, 85
Columbian Exposition, Chicago, 22, 25, 27, 31
Columbus caravels, 24, 25, 26-27
Columbus four hundredth anniversary celebration, 22-25
Congressional Reception, 149-50
Connally, Senator Tom, 215, 216
Connaught, Duke of, 73, 88
Constellation, U.S.S., 15
Constitution, U.S.S., 15
Cooke, Charles L., 49
Coolidge, Calvin, 126, 129-31
Coolidge, Mrs. Calvin, 131
Cowan, Ruth, 178-79, 296, 297
Cowles, Mrs., 45
Craig, General Malin, 195
Craig, May, 297
Crane, Charles, 106
Crane, Senator Murray, 43
Creel, George, 62, 94
Crim, Howell G., 140, 141
Curie, Eve, 170
Curie, Marie, 127
Curzon, Lord, 77, 78

Cust, Sir Charles, 73, 76, 86
Cutts, Alice, 19

Da Gama, Admiral, 33-34
Dall, Anna Eleanor, 151
Dall, Curtis, 151
Daniels, Jonathan, 245, 246, 258
Daniels, Josephus, 170
D'Aosta, Duchess, 80, 84
David, Ross, 65
Davidson, Jo, 243
Davis, Jefferson, 36-37
Davis, Norman, 115
Debutante dances, 166-67
De Gaulle, General Charles, 253
Delano, Frederick A., 171, 196, 269
Departmental Reception, 263
Dill, Sir John, 211
Diplomatic Circle, 136-37
Diplomatic Dinner, 259-60
Diplomatic Reception, 147-48
Dmitri Donskoi, 25
Dodge, Cleveland, 50
Dolgorouky, Princess, 25
Dougherty, Richard E., 280
D'Oultremont, Countess, 115
Drake, Mrs. Edward, 31
Drum, Major General Hugh A., 195
Dun, Mrs. Angus, 269
Dun, Right Reverend Angus, 242, 247, 248, 267

Early, Stephen T., 195
Edgerton, Major General Glen E., 280
Edinburgh, Duke of, 276-77, 288
Edward, Prince of Wales (Duke of Windsor), 123-24, 212
Eisenhower, General and Mrs. Dwight D., 262-63
Eldon, Earl of, 189, 194
Elizabeth, Princess, 276-77, 288
Elizabeth, Queen, 170, 186-206, 210, 289-90
Elphinstone, Mrs. Andrew C. V., 276-77
Esterhazy, Countess, 38
Eustis, American Ambassador in Paris, 31
Evans, Commander, 117

Fall, Albert B., 129
Farley, James A., 195
Fish, Mrs. Stuyvesant, 30

Flanders, 115
Fleeson, Doris, 257, 297
Foch, Marshal Ferdinand, 70, 102
Forbes, Dora Delano, 171
Forrestel, Rear Admiral Emmet, 289
Fort Wadsworth, 17
Frazier, Mr., 94
Furman, Bess, 296-297, 300

Galt, Edith Bolling, see Mrs. Woodrow Wilson
Galvin, Mrs. William, 238
Ganymede, 75, 77
Garfield, James, 154
Garner, John Nance, 194, 196
Geaney, Mrs. Victoria, 270
Genoa, Duke of, 84
George, David Lloyd, 59, 86, 87, 91, 104, 105, 106, 107, 112, 121
George, King of Greece, 207
George V, King, 73, 75, 77-79, 186
George VI, King, 170, 186-206, 214, 289-90
George Washington, steamship, 92, 96, 135
Gerstenfeld, Dr. Norman, 267
Goelet, Mrs. Ogden, 30
Gould, Anna, 33
Grant, Ulysses Simpson, 9-10, 11, 13
Grayson, Admiral Cary, 61, 62, 64, 73, 74, 76, 77, 86, 88, 91, 95, 103, 106, 118, 131, 132
Grayville, Illinois, 127, 137, 175-79
Grey, Viscount, 123
Gridiron Club, 172
Gridiron Widows' Party, 172-74
Griffin, Isabel, 297
Gulick, Mrs. Mason, 52, 236, 237

Hagner, Belle, 35, 41, 45-46, 255
Haig, Sir Douglas, 79
Halifax, Lord and Lady, 212, 219
Halsey, Edwin A., 241
Halstead, Admiral, 99
Hamilton, Mrs. Schuyler, 29
Hamlin, Charles, 136, 206
Hankey, Sir Maurice, 112
Harding, Mrs. Warren G., 127
Harding, Warren G., 126, 127, 131, 246
Harlan, Laura, 41, 127
Harlow, Lieutenant Charles, 15
Harrison, Benjamin, 26

Harts, General, 76, 77, 84, 99, 103, 116
Hassett, William D., 203, 258
Havenith,, Helen, 118
Hay, John, 41
Hayes, Rutherford B., 10
Healy, Secretary of Irish Legation, 189
Helm, Rear Admiral James M., 19, 56-59, 61, 122, 125, 126, 134, 175, 235
Helm, U.S.S., 235-36
Herbert, Secretary of War, 27
Herdics, 37-38
Herschell, Lord, 77, 86
Holcomb, Major General Thomas, 195
Hooker, Major Harry, 245
Hoover, Herbert, 115, 126, 131-32, 133, 164
Hoover, Mrs. Herbert, 132-33, 172, 283
Hoover, I. H. (Ike), 61, 64, 68-69, 70, 105, 112, 140
Hopkins, Diana, 200, 209
Hopkins, Harry, 195, 209, 210
Horner, Henry, 176
Hornet, U.S.S., 57
Houghteling, Mrs. James, 167
Houghteling, Margaret, 167
House, Edward M., 50, 60, 69, 71, 104
Howe, Louis, 173
Hoyt, Mrs. Lydig, 201
Huang, J. Z., 215, 216
Hudson-Fulton celebration, 58
Hughes, Mrs. Charles Evans, 194, 196
Hull, Mrs. Cordell, 173
Hunt, Jane, 125
Hunt, Nellie, 41
Hyde Park, New York, 187, 201-06, 208-09, 248

Ickes, Harold, 181, 195
Idaho, U.S.S., 58
Infanta Eulalia, 103
Irving, Lieutenant, 116, 118
Isham, Mrs., 285

Jackson, Andrew, 37, 264
Jaffray, Mrs., 55
Jamestown, Rhode Island, 29
Jefferson, Thomas, 252
Jellicoe, Admiral, 78, 79
Joffre, Marshal Joseph J. C., 54
John Rodgers, lighthouse tender, 17-18
Johnson, Alice Frein, 296

Johnston, Harriet Lane, 37
Jones, Jesse, 241
Judicial Reception, 148
Juliana, Queen, 207, 208-09, 210, 214, 276, 279, 281, 286-91
Jusserand, Jules, 66, 127

Kennedy, Francis A., 95-96, 101
Keppel, Sir Derek, 76, 77, 79
Kerensky, A. F., 54
Kerr, Mr., 105
Keyes, Sir Roger, 73, 211
Kilbourne, Lieutenant Commander, 21
Kortright, Elizabeth, 6
Kortright, Hester Mary, 6
Kortright, Captain John, 6
Kung, L. K., 218, 219, 221
Kung, Miss, 218-19

Lafayette, Marquis de, 112
Lamont, Thomas, 104, 122
Lansing, Mrs. Robert, 32, 54, 67, 91, 92, 120
Lanti, Duc de, 87
Lascelles, Alan, 194
League of Nations, 91, 94, 97, 122
Leahy, Admiral William D., 195
Lee, Captain Phillips, 265
Lee, Robert E., 265
Lee House, 264-65, 273
Legh, Lieutenant Colonel Piers W., 194, 201-02
LeHand, Marguerite, 140, 187, 196
Lehman, Herbert, 201, 205
Leslie, Earl, 144
Leygues, M., 99
Lincoln, Abraham, 264, 285, 299
Lincoln, Jesse, 284-85
Lincoln, Robert, 284-85
Lindsay, Sir Ronald and Lady, 181-82, 189, 190, 192-93, 198
Litvinov, Maxim, 182-83
London, England, 34, 72-79
Long, Breckinridge, 49
Louise, Princess, 77
Low, Ivy, 183
Lynn, David, 241

MacArthur, General Douglas, 214
MacDonald, Ishbel, 170
Mackenzie King, W. L., 189, 194, 202
Mafalda, Princess, 82
Magee, Reverend John, 247

Magee, Ralph, 47
Malaprop, Mrs., 44
Mare Island Navy Yard, California, 18, 19-21, 56, 57
Marie, Queen of Roumania, 103-04
Marler, Sir Herbert, 189, 195
Marshall, Vice-President, 123
Martha, Crown Princess of Norway, 207, 208
Mary, Princess, 73, 76, 77
Mary, Queen, 73, 75, 77, 78-79, 186
Masaryk, Alice, 106
Mason, Earl, 16
Mason, Edith, 16
Mason, Lion, 16
Mason, Mrs. Livingston, 15-16
Mason, Marguerite, 16
Mayes, John, 126-27, 144
Mayflower, yacht, 54, 199
Mayo, Admiral, 65
McAllister, Ward, 28
McBride, Colonel Harry, 266
McCabe, John Lincoln, 144, 154
McIntire, Rear Admiral Ross T., 196
McKellar, Senator Kenneth D., 280
McKinley, Mabel, 36
McKinley, President and Mrs., 36
McLean, Edward B., 129
McManus, General, 62
McReynolds, Mrs. Sam D., 195
Meigs, Mrs. Edward B., 270
Mellett, Lowell, 258
Meloney, Mrs. William Brown, 127
Mercier, Cardinal, 114
Merryman, Mrs. D. Buchanan, 269
Mesta, Mrs. Perle, 269
Millay, Edna St. Vincent, 174
Miyanoshita, Japan, 11
Moffett, Admiral William A., 18
Moncheur, Baron, 114
Monroe, James, 6, 159
Montgomery, Ruth, 297
Moreno, Commander, 82
Morgan, Gerald, 201
Morgan, J. Pierpont, 194
Morgenthau, Mr. and Mrs. Henry, 195, 201, 204
Morgenthau, Joan, 167
Muir, Raymond, 140
Murat, Prince and Princess, 60, 70, 90, 97, 98
Murphy, Frank, 195
Myers, General John T., 19

Naval Academy, Annapolis, 15, 18-19, 57
Naval Ball, Madison Square Garden, 28
Naval Rendezvous of 1893, 25-27
Nesbitt, Henrietta, 140
Newark, U.S.S., 21-22, 25, 34
Newport, Rhode Island, 15-16, 29-31
Niblack, Mrs. Albert P., 269
Nieuport, Belgium, 114, 115
Niles, David, 243
Nunburnholme, Lady, 191, 194, 201

O'Boyle, Archbishop Patrick, 267
Odum, Reathel, 253-54, 255, 256, 257, 265, 288, 296
Olaf, Crown Prince of Norway, 207, 208
Orlando, V. E., 87, 105, 112
Orndorff, Irene, 291
Orr, Douglas W., 280
Owen, Ruth Bryan, 183

Packer Institute, 21
Paderewski, Ignace, 51, 104
Page, T. J., 22
Panama, 13
Paris, France, 31-34, 67-71, 86-98, 100-08, 109-13, 118-22
Paris Peace Conference, 60, 91-98, 102-08
Parish, Henry, 196, 199
Parsons, Mrs. Geoffrey, 90
Patricia, Princess, 77
Patten, Mary, 53, 130
Pearl Harbor, attack on, 207
Perdicaris, Mr. and Mrs. Ion, 41-42
Perkins, Frances, 184, 195
Pershing, General John J., 109, 110
Peter II, King of Yugoslavia, 207
Phillips, William, 49
Pichon, 88
Pittman, Key, 195
Poincaré, President and Madame, 67, 69, 86, 97, 100, 122
Poor, Lindsay, 35
Portsmouth, New Hampshire, 14-16
Pound, Sir Dudley, 211
Press conferences, 169-72, 221-23, 245, 256-58, 285-88
Prokofiev, Sergei, 182

Quirinal Palace, 80, 81, 83, 84, 113

Randolph, Mary, 130
Read, General Meredith, 31
Reading, Lord, 73, 79
Redmond, Robert, 270
Refugee royalty, 207-09
Reid, Mrs. Whitelaw, 104
Richardson, Rear Admiral James O., 196
Richmond, Staten Island, 6-9, 34-35, 36
Richmond, U.S.S., 9, 10, 12-13
Riley, Elizabeth, 40
Rockwell, William, 144, 154
Rodman, Admiral, 65
Rogers, Edith Nourse, 181-82, 185, 195, 216
Rohan, Prince de, 92
Rome, Italy, 80-85
Roosevelt, Alice, 167
Roosevelt, Anna, 151, 173, 245
Roosevelt, Eleanor, 167
Roosevelt, Elliott, 196
Roosevelt, Ethel, 167
Roosevelt, Franklin Delano, 4, 133, 134, 135-36, 137, 146-47, 148, 152, 175, 176, 178, 189-206, 209, 211, 214, 217, 218-19, 224, 235, 240-48, 263, 281, 299, 300
Roosevelt, Mrs. Franklin Delano, 51, 53, 90, 133, 134-35, 137-39, 141-45, 146-47, 148, 151-52, 154, 160-63, 166-68, 169-75, 176-79, 185, 189-206, 208-09, 212-23, 224-25, 229, 234, 237-39, 240-49, 251, 257, 271, 280
Roosevelt, Franklin D., Jr., 196
Roosevelt, G. Hall, 196
Roosevelt, Mrs. J. Roosevelt, 201
Roosevelt, James, 196, 206
Roosevelt, Mrs. James, 171, 201, 255
Roosevelt, Quentin, 90
Roosevelt, Theodore, 35, 36, 39, 41, 42, 85, 134, 283, 284
Roosevelt, Mrs. Theodore, 46
Roper, Mrs. Daniel, 183
Rosen, Baron, 43-45, 182
Rosen, Elizabeth, 43, 44-45, 182
Ross, Charles, 256, 258
Rowley, Edithe, 144, 291
Ryan, Right Reverend Monsignor John A., 242

Sandhurst, Lord, 88

San Francisco, U.S.S., 20-21, 25, 29, 235
Santa Barbara, California, 21
Saunders, Paul, 290
Schemerhorn, Captain Jake, 18
Schindler, N. P., 95-96, 101-02
Scott, Mary, 20
Seaman, Billopp Benjamin, 6
Seaman, Emma Hester, 6, 8, 15, 16, 19, 27, 31, 35
Seaman, Henry John, 6, 16-17
Seaman, Katharine, 6
Seaman, Katharine Sarah, 6
Searles, Wilson, 141
Seymour, Lady Katharine, 190-91, 194, 198-99, 201
Shanghai, 11
Shonts, Theodore, 43
Simmons, John Farr, 289
Sims, Admiral William S., 65
Sinclair, Harry, 129
Smith, Kate, 198
Smith, Margaret Chase, 297
Smith, Merriman, 290
Smuts, General Jan Christian, 91
Southgate, Richard, 142, 160
Spring Dance, 174-75
Spring-Rice, Sir Cecil, 45
Squire, Helen, 41
Stein, Gertrude, 234
Stevenson, Vice-President Adlai, 28
Steward, George F., 194
Strayer, Martha, 297
Sullivan, Timothy D., 58
Summerlin, George T., 187, 196, 244, 246
Sutherland, Duchess of, 73, 75, 77
Swanson, Mrs. Claude A., 195

Taft, Helen, 167
Taft, Mrs. Robert, 292
Taft, William Howard, 48
Tammany Hall, 58
Tardieu, André, 87
Taylor, Mrs. Myron C., 201
Teapot Dome scandal, 129
Tellegen, Marie Ann, 288, 289, 290, 291
Third Lighthouse District, 16-18
This I Remember, Roosevelt, 169
Thompson, Commander C. R., 209
Thompson, Huston, 49

Thompson, Malvina, 135, 137, 142-44, 147, 163, 169, 171, 172, 173, 176, 178, 187, 190, 192, 193, 194, 196, 199, 202-06, 207, 209, 212, 217, 219, 221, 222, 225, 229, 233, 245, 246, 248, 250, 253, 254, 299
Thomson, Mrs. James, 270
Tibbett, Lawrence, 188
Toklas, Alice B., 234
Tolley, Adrien B., 144, 154, 156, 187, 188, 241, 246, 248, 267, 268-69, 288, 295, 296
Tompkins, Minthorne, 8
Tompkinsville, Staten Island, 16-18
Tracy, Benjamin F., 43
Treaty of Versailles, 119-22
Trenton, U.S.S., 20
Troyanovsky, Ambassador, 182
Truitt, Mrs. Max, 268
Truman, Harry S., 4, 136, 214, 246, 250-51, 252, 261-62, 263, 264, 266, 269, 272-73, 274-76, 277-78, 279, 292, 297-98
Truman, Mrs. Harry S., 135, 169, 243, 248, 250-53, 255-56, 258-62, 263, 264, 265-66, 269, 270-72, 274, 275-76, 279, 280-81, 284, 286-88, 291-92, 296-97, 298
Truman, Margaret, 227, 254-55, 256, 263, 269, 272, 273, 282, 292, 296
Truxtun, U.S.S., 40
Tucker, Henry St. George, 201
Tufty, Esther, 297
Tully, Grace, 140, 221
Tumulty, Joseph, 61, 62
Tyrrell, Sir William, 123-24

Udini, Prince, 54, 84
Uhlan, 32
United Nations, 244-45

Vandalia, U.S.S., 20
Vanderbilt, Cornelius, 10
Vanderbilt, Gladys, 30
Vanderbilt, William Henry, 10
Vaughan, Mrs. Harry, 270
Venizelus, Mr., 104
Verdun, 116-17
Very, Mrs. Edward, 38
Victoria, Princess, 77
Victoria, Queen, 87-88, 124, 206
Villa Savoia, 80, 82

Viviani, 54
Von Brockdorff-Rantzau, 107

Walker, Admiral J. Grimes, 16
Wallace, Mrs. David, 255, 275, 284, 292
Wallace, Henry A., 195
Walsh, Thomas J., 129
Warren, Mrs. Charles, 269
Watson, General Edwin M., 195, 241
Wedel, Baroness, 112-13
Welles, Sumner, 195
Wells, Isabelle, 270
West, J. B., 141
White, Henry, 87, 88, 89-90, 100-01, 107, 121, 194
White House Profile, Furman, 300
White House reconstruction, 279-92
Whitlock, Mr., 118
Wilhelmina, Queen, 170, 207, 208, 214, 215, 221
Wilkinson, Howard, 247-48
Williamsburg, yacht, 274
Wilson, Henry, 65
Wilson, Margaret, 46, 49, 52, 65, 67, 69, 70, 80, 83, 84, 114, 115, 118, 120

Wilson, Mrs. Orme, 270
Wilson, Woodrow, 32, 46-48, 50, 51, 55, 59-71, 72, 73-85, 86-94, 96, 97-98, 99-100, 102, 103-05, 106, 107, 109, 110, 111, 112, 113-14, 116, 118, 119, 121, 122, 123-24, 129, 130-31, 139, 186, 214, 244, 247, 300
Wilson, Mrs. Woodrow, 46, 47-48, 50, 51, 52, 55, 59-71, 73-85, 86-94, 97, 101, 103-04, 105, 106, 107-08, 110, 111, 112, 114, 115-16, 117, 118, 119, 122, 123-24, 125, 129, 135, 186, 195, 228
Winslow, Lorenzo S., 280
Woodward, Stanley, 215, 216
World's Fair, New York, 187
Wouters, Mme. de, 118

Yokohama, Japan, 11-12
Yolande, Princess, 82
Young, John Russell, 11
Young, Warren S., 154
Yourievski, Prince, 25
Ypres, 116-17

Zeebrugge, 117-18

CPSIA information can be obtained
at www.ICGtesting.com
Printed in the USA
BVHW041808151221
624132BV00014B/952